homely
ballads
and
stories
in
verse

homely ballads and stories in verse

The Poetry of Mary Sewell

Edited, with an introduction,
by Thomas Ruys Smith

Contents

W.T. BASHFORD,
PHOTOGRAPHER.

Mary Sewell.
ARGYLE HOUSE.
PORTOBELLO.

Image courtesy of Norfolk County Council at www.picture.norfolk.gov.uk

Before *Black Beauty*:
Looking for Mary Sewell

Thomas Ruys Smith

"The story of one who, in her sixtieth year, deliberately set
herself to master the art of moving human hearts by simple,
telling, faultlessly flowing verse; and who succeeded in
producing metrical tales which have sold by the million,
and still circulate by the thousand, is surely worthy of note
amongst the curiosities of literature. But the earnest, effective
life-work of Mary Sewell [...] has far higher claims on our
attention."

Wesleyan-Methodist Magazine, 1889[1]

Black Beauty casts a long shadow: one of the bestselling books of
all time, our ongoing infatuation with the horse that still gallops
through our collective imagination has almost obscured those
people who helped bring him into the world in 1877. Housebound
in Norfolk after many years of ill health, Anna Sewell wrote her
groundbreaking animal rights novel throughout the last years of her
life, finally seeing it into print six months before her death in 1878.
If her mother, Mary Sewell, is remembered at all in the twenty-first
century, it is as Anna's carer and amanuensis, taking dictation from
her daughter when she was too sick to hold a pen herself. Mary

would certainly never have quibbled with being allotted that place in history by fate and circumstance, and she evidently took intense pleasure in her daughter's literary successes. As one of her close friends put it, "the devoted mother could rejoice, even in the midst of the anguish of parting, over the welcome given by thousands of readers to her darling's dying work."[2]

Yet one of the things that *Black Beauty*'s triumphs have obscured from us is the extraordinary life and career of Mary Sewell herself. When her daughter's world-changing book met its enthusiastic public in 1877, Mary was already eighty years old. Like her daughter, Mary began and ended her life in Norfolk, but she saw much of the world in between times. By her own reckoning, in a short autobiographical sketch she wrote for her grandchildren in the 1880s, she had witnessed society change around her indelibly in that profound period of flux: "The years through which I have lived have been some of the most interesting in our country's history. I came into the world in the year 1797—about the time of the great French Revolution—and from that time to this includes the grand march of commerce, science, and invention, including the lives of some of the first historical characters."[3] By such a measure, her own biography might seem less momentous. Even her friend and biographer Mary Bayly judged her to have led a "quiet and uneventful life," albeit one "invested with a charm and dignity all its own."[4] Yet for decades, Mary Sewell worked tirelessly in communities across the country to improve the lives of those that the grand march of history had left behind—the enslaved, the poor, the sick, animals subjected to cruelty. "Her sympathies flowed out to every living thing," as another friend put it.[5] For that work alone she deserves to be considered a figure of local and national importance in the field of philanthropy. But there was still more to Mary Sewell: quietly, without fanfare, before the singular success of *Black Beauty* consigned her to a secondary role in her own story, she was one of the most popular and successful poets in Victorian Britain. As one newspaper applauded in 1861, Mary Sewell's name had been raised "to so high an eminence, both as a philanthropist and a poet."[6] Once, her work was known and loved by millions. Now, in this collection, we can finally rediscover her forgotten verses anew.

To help us rescue Mary Sewell and her work from obscurity, we have her own words to help us. As well as the autobiographical sketch that covers much of her early life in Norfolk and beyond, in later life she wrote a non-fiction guide to practical charity work— *'Thy Poor Brother': Letters to a Friend on Helping the Poor* (1863)—which gives us a sense of her decades of humanitarian exertion. For much of our understanding of Mary, however, we are dependent on another mother and daughter collaboration. After Mary Sewell's death in 1884, her friends Mary and Elisabeth Boyd Bayly took on the task of narrating her life to the public and honouring her literary achievements. According to Mary Bayly, this labour of friendship presented a daunting prospect: "The materials at hand for use were by no means abundant. The bulk of her family correspondence had been destroyed and she had not escaped the sorrow—the lot of most who live to an advanced age—of seeing her earlier friends drop one by one by the way. There are now few living who remember anything of her earlier life." Mary Bayly's own relationship with her subject "did not begin until she was upwards of sixty years of age." But though late blooming—like many things in Mary's life—their friendship resulted in "a very near and intimate acquaintance."[7] And so, across a number of years, mother and daughter Bayly produced a series of publications that remain our best and, in many ways, only guide to Mary's experiences. In 1885, the year after Mary's death, Elisabeth published a glowing obituary in *The Sunday Magazine*. The following year, Elisabeth helped into print a two-volume selection of Mary's poems and ballads that Mary herself had been planning before her death.[8] Then, in 1889, Mary Bayly's definitive *Life and Letters of Mrs. Sewell* finally provided readers with a full account of her life, including a tribute to Mary's literary work by Elisabeth which still remains the best guide to her writing career. More recently, Mary has also featured prominently in important biographies of Anna Sewell and *Black Beauty* by Susan Chitty (1971), Adrienne Gavin (2004), and Celia Brayfield (2023)—but mostly, inevitably, as a prominent part of her daughter's story and her daughter's artistry.[9] In this collection, however, it is finally time to focus on Mary Sewell's life and career before *Black Beauty* trotted into view. In particular, I want to shine a spotlight on the poetry that made Mary a household name but which has rarely been taken seriously since her death in 1884. But since that story itself doesn't begin until 1858, when Mary was sixty, it is first necessary to get a sense of the life that made the poet.

Mary was born into a family with deep Norfolk roots, but she herself came into the world in Sutton, in Suffolk, where her Quaker parents, John and Ana Wright, were then farming. Before she was two, they moved to another farm, at Felthorpe, close to Norwich, where the family remained for around a decade. Her mother took on the role of "the lady of the village."[10] "Shall I say it was the happiest part of my life?" Mary pondered in her autobiography, "No, I will not do that, although my memory can recall very few shadows that rested upon it."[11] Despite the backdrop of the Napoleonic Wars and the threat of invasion from France, Mary was free to explore her family's eight hundred acres: "to us it was a delightful pleasure-ground [...] We needed no one to provide amusement for us." This idyll didn't insulate Mary from the harsher realities of rural life, however. She and her siblings tried to avoid walking down one lane in their village: "The report current was, that a man of the name of Brand had killed himself in that lane, and if any one drove down it after nightfall, they would see a man without a head running along by the side of the cart." The shifting nature of country life was also apparent, even to a child: John Wright introduced a threshing-machine to his farm, which promptly mangled one man's arm and killed a woman. Mary remembered walking through the village in the aftermath of those incidents: "Instead of the greetings and curtseyings common on such occasions, there was a dead silence [...] I felt the weight of the solemnity painfully oppressive." Mary also came face-to-face with the travails of those who were less fortunate: "A very poor family had removed into the village, and my father did all he could to find the man and his family employment." When one of the children was hired to dig a hole in the Wrights' orchard, Mary and her sister Elizabeth contrived a way to give the boy some extra money—her first act of charity. Not that she was a paragon: she also remembered, on a rare shopping trip to Norwich, "secretly getting into debt" over the purchase of some doll's house furniture from a toy shop: "this penny hung about our necks for weeks, attended with the most anxious fear lest the man should see my father and tell him of it." Then came her education: after the local dame school, Mary was put under the charge of "a bright young governess" who opened new vistas for her pupils: "She was specially clever in teaching history, and giving it the charm of reality [...] She introduced us to a much more stirring kind of poetry than we had known before." Once a week a French tutor visited from Norwich, as did a drawing-master.

Change soon came: crop price fluctuations caused by the end of war in Europe meant that her father's farming career "found a sad reverse." He liquidated his resources at Felthorpe—Mary remembered his "anxious, almost agonized" face on auction day "when he saw his beautiful farm horses and other stock selling far below their value"—and went into business with a shipowner at Great Yarmouth. Nearly thirteen, Mary took a "heartaching look round on the dear old place where all my life had hitherto been spent," and set off for her new life on the Norfolk coast "full of hope and curiosity"—a hallmark of her peripatetic life. Their new residence brought them into close contact with a number of other Quaker families—"all in trade, and thoroughly respectable." The leading Elders of this "pleasant, sociable community" were William Sewell and his wife Hannah, the proprietors of a grocer's shop in the market-place. Sewell opened his house to young Quakers, "promoting in every way their intellectual studies"; the boys and girls founded separate groups dedicated to cerebral pursuits, and Mary was a member of the Agenorian Society. The charms of these new associations did not come without their restrictions. Mary's mother, for example, had "rather a taste for dress" in a way that stuck out in a community concerned with "plainness of speech, behaviour, and apparel." When she ordered striking sage green pelisses for her four daughters from a fashionable dressmaker in Norwich, trimmed with swansdown, she caused a minor scandal: Hannah Sewell visited the Wrights to warn Mary's mother of "the danger of leading other young girls into the temptation of dress." The swansdown was promptly removed. Mary also engaged in her own quiet rebellion, one that held evident significance for her later career. After a year at a boarding school in Tottenham, she developed consuming literary passions:

> My great delight was in poetry, and the works of Moore, Southey, Byron, Scott, and others, continually coming out, gave me a perpetual feast. For two years I think I read little besides, learning whole books, and repeating them to myself in the silent meetings. I do not think I derived any harm from this almost exclusive attention to poetry. Quaker girls have little excitement in their quiet lives, and these works afforded to the craving imagination all the excitement and variety it needed. There were other books that Elizabeth and I read and half-studied together, and with drawing, and attending the various meetings of the Agenorian Society, our time passed pleasantly enough. We every now and then got a novel from the circulating library, but this being forbidden fruit, we devoured it in our bedroom.

The Wrights' life at Yarmouth was disrupted by two calamities: first, John Wright was swindled by his business partner, losses that he never managed to recoup. Second, John also invested in steamboats operated by his brother Richard—the first river steam-packet service in England, running between Yarmouth and Norwich. In April 1817, one of the steamboats exploded, with a significant loss of life. The *Norfolk Chronicle* reported: "the vessel was literally blown to atoms." Eight passengers were "instantaneously killed", six were transported to hospital, "miserably wounded."[12] John was ruined. After "grave consultations" with her siblings about what they could do to help, Mary took up a position as a teacher at a school in Essex. Though she soon "felt pretty much at home", she found it hard to adjust to the change in her status which saw "the servants call you familiarly by your name as if you were one of them." Her sisters Elizabeth and Anna also found teaching positions. "We were scattered about," Mary recalled, "each of us with our own difficulties, every one doing their best, no one adding to the other's burdens." On a visit home to her parents' new farm at Buxton, near Norwich, the seeds of another profound change were planted. Mary began a long—and, it seems, rather reluctant—courtship with Isaac Sewell, son of William and Hannah. "My heart had never been entangled," Mary recalled, "and was not at all ready to put on chains." Or to put it more bluntly, "there was no spark upon the tinder" to ignite Mary's "enthusiastic and sentimental" heart. After a long correspondence, Mary finally succumbed. She was 22. Looking back on her life at the age of 84, Mary judged, "I am sure I made no mistake—a kinder husband or better father could rarely be found." Certainly, she concluded, their life had not been "dull." They were married in 1819 at the Quaker Meeting House at Lammas and moved into a small house in Yarmouth—a building that still stands and, known as Anna Sewell House, is run by horse welfare charity Redwings as a site dedicated to Anna's life and work. Anna herself was born there in 1820—"an unclouded blessing," as Mary put it, "for fifty-eight years the perennial joy of my life." More change soon followed: in what would become a familiar pattern of their married life, Isaac's business ventures ran into trouble and the family was forced to relocate. Though Mary "abhorred the idea", the Sewells moved to London. She found "Great London" to be "like a huge cage, with iron bars [...] I loathed, and hated the place."[13] Their first attempt at running a shop in Bishopsgate was a dismal failure, personally and profession-ally. "The want of fresh air, the high stairs, the noise, and incessant work began to tell upon me," Mary recalled; "before two years it was broken up, and so was I." In the midst of this fresh disaster, her son Philip was born—"a blessing to me every day of his life."

A doctor advised the Sewells that Mary "must leave London", and so they decamped to Dalston for a decade. Isaac became a "traveller to a large lace manufactory at Nottingham." They had a small house, enough to eat, one servant, and were "exceedingly happy." It was at Dalston that Mary properly charted the course of her life as it would unfold over the coming decades. She wrote her first book: *Walks with Mamma* was an illustrated book for young children composed entirely in words of one syllable, published anonymously in December 1824. Mary was motivated, she remembered, by the desire to "earn money [...] for the purchase of books to help me in the chil-dren's education." She sold it for £3, "a little fortune for me then." This was no mean feat: her publisher was John Harris, the premier retailer of books for young readers in the early nineteenth century.

Harris produced at least two editions of the book and it was still in print decades later.[14] The British Library's copy of *Walks With Mamma*, complete with coloured illustrations, was published by Grant and Griffith, who took over Harris's firm in 1843, and is likely to date from the 1850s. Immediately, Mary's ability to innovate with a reduced palette of single-syllable words is clear. What's also striking about her sketches of nature walks between young "Ann" and her mother is their concern for animals, including a long passage dealing with the proper treatment of horses:

> Well, now what shall I show you, my dear? Oh, look in at this door, and you will see the new horse which your aunt bought last week. See, how still he stands in the stall, to eat his corn and hay; while James, the boy-groom, rubs him down, and combs out his mane and tail. Some grooms have had sad kicks from a horse, and some have lost their lives; but James seems to have no cause for fear. The horse is of great use to us, and we ought to take care that he is well fed and kept nice and clean; and it is a sad thing when men or boys vex or hurt him. If we had no horse, we could not ride out in our chaise; our men could not plough the fields; nor could we send so much corn at one time to the mill; but you know we have a grey horse, that runs in the chaise; two black ones, which draw the plough; and a brown one, which takes our wheat to be ground, and brings back the flour to our house; whilst the horse which you see here is kept for your aunt to ride on.[15]

Then, Mary properly turned her attention to philanthropy. She joined the Anti-Slavery Association and became involved with prison reform in Shoreditch. She was roused into action by "the sufferings of little chimney-sweepers", and there was also, of course, "a great deal of visiting the poor." This was the true beginning of a lifetime of significant charitable activity, a thread that ran through her existence whatever the frequent reversals of her own family's circumstances. As she would modestly document in *Thy Poor Brother*, wherever Mary found herself she set about to see what good works needed to be done: teaching, visiting the poor, visiting the sick, visiting workhouses and prisons, addressing mother's

An advertisement for Mary Sewell's first book, *Walks With Mamma*,
published in *Saint James's Chronicle*, December 14 1824.

15

meetings, promoting temperance, and undertaking a whirl of other benevolent activities. At times, Mary's philanthropic world might evoke Elizabeth Gaskell's account of the "Amazons" of *Cranford* (1853) and their activities: "obtaining clear and correct knowledge of everybody's affairs in the parish [...] keeping their neat maid-servants in admirable order [...] kindness (somewhat dictatorial) to the poor, and real tender good offices to each other whenever they are in distress."[16] Yet, if some of that rings true, to her friends Mary was famous for the warmth and empathy she brought to her work. As Elisabeth described: "One can just imagine Mrs. Sewell, after gaining a welcome from the worst ward of the workhouse, saying, 'Come, then, let us sit down and talk together; tell me your troubles and let me see if I can help you.' In *listening* lay her great power of dealing with humankind."[17] The most important lesson Mary strove to impart to would-be charity workers was a simple one: "In the more important features of characters, such as religion, morality, worth, and affection, the rich and the poor stand upon a level."[18] She censured those who tried to "domineer and usurp authority, as if they had the right to rule in a poor man's house," those who "find fault without reason," and those who dealt "especially harsh judgments on the conduct of the lower classes." And she cautioned against the desire to "inquisitively pry into their private history."[19] Mary understood, too, "that the mental anguish of many of these poor men and women, is, out of all proportion, greater than any amount of physical sufferings they may have to endure."[20] Those same precepts—that deep sense of leveling compassion—would go on to inform her poetry four decades later.

Before long, the Sewells were on the move again. They took over an old coach-house and stables in Stoke Newington which had four acres of meadow land. They kept cows, but "prosperity never came." Their milkwoman "turned out to be a thief." They took in lodgers, "but this proved neither pleasant nor profitable." And after much internal wrangling, Mary left the Quakers, and was subsequently "very lonely—almost all my friends and acquaintances were Friends, and there was, as might be supposed, much misgiving." She experimented with a variety of other modes of worship, and the bedrock of her active faith is apparent in almost all of her verses; but to quote one of her friends, "she never gave her heart to any other denomination." As she put it in later life, "my chains were all broken." Worse was to come. Running home from school one day in a shower of rain, Anna fell and, as Mary phrased it, "sprained her ankle." Whatever the true nature of Anna's injury, it marked the beginning of a "life of constant frustration." The injury never healed properly, Anna's mobility was severely impaired, and much of Mary's life would be devoted to caring for her daughter as her health fluctuated. And it was time to move again. Isaac took on a new role as the manager of "the London and County Joint-Stock Bank, which was to be opened at Brighton." Moving to the town in 1836, it doesn't seem that Mary's life in Brighton was one of unalloyed joy. Since her autobiographical sketch breaks off at this juncture, we are left without Mary's own narration of events. However, in *Thy Poor Brother*, she did recollect a dispiriting early morning walk along the pier: "I had risen earlier than usual, for I had many troubles on my mind, and I wanted to be alone. A thick gloom was spread over the whole face of nature; the wind was wild and cold, the sky a leaden grey, and the sea rolled its heavy discoloured waves with an angry growl upon the shore [...] Nothing spoke of hope."[21] After nearly a decade in Brighton, they moved to Lancing in 1845; in 1849 they moved to Hayward's Heath; in 1853 they moved to Grayling Wells, near Chichester; they even visited Philip in Spain—but as Mary Bayly lamented, only scanty records remain from these times which left "fewer traces than any other part of Mrs. Sewell's life."[22] In April 1857, though, Mary wrote to a friend with significant news of a familiar sort:

> My good husband has resigned his position in the Bank [...] We are able to live without his being in much more business than attending to his own; but I am afraid he will find leisure wearisome. We shall have to be more careful, of course, than we have been, and that is never very pleasant, is it dear?[23]

But Mary herself was on the brink of her own transformation. As Mary Bayly put it, she was about to embark upon "the discovery of a new existence—a new era, though it came as quietly as the leaves unfold in spring."[24]

In the late 1850s, Mary began to write in earnest. As Elisabeth put it, "The Muse kept captive for nearly sixty years" was finally unshackled.[25] According to the Baylys, Mary's turn to poetry took place while Anna was on an extended stay at a German health spa. In Elisabeth's account, "She described to me how the emptiness of her life in Anna's absence tempted her on to write, till several ballads were accomplished."[26] What had begun as a response to one kind of loneliness was spurred on by a different type of solitude when the family moved to the isolated Blue Lodge in the village of Wick, almost equidistant between Bath and Bristol. It was, Mary described to a friend, "a long way from *everything*, with neither postman, carrier, omnibus, nor rail, neither shop, needle-woman, nor charwoman to be had, so that everything has to be done and obtained with the greatest difficulty."[27] The time and space afforded by the lack of visitors was, at least, helpful for her burgeoning writing career. As much as Mary's first flush of poetic inspiration was a response to circumstance, it was evidently the product of much thought and experience—or as Elisabeth put it, "threescore years of training for it by using her imagination as a power of sympathy."[28]

Mary Sewell herself could be dismissive about her own artistic relationship to her work. Walking with a friend after her poetry had found an enthusiastic audience, inundated with praise from friends and admirers, Mary responded "almost reproachfully" to the playful suggestion that such success might go to her head: "'I have *nothing* to be proud of; it all came in answer to prayer.' 'Yes,' she added immediately after, 'even the rhymes.'"[29] This was a typical gesture for women writers of this generation, especially those publishing with a righteous cause in mind. Famously, Harriet Beecher Stowe claimed to have been similarly inspired to compose *Uncle Tom's Cabin* (1851): "It all came before me in visions, one after another, and I put them down in words."[30] To others, however, Sewell made it clear that there was a great deal of method that underpinned the divine inspiration. According to Elisabeth, Mary "loved to compose out of doors" while walking—like Dickens. But her requirements were precise:

her preference was for the long, straight path in her garden at Wick: "'A crinkle-crankle walk is dreadful,' she said; 'it cuts off all one's rhymes.'" For further inspiration, she thought back to the poetry that she had memorized as a teenager: "all the Byron at Friends' meeting trained me well in rhythm."[31]

Mary's choice of poetic form was also telling. She consciously labeled her poem as ballads or stories in verse. This was a gesture that put her in touch with centuries of popular poetic tradition, rooted in the rhymes and songs that had long been part of people's lives. As Patricia Fumerton and Anita Guerrini have described:

> Although ballads were originally an oral genre dating back to medieval times, the invention of printing led to an explosion of printed ballads in the sixteenth and seventeenth centuries [...] By far the most printed medium in the literary marketplace of London, all such broadsides were vehicles of mass communications [...] Indeed, one could not travel anywhere in the city of London without hearing ballads sung on street corners or broadsides pasted up on posts and walls. Ballads and their broadside brethren thus touched all levels of society; Shakespeare, for one, cites ballads in almost every play he wrote.[32]

Printed in their millions, adaptable and ubiquitous, ballads encompassed all aspects of life. As Robin Ganev enumerates, they could be written "to commemorate an event, to spread news, to voice grievances, or simply to entertain."[33] Murders abounded, mostly yoked to tragic love, as did news of military triumphs and tragedies; some were funny, many were sad and sentimental. When Mary was a romantically minded young girl committing the poetry of Walter Scott and others to memory, the ballad was a form in flux. As Peter Jimack has noted, engagement with the "popular ballad" was "central" to the development of British Romanticism.[34] Scott himself was a key figure in an antiquarian revival of interest in the form; his obsession with the "natural pathos" and "rude energy" of the examples that he avidly collected both as printed broadsheets and "among the peasantry of Scotland" resulted in his ballad collection *Minstrelsy of the Scottish Border* (1802).[35] Similarly, Wordsworth and Coleridge's

Lyrical Ballads (1798)—their earthshaking experiment in translating the lives and "the language of conversation in the middle and lower classes of society" into "poetic pleasure"—announced its engagement with the form in its very title.[36]

If Mary was steeped in these romantic traditions, no less influential for her own poetic career must have been the model of Hannah More. In 1795, More took on the project of editing and writing a series of Cheap Repository Tracts which attempted to use the ballad form to subvert what she saw as its unwholesome hold on the imaginations of the poor. Her aim was to supplant "the corrupt and vicious little books and ballads which have been hung out at windows in the most alluring forms, or hawked through Town and Country, and have been found so highly mischievous to the Community, as to require every attention to counteract them." If ballads were a bad influence on the poor, as More believed them to be, her Cheap Repository Tracts sought to counter the "poison continually flowing thro' the channel of vulgar and licentious publications" and instead instill godliness, thrift and virtuous behaviour in her readers (as well as attempting to quell social unrest).[37] Her 1796 ballad "The Hackney Coachman; or, The Way to Get a Good Fare", for example, yoked a message of hard work, temperance and piety to a plea for kindness for working animals:

> I am a bold Coachman and drive a good Hack,
> With a coat of five capes that quite covers my back;
> And my wife keeps a sausage-shop, not many miles
> From the narrowest alley in all broad St. Giles.
> [...]
> Tho' my beasts should be dull yet I don't use them ill;
> Tho' they stumble I swear not, nor cut them up hill;
> For I firmly believe there's no charm in an oath
> That can make a Nag trot when to walk he is loth.
>
> And tho' I'm a Coachman, I'll freely confess,
> I beg of my Maker my labors to bless;
> I praise him each morning, and pray every night,
> And 'tis this makes my heart feel so cheerful and light.[38]

They sold in their millions. Mary's ballads, then, stood in a remarkable lineage of popular literature.

After Mary had completed the initial composition, plodding up and down her garden at Wick, next came lengthy rounds of revision. Her acquaintance James Fleming, who would go on to become chaplain to Queen Victoria and Edward VII, provided an invaluable insight into Sewell's editing process and the sense of craft that she clearly brought to her poetry—and the multiple layers of pruning to which she subjected her verses:

> I asked Mrs. Sewell one day—"How do you make your ballads so simple?" She replied—"This is my plan:—I first write one as it comes to my mind. I then put it away for two or three days, and go over it carefully, cutting out all words that seem to me at all difficult, and I put it away. Then I take it out again, and try to substitute words of two syllables for words of three; and afterwards, words of one syllable, if possible, for words of two.[39]

This commitment to always simplify, embedded in her first publication back in 1824, was profound—and infamous to those that knew her. Elisabeth tells us: "It was remarked to one of Mrs. Sewell's grandchildren that 'mirk' would have been a better rhyme than 'dark' in one of her 'Stories in Verse.' 'But grandmother would never have used that word,' she said, 'because it is not one that poor people are accustomed to.'"[40] More characterfully, Mary once curtly corrected one acquaintance who referred to "an apiary" in her presence: "It's a *bee-hut*."[41]

Finally, Mary's poems had to find favour with their ultimate judge: Anna. Even though Mary had begun her new literary career during her daughter's absence—perhaps conspicuously so—she was always adamant about the vital role that Anna played in the composition process. In Mary's own statement: "I have never made a plan for anything without submitting it to her judgment. Every line I have written has been at her feet before it has gone forth to the world."[42] In Elisabeth's framing, Mary "originated" while "the frail, ripe-judging daughter weighed the product."[43] Not that Anna was a gentle critic. "Oh, if I can only pass my Nannie," Mary confessed, "I don't fear the world after that."[44] Mary Bayly observed the truth behind this statement at first hand, a fascinating glimpse of the intimate collaborative process that developed between the two women:

> I was once with Anna when her mother read aloud to us something she was preparing for the press. It was beautiful to witness the intense love, admiration, and even pride which beamed in the daughter's face, but this in no wise prevented her being, as I thought, a very severe critic. Nature has bestowed on her a remarkably sweet-toned and persuasive voice. I think I hear her now, saying, "Mother dear, thee must alter that line," or "Thee must put a fuller word there, that will give out more of thy meaning." The point was seldom disputed: the faulty line would be changed, and the stronger word inserted.[45]

When it was finally time for her poems to meet the world, Mary aimed high. She first showed them to Henry S. King—a family friend who, in Mary's opinion, was "the most refined man" whose tastes were "perfect." Mary sat in "fear and trembling [...] while he turned over the leaves" of her ballads until King gave his judgment: "This will do."[46] Handily, this was not just a friendly endorsement. King was connected to the influential publishing firm of Smith, Elder & Co: after achieving extraordinary success with the publication of *Jane Eyre* (1847), their roster of authors included Victorian superstars like Thackeray, Elizabeth Gaskell, Anthony Trollope and Robert Browning. And in 1858, with the publication of *Homely Ballads for the Working Man's Fireside*, Mary Sewell joined their ranks. Immediately, Mary met with acclaim. The *Literary Gazette* judged: "Very good verses for the most part, conveying many useful lessons."[47] The *London Sun* found the collection "simple and pleasing in style [...] The moral is excellent, without being brought too prominently forward, and the ballads tell of the joys and troubles of everyday life."[48] The *Morning Post* found that Mary's poems "illustrate some sterling home truths and fine sentiments in the simple but impressive style of our old English ballads."[49] Smith, Elder & Co. would also publish a sequel volume: *Stories in Verse for the Street and Lane* (1861). But they weren't to have sole ownership of Mary's work. Her friend

Sarah Stickney Ellis wrote to another acquaintance in 1859, "Mary Sewell is doing wonders with her little poems [...] Two publishers are wanting to have them, and they bid one against another so that she enjoys the full pleasure of her own plentiful pocket-money."[50] The Norwich-based firm Jarrold and Sons presumably gave Mary an offer she couldn't refuse—perhaps helped along, as Adrienne Gavin judged, by their "Norfolk connection" or their "temperance connections"—since they would release almost everything else that Mary published.[51]

And there was certainly plenty to publish: for the next few years Mary was extraordinarily prolific. In 1859, Jarrold and Sons released Mary's innovative verse-novel for younger readers, *The Children of Summerbrook: Scenes of Village Life*. In 1860 came Mary's most popular poem, *Mother's Last Words*, first released on its own as one of Jarrold and Sons' "Household Tracts for the People, Twopence Each"—before being endlessly repackaged in illustrated gift editions and in combination with her other poems. The *Norfolk News* pronounced it "exquisitely beautiful" and predicted that copies of Mary's poems would soon "be found in almost every home in the land."[52] In 1862, Mary released an epistolary novel aimed at young girls contemplating a life of household work: *Patience Hart's First Experience in Service* ("the best book for a young domestic servant that we ever saw", according to *The Nonconformist*).[53] She released non-fiction, too: in 1863, she published two books which exemplified the different sides of her progressive concerns—local and global. The first was *'Thy Poor Brother': Letters to a Friend on Helping the Poor*, her advice-book drawn from decades of experience "as it has impressed itself upon her in the common round of life and duty."[54] The second, released while the American Civil War was entering a pivotal phase, was the abolitionist pamphlet *An Appeal to Englishwomen*—written in response to "the cry of the American slave" that "rolled on the waves of the wide Atlantic, breaking helplessly, almost hopelessly, on our shores."[55] Though she would never again be as productive as this extraordinary five year period, Mary would continue publishing for the rest of her life—even including a new verse collection, *The Suffering Poor*, that was released in December

1883 when Mary was 86, just a few months before her death. As the *Norwich Mercury* reported, this final flourish from "the well known authoress" would "doubtless be read at many a village entertainment during the winter." All the profits were to be "devoted to the help of the outcast poor in the East of London."[56]

As that short summary makes clear, there was a driving sense of both purpose and audience that ran throughout Mary's poetic career. She made those concerns explicit in a Preface to her first collection of *Homely Ballads*. As well as writing to benefit the poor both directly and indirectly, Mary also had ambitions to write poetry that would capture the interest of "the noble-hearted, patient, and industrious workers in our native land":

> The Author believes—and her opinion is confirmed by others intimately conversant with the minds of the working classes in different parts of the country—that there exists amongst them generally, an instinctive love and appreciation of simple descriptive poetry; and that, both morally and intellectually, it is of more importance to them to have the imagination cultivated and refined by the higher sentiment of poetry, than it can be to those who have the advantage of a liberal education; to the one, it is a luxury - to the other, an almost needful relaxation from the severe and irksome drudgery of their daily lot.[57]

There are, of course, a multitude of judgements and assumptions embedded in this passage—the imposition of narrow social and cultural values down the social scale that would even elicit some criticism at the time of their publication. That was the kernel of Anthony Trollope's politely devastating review of Mary's work—an evisceration that has, until now, unfairly served as her literary epitaph. Using Mary's temperance poem *The Rose of Cheriton* (1867) as a strawman to attack the wider popularity of "small pietistic books which have come in my way", Trollope argued that simplistic sentimental verses which attempted to preach to the poor with little understanding of their lives and without much in the way of practical instruction were both an artistic and moral failure:

Tom the good rustic, and Dick the wicked rustic, have an argument together about going to church, in which every word spoken by Tom is taken for granted as being gospel truth, and in which Dick, though he argues stoutly for the sake of the length of the story, knocks under at last in a way which makes one feel that wickedness is very easily overcome. These little works generally amount to nothing more than reiterated assertion that a godly life is the proper life to lead; and so far they would be true, were it not that they make a godly life to consist in such a renunciation of worldly things as to ordinary men and women is manifestly impossible; but they contain assertion only, and tell the reader nothing which will make a godly life either more easy to him, or more profitable in his sight, than it was before.[58]

In a similar vein, we might consider the fact that plenty of working class poets were forging poetic statements about their own lives in this period, without Mary's easier access to publishers. As Florence Boos has revealed, "Victorian proletarian women wrote thousands of lines of poetry" but "most mainstream editors and reviewers ignored their contributions, and class-based condescension and malign neglect silenced their poetic efforts."[59] Still, having spent decades in the company of her poorer neighbours around the country, Mary understood those tensions all too well. She even vocalised them in one of her most righteously angry poems, "The Working Woman's Appeal", in which her eponymous heroine is visited by a former employer who understands nothing about the lives of ordinary people:

She only knew of cottages
That poets write about;
Where work is pleasant exercise
Both in the house and out,
And children all have curling hair
Like cherubim, no doubt.

Confronted with the ramshackle reality of her former employee's cottage on washday, the "mortified" visitor can only offer a lecture and a "freezing look": "She could not sympathize at all, And so she went away."

Mary could certainly sympathise; and, for all of Trollope's criticisms, that sympathy clearly struck a profound nerve in Victorian culture. To say that Mary was a popular poet is in many ways an understatement. At the time of her death, according to Elisabeth Boyd Bayly, the sales figures of Mary's most popular volumes were as follows: "'Homely Ballads' is now in its fortieth thousand; 'Children of Summerbrook,' thirty third thousand. 'Stories in Verse' was not published complete until 1869, since when 19,000 copies have been printed; but the ballads had been selling as Household Tracts long before that time."[60] How does that compare with other poets from the same period? Richard Altick, in his groundbreaking *The English Common Reader* (1957), attempted to tabulate the bestselling books of the nineteenth century. Going by his calculations, Mary's sales figures were certainly comparable to some of Tennyson's collections: the first volume of *Idylls of the King* (1859), the poem that secured his affection with Victorian readers, sold around 40,000 copies in its first edition. By contrast, Mary's reach far outstripped the likes of Robert Browning, who sold only a few thousand copies of most of his publications.[61] So by that metric alone, Mary Sewell should be judged as one of the bestselling Victorian poets. But as Elisabeth hints, those figures counted only single volume collections of her poetry. Many of her sales came from cheap pamphlets and tracts, perhaps containing a single poem alongside a woodcut illustration for a penny or two, much more easily accessible to the poor. And what little we know of those sales figures is astonishing. Elisabeth writes: "In November 1860 'Mother's Last Words' appeared, and had a sale unprecedented in the history of ballads. It has now reached one million and eighty-eight thousand [...] 'Our Father's Care,' the story of a little water-cress girl, followed in 1861, and is now in its 776th thousand."[62] When Elisabeth uses the word "unprecedented" here, we should certainly pause over its significance. It may be surprising that the most popular poet in Victorian Britain was American author Henry Wadsworth Longfellow. Like Mary, his poems were readily available in cheap editions accessible to the poor: the lack of international copyright meant that publishers could flood the market with his work. Like Mary, both his long narrative poems and shorter lyrics found an enthusiastic working class audience: when he was granted a meeting with Queen Victoria in 1868, she famously remarked, "I noticed an unusual interest among the attendants and servants. I could scarcely credit that they so generally knew who he was. When he took leave they concealed themselves in places from which they could get a good look at him as he passed."[63] According to Altick's best calculations, two of Longfellow's main English publishers sold "over 1,126,900 copies of Longfellow's various volumes to 1900."[64] If Mary was not quite that successful, we still need to appreciate that the extraordinary reach of her most popular verses was truly comparable only to the most beloved poet on both sides of the Atlantic in this period.

Besides, partial sales figures can still only tell us so much about her popularity. As she must have intended, her verses became fully embedded in the charitable efforts of countless philanthropic volunteers across the country. As an enthusiastic reviewer of *Homely Ballads* put in the *English Woman's Journal* in 1860, having been "riveted" by its contents after stumbling upon a copy in a circulating library during a downpour of rain, "to test their true worth they should be read aloud at some poor 'Mothers' Sewing Meeting,' or at a Christmas gathering of the poor, by some kindly-hearted reader mentally *en rapport* with the authoress."[65] It was a test that they apparently passed: her poems found a secure place in public readings, both formal and informal, that were allied to programmes of reform. And while we don't have any unmediated working class voices attesting to their love for her poetry, we have plenty of observations from a variety of correspondents that Mary's poems did engage the audience that she most hoped to entertain. Her friend James Fleming noted that when he held a series of penny readings in Bath, the assembled company "liked nothing so well as Mrs Sewell's ballads. They listened with wrapt attention."[66] Another correspondent told Mary, "I am now engaged in reading to the sick and suffering in a Hospital, and I am so delighted with the effect of your poems that I shall circulate as many of your good and excellent books as possible, besides sending them to clergymen for their country parishes."[67]

Sewell also struck a chord with more unexpected audiences. "I may add that your little books are great favourites among seamen," wrote one ship's captain, "I have often been asked to obtain them for different sailors. Some very rough fellows have been greatly impressed for good by our readings."[68] Perhaps most powerfully of all, in the *North British Review* in 1865 a contributor testified to the emotive power of *Mother's Last Words*: "We have seen a class of adult criminals [...] roused, interested, awakened to life, to intelligence, to affection, through the mere reading aloud of this simple story. We have known them follow its course with eager, attentive eyes, with broken exclamations, with sobs, with floods of tears, as if there lay within some spell, with power to restore them, were it but for a moment, to their share in all that is most holy and tender in our common nature."[69] Newspapers from across the country also attest to the embedding of Mary's poetry in assorted communal gatherings. In 1878 in the Norfolk town of Sheringham, for example, a meeting of temperance organization the United Band of Hope was enlivened by "four girls who recited 'Mother's Last Words,' by Mrs, Sewell, which was arranged for the occasion, as a service of song, by Mr. R. Bishop. It greatly interested the audience, and a request was made that it be repeated at the next monthly meeting."[70] Like Longfellow, Mary crossed the Atlantic too. The American Sunday-School Union released an edition of *Mother's Last Words* for its young audience in the 1860s, and a variety of American editions of her poems were in circulation.[71] A New York edition of *Mother's Last Words* from 1863 marveled on the title page, "There have been SEVENTY THOUSAND copies of the following little ballad sold in London in a short time."[72] Elisabeth summarised, "It is interesting to see, what a great variety of people, of all ranks and ages, found a charm in these ballads."[73] As the *Brighton Herald* simply put it, "her works are printed by hundreds of thousands, and have a world of readers not inferior to any poet or poetess of the present day."[74]

***

As rich and as populated as it was, that world did not survive long. Her profound popular charm failed to breach the border of the twentieth century. When Mary's poems have been noticed at all over the last century or so, they have generally been dismissed as a curious adjunct to the legend of *Black Beauty*. To use John Sutherland's term, Mary's works have been classed as "ultra sentimental"—and accordingly ignored.[75] For Susan Chitty, following Mary's own humble self-judgement, Mary was simply "a versifier rather than a poet."[76] Yet what if, to borrow Jane Tompkins' influential words, we stop seeing Mary's popular poetry as "degraded attempts to pander to the prejudices of the multitude" and rather position them as "providing men and women with a means of ordering the world they inhabited"—and perhaps changing that world too. Taken in context, Mary's poems are hardly unusual for their use of sentiment in a period during which popular culture was driven by empathetic sympathy and effusions of emotion. It is no coincidence that the most popular novel of the era—indeed the century—was Harriet Beecher Stowe's anti-slavery novel *Uncle Tom's Cabin* (1851), a text which allied political protest to emotive sympathy just as Mary did. And we might say of Mary's poetry what Tompkins has judged of Stowe's work: "her language had power to move hundreds of thousands of readers in the nineteenth century because they believed in the spiritual elevation of a simple childlike idiom."[77]

Even allowing for the fact that sentiment was the *lingua franca* of Victorian popular culture, and that the cultural currency of tears was profoundly powerful, we must also start to understand that for her contemporaries, Mary's use of sentiment was not what made her ballads noteworthy. Rather, it was their toughness. Their homely framing was disarming; arguably the most perceptive criticism ever directed at Mary's poems can be found in a three word judgment from Elisabeth Boyd Bayly: "They have *claws*."[78] Even more telling was the shocked reaction of Mary's brother John after reading *Homely Ballads* for the first time: "Why, Mary! what company have thee kept?"[79] Her poems were the product of decades of close observation of what it meant to be poor in Victorian Britain. They are, therefore, often vivid in their intimate, grimy details of everyday suffering—like the "desolate room" that Peggy encounters in "A Religious Woman":

> The cinders were cold in the rusty grate,
> As if they had never burn'd;
> The poker and tongs had fallen about,
> The fender was overturn'd.
>
> And pewter pots on the table stood,
> In circles of porter stain;
> And tobacco-ashes, and broken pipes,
> For days might there have lain.
>
> And ragged old bits of carpet and mat
> Were kick'd up here and there;
> A medicine bottle and broken mug
> Were standing upon a chair.

Rarely are Mary's ballads romanticized in their vision of what this suffering looked and felt like. If Mary has a soft spot, it is in her preference for the country over the city, and the past over the present. "In the city," the mother from "The Common" warns her son, "there are quarrels, / Swearing, stealing, care, and want, / Drunken husbands, wretched women, / Children disobedient." In the country, however, all is "peace, and sweet contentment." In "Sixty Years Ago", too, Mary extols the time when the "great mill cities had not risen" and rural labourers apparently thrived on "hardy vigour and on frugal fare." Presumably, not all of her neighbours would have agreed. There are other moments when Mary can seem far away from us in her attitudes—the occasional hints that, ultimately, working people should know their place, obey their masters and mistresses, and wait for their ultimate reward in the next life. "A servant's duty always is / To listen and obey," Mary tells us approvingly in one poem. But at times she can feel chillingly contemporary in her encapsulation of the impossible positions her characters are forced into by poverty, collapsing the distance between Victorian Britain and the present moment. Often, these verses are palpably angry about the lives of ordinary people, and they are campaigning in their desire to make those lives better. But they are also funny, and poignant, and dramatic and even sensational, qualities which leaven the sentiment, piety and moral didacticism. And they are rarely simply pretty. As Elisabeth put it, Mary "had small interest in beauty apart from character. Wild plants in the hedgerows, forcing their way through difficulties, were much more interesting to her than prize specimens at a flower-show."[80] Even Trollope had to admit, after he had dealt out his blows, "Mrs. Sewell must be put in a very different category from that in which we should class the general writers of such little books."[81]

Mary's most powerful poems are concerned with the lives of women trapped in poverty. In both "The Working Woman's Appeal" and "A Sad Story", Mary presents the reader with robust laments from working class women, and it is impossible not to imagine that countless conversations with real women stand behind these verses. They remain shocking in their presentation of a kind of poverty that is all too familiar: high rents, rooms which are "damp and cold", expensive food, little work, pandemic diseases, suspicion and scorn from those better off. The questions posed by the narrator of "A Sad Story" still echo down the years:

> "It passes me to understand
> Why things should go this way;
> Why some folks' life is chained to work,
> And some do nought but play
> [...]
> "Oh! what a little thing would make
> A toil-worn woman glad!—
> But all the round of day and night,
> Is only sad, and sad;
> Shut out of light, and air, and room;
> And pay and victuals bad.

Taken together, they remain—however inevitably mediated by Mary—some of the most vital and unvarnished portraits of Victorian working class women's experiences.

No less moving and evocative is "Crazed", a dramatic monologue from a woman descending into madness because of the pressures of grief and poverty:

> "I do not know—the world is cold;
>   Then stranger people came
>   And took me from my little babes;
>   My brain was turned to flame—
>   And then! I cannot tell you what
>   Of my poor soul became.

Though some noble husbands feature in these verses, Mary is adamant that men are at the root of most of these women's problems—specifically, brutal, drunken men. "Cruel men are wicked," warns the mother in "The Common", neatly summing up the emotional heart of many of these verses. Mary, always campaigning for temperance, pulls no punches when picturing the consequences of their actions. The dying mother in "The Drunkard's Wife" powerfully complains of her abusive husband, "He valued us no more / Than this damp bed of filthy straw, / That lies upon the floor." Yet Mary is also able to inhabit the consciousness of just such a cruel man in "The Guilty Conscience", a haunted, blood-soaked murder ballad that would probably have shocked the likes of Hannah More. "The Drunkards" is equally potent in its examination of the intersections of masculinity, alcohol and violence.

The fate of poor children also occupies Mary's attention, never more famously than in *Mother's Last Words*, an account of what happens to two boys left alone in London after the death of their mother. There is—as there often is in these poems—a Dickensian quality to the boys' attempts to scratch a living as crossing sweepers in London; inevitably, their efforts evoke the figure of Jo from *Bleak House* (1852-3) who, "Knows a broom's a broom, and knows it's wicked to tell a lie."[82] But Mary's poem also prefigures the kind of stories made wildly popular by American author Horatio Alger after the publication of *Ragged Dick* in 1867—another story of street children attempting to make their lives better in the face of apparently insurmountable odds, sustained by faith and good character.

Mary not only wrote about children, she also wrote verses explicitly aimed at them. Indeed, *The Children of Summerbrook*—included here in its entirety—is one of Mary's most stylistically innovative publications, since it is a verse-novel for younger readers. The verse-novel was, as Stefanie Markovits has explored, "a distinctively Victorian literary form." Poets as diverse as Elizabeth Barrett Browning (*Aurora Leigh*, 1856) and Coventry Patmore (*The Angel in the House*, 1854-1862) had helped to popularise this style of long narrative poem which, as Markovits elucidates, was a stylistically "mixed form" which often attempted "to resolve tensions between the novelistic (present, objective, real) and the poetic (past, subjective, ideal)."[83] For Mary to shape a verse-novel about the lives and experiences of a group of children in a village in the Sussex Downs across the changing seasons—to imbue those quotidian lives and experiences with a touch of the heroic suggested by her choice of poetic form—was one of her many quietly radical and unrecognised literary gestures in these poems. The *Brighton Herald* rightly dubbed it "quite a child's epic."[84]

For those who are interested to think about the ways in which Mary's poems might prefigure the concerns of *Black Beauty*, it is immediately evident that Mary's circle of sympathy also extended to animals. The unthinking boys who commit acts of animal cruelty in some of these poems, particularly "The Chaffinch's Nest", Mary clearly suggests, will grow up to become the destructive drunken men who populate many of her other poems. Yet those animals are also empowered to talk to us in these verses: alongside the chaffinches, dogs, bees and spiders are able to speak. The birds in "The Boy and the Rook" particularly upbraid the behaviour of humans, finding them "far beneath ourselves" because "they are so mean." *Black Beauty* fans may also find it tantalizing that in "Abel Howard and his Family", young Tom Howard is praised by a groom searching for an apprentice in ways that seem to anticipate the attitudes of Black Beauty's friend John Manly in Anna Sewell's novel:

A better lad I ne'er set eyes upon.
[...]
The very horses are so fond of him.

I've mark'd it scores of times, and found it suit,
And judge a boy as he will treat a brute.
Suppose I see him speak a pony fair,
Rubbing his nose, and stroking down his hair,
Driving the sheep, and keeping back the dog,
Feeling a man although he does not flog,
Walking with patient step behind the cows,
Leaving a donkey quietly to browse;
I'd trust that boy to have a kindly heart,
And that of men, I think, the better part.

Women, children, animals; faith, temperance, charity, hope: Mary's overarching vision in these poems might be summed up in a line from "The Traveller and the Farmer": "I hate all oppression, and grinding, and strife." Taken together, they give us a remarkable, forgotten portrait of everyday Victorian life, and a compelling window into a lost dimension of Victorian popular culture. At times, their ability to move readers remains undiminished. And we should also appreciate that there is another quiet radicalism at work in these verses. In opposition to a culture dominated by a Gradgrindian devotion to facts and austerity and bare utility, Mary made the case that literary pleasure had a role to play in the lives of the poor—not as a wasteful luxury, but as a vital necessity. The *London Sun* recognised the importance of this aspect of Mary's work in 1861, in a review of *Stories in Verse*. Her "most excellent" poems charted a course between those who felt that charity was simply a "pound, shilling, and pence affair" and those who "inundate the dwellings of poverty with tracts, filled with terrible denunciations against sinners." Mary, however, understood that the poor were "fellow-creatures with faculties to cultivate," and accordingly addressed them "in a friendly spirit."[85] Even today, as libraries close, books are banned and literacy rates fall, such arguments can feel revolutionary.

***

After a sojourn in Bath, in 1867, Mary, Anna and Isaac returned to Norfolk after an absence of four decades. Philip's wife had died the year before, and in part the move seems to have been inspired by the desire to help Philip raise the seven children she left behind—at least until he remarried in 1870. They settled into a house at Old Catton, not far from Norwich, surrounded by assorted relatives. In Mary Bayly's words, "It was the last move; the little white house became the home of seventeen years [...] all who went there cherished the memory of its graceful, heartfelt hospitalities."[86] As ever, Mary and Anna busied themselves with a variety of good works amongst local women and children, temperance activities, and a close familial involvement in the Reformatory for Juvenile Offenders based at Buxton. A fragmentary diary kept by Anna gives a sense of their busy domestic life and work in this period:

August 9.—Mrs. Riches' class of thirty girls came to tea.

Sept 1.—We gave a tea and frolic to thirty-four children, Miss H.'s Band of Hope [...]

Sept. 13—Mother's Sun Lane Infants (50) had tea and play [...]

Nov. 6.—Mother's Sun Lane School was inspected by Mr. S. The week previous she went every day, and since then goes one day each week, taking her dinner at Mrs. A——'s. She is trying a new plan of teaching to read without spelling, but making words with loose letters. She is also making clothes for the R——'s. Little Caroline R. comes three days a week. Mother gives her two lessons a day.

Nov. 11.—Mother also began a class for the girls of Miss H.'s Band of Hope on Saturday mornings every other week.

Jan. 1, 1872.—Mother went, with our children, to St. Faith's Union, and gave toys and presents [...]

Jan. 26.—I am quite poorly with pain.[87]

As that last entry suggests, Anna's health deteriorated markedly in the 1870s, as did Isaac's. By 1871, Anna was housebound. And so she began a new endeavour: "I am writing the life of a horse," she noted in her diary on November 6 1871—and the rest is history.[88] Over the next six years, Mary would prove to be as intrinsic to *Black Beauty*'s composition as Anna had been to her mother's poetry: Mary took dictation when Anna was too weak to write herself; and it would be Mary's publisher, Jarrold and Sons, who would eventually release Anna's book in late November 1877. The publication of *Black Beauty* was a world-changing moment, an extraordinary literary legacy for Anna—and her mother—that would stretch into the twenty-first century. But for Mary, its appearance was merely a prelude to far more profound changes in her own world. Having nursed them both for many years, Anna, her "jewel", died in April 1878, and Isaac died in November.[89]

Mary remained unbowed in the face of grief. Elisabeth Bayly visited her around this time: "The world was going on," she wrote to her mother about their mutual friend: "she was intensely interested in it, and wanted to live, and see what would happen next."[90] Another close friend remembered her last visit to see Mary in Old Catton in 1882 and, at the age of 85, found her "brave spirit" equally "unabated": "The main business of her life still lay among the poor, the down-trodden, the neglected, and she discussed plans of amelioration with all her old ardour, though with less of sanguine expectation."[91] Mary's letters amplify that, even in the weeks before her death, she remained deeply interested and engaged with the world's problems—and equally committed to their improvement. She worried about the state of "the slums of Norwich", the downturn in the shoemaking industry, the state of local schools. She was reading an "elevating and invigorating" collection of sermons by American clergyman Philiips Brooks, and debating the merits of the political philosophy of another American, the bestselling journalist and campaigner Henry George.[92] Even after a period of illness in the early months of 1884, Mary was still not resigned to leaving the world behind, even though, she noted to a correspondent, "I believe this does not *sound right* at my age, when I ought to be longing to depart." Instead, she felt it was time to begin again, again: "I think I have now started afresh, and there is so much to do, even for the aged, I really grudge to be idle." To Mary, "life and thought and action" simply remained "so intense and interesting, and so various."[93] Death, she felt, was "postponable, whilst there is any capacity left to help or comfort anyone." On June 10th 1884, she could postpone it no longer.

The *Norwich Mercury* wrote, "Though widely known for her literary efforts, she was much more beloved and honoured in the sphere in which she moved, for her kind unostentatious and effective exercise of those strong feelings of philanthropy and charity to the poor, which were perhaps the most powerful elements of her being."[94] Mary Bayly went to visit her friend's grave on a bright November day later that year. Standing before Isaac and Anna and Mary, she found the air "wonderfully soft and genial"; she listened to the robins sing "as if there was no such thing in the world as death."[95]

What would Mary Sewell be doing in the twenty-first century? Unquestionably, she would be helping those who needed her help. She might be saddened that the issues which were besetting the world in the 1850s were, mostly, still with us today—"I am so very anxious about the state of our country," she lamented just before her death, and would undoubtedly have cause to lament again, "one cannot help believing there is much amiss, much that needs alteration."[96] But she wouldn't pause long for lamentations. She would undoubtedly be running foodbanks, supporting refugees, helping neglected animals—and maybe even writing poetry about the lamentable state of the country. After Mary's death, one of her surviving childhood friends tried to articulate her sense of loss: "It was pre-eminently in the little things of life, the small everyday troubles and difficulties and pleasures, that the thought would occur, 'Oh! if I could only tell Mrs. Sewell this!' [...] And so she is an everyday loss; and while we feel the world is poorer since she has been taken, we still feel ourselves the richer for having known her and claimed her as a friend."[97] Today, our sense of so many things—Victorian popular literature, the lives of the poor in the middle of the nineteenth century, Norfolk's cultural heritage, the literary apprenticeship of Anna Sewell, and much more besides—will be richer for the rediscovery of the extraordinary Mary Sewell.

Endnotes

1   "G.M.A.", "'Fruit in Old Age': Gleanings from the Life and Writing of Mary Sewell", *Wesleyan-Methodist Magazine* (December 1889), 892–902, 892–3.

2   Mrs [Mary] Bayly, *The Life and Letters of Mrs Sewell* (London: James Nisbet & Co., 1890), 170.

3   Bayly, *Life and Letters*, 1–2.

4   Bayly, *Life and Letters*, v.

5   Elizabeth Boyd Bayly, "Mary Sewell", *The Sunday Magazine* (September 1885), 562–566, 562.

6   "Stories in Verse", *John Bull*, January 26 1861, 12.

7   Bayly, *Life and Letters*, v.

8   Mrs. Sewell, *Poems and Ballads* (London: Jarrold & Sons, 1886), 2 volumes.

9   Susan Chitty, *The Woman Who Wrote* Black Beauty*: A Life of Anna Sewell* (London: Hodder and Stoughton, 1971); Adrienne Gavin, *Dark Horse: A Life of Anna Sewell* (Thrupp, Gloucestershire: Sutton Publishing Limited, 2004); Celia Brayshire, *Writing* Black Beauty*: Anna Sewell and the Story of Animal Rights* (Cheltenham: The History Press, 2023).

10 Unless otherwise noted, all of the quotations in this account of Mary's early life are taken from the autobiographical reminiscences that she recorded for her grandchildren in the last years of her life. Reprinted in Mrs [Mary] Bayly, *The Life and Letters of Mrs Sewell* (London: James Nisbet & Co., 1890), 1–76.

11 Bayly, *Life and Letters*, 17.

12 *Norfolk Chronicle*, April 5 1817, 2.

13 Mrs Sewell, *'Thy Poor Brother': Letters to a Friend on Helping the Poor* (London: Jarrold and Sons, 1863), 138–9.

14 See Marjorie Moon, *John Harris's Books for Youth, 1801–1843* (Cambridge: Published for the author by Five Owls Press and sold by Alan Spilman, 1976), 133.

15 [Mary Sewell], *Walks With Mamma* (London: Grant and Griffith, no date), 37–38.

16 [Elizabeth Gaskell], *Cranford* (London: Chapman and Hall, 1855), 1–2.

17 Elisabeth Boyd Bayly, "Mary Sewell", 565.

18 Mrs Sewell, *'Thy Poor Brother': Letters to a Friend on Helping the Poor* (London: Jarrold and Sons, 1863), 16.

19 Sewell, 'Thy Poor Brother', 18–19.
20 Sewell, 'Thy Poor Brother', 131–2.
21 Sewell, 'Thy Poor Brother', 96.
22 Bayly, Life and Letters, 127.
23 Bayly, Life and Letters, 129.
24 Bayly, Life and Letters, 129.
25 Bayly, Life and Letters, 143.
26 Bayly, Life and Letters, 133.
27 Bayly, Life and Letters, 164–5.
28 Bayly, Life and Letters, 131.
29 Bayly, Life and Letters, 147.
30 See David Reynolds, Mightier Than the Sword: Uncle Tom's Cabin and the Battle for America (New York: W. W. Norton & Company, 2011), 33–4.
31 Bayly, Life and Letters, 136.
32 Patricia Fumerton and Anita Gerrini, "Introduction: Straws in the Wind", in Patricia Fumerton and Anita Guerrini eds, Ballads and Broadsides in Britain, 1500–1800 (New York: Routledge, 2017), 1–12, 1–2.
33 Robin Ganev, Songs of Protest, Songs of Love: Popular Ballads in Eighteenth-Century Britain (Manchester: Manchester University Press, 2010), 3.
34 Peter Jimack, "England and France in 1798" in Richard Cronin ed, 1798: The Year of the Lyrical Ballads (London: Macmillan Press, 1998), 151–169, 167.
35 [Walter Scott], Minstrelsy of the Scottish Border (Edinburgh: James Ballantyne, 1803), 3 vols, 1: cxvi, cxxv.
36 [Samuel Taylor Coleridge and William Wordswoth], Lyrical Ballads, with A Few Other Poems (London: J. & A. Arch, 1798), i.
37 Quoted in David Stoker, "Street Literature in England at the End of the Long Eighteenth Century" in David Atkinson and Steve Roud eds, Street Literature of the Long Nineteenth Century: Producers, Sellers, Consumers (Cambridge Scholars Publishing, 2017), 60–98, 92.
38 [Hannah More], The Hackney Coachman; or, The Way to Get a Good Fare (London: J. Marshall, 1796) 1, 5–6.
39 Bayly, Life and Letters, 336.
40 Bayly, Life and Letters, 137.
41 Bayly, Life and Letters, 300.
42 Bayly, Life and Letters, 133.
43 Elisabeth Boyd Bayly, "Mary Sewell", 566.
44 Bayly, Life and Letters, 133.
45 Bayly, Life and Letters, 248.
46 Bayly, Life and Letters, 132.
47 "Short Notices", The Literary Gazette, October 2 1858, 432.
48 "Literature", The London Sun, November 15 1858, 2.
49 "Literature", The Morning Post, October 9 1858, 3.
50 Quoted in Gavin, Dark Horse, 133.
51 Gavin, Dark Horse, 133.
52 "Mrs. Sewell's Popular Ballads", Norfolk News, February 8 1862, 6.
53 "Brief Notices", The Nonconformist, September 17 1862, 19.
54 Sewell, 'Thy Poor Brother', iii.
55 Mary Sewell, An Appeal to Englishwomen (London: Jarrold and Sons, 1863), 1.
56 "Literary Jottings", Norwich Mercury, December 15 1883, 3.
57 Mary Sewell, Homely Ballads for the Working Man's Fireside (London: Smith, Elder and Co., 1858), n.p.

58 Anthony Trollope, "The Rose of Cheriton, by Mrs Sewell", *The Fortnightly Review* (February 1867) 252–255, 253.

59 Florence S. Boos, *Working-Class Women Poets in Victorian Britain: An Anthology* (Peterborough, Ontario: Broadview Press, 2008), 13–15.

60 Bayly, *Life and Letters*, 146.

61 See Richard D. Altick, *The English Common Reader: A Social History of the Mass Reading Public, 1800–1900* (Columbus: Ohio State University Press, 1998 (1957)), 386–7.

62 Bayly, *Life and Letters*, 146–7.

63 Quoted in Amy Cruse, *The Victorians and Their Books* (London: George Allen & Unwin, 1935), 242.

64 Altick, *English Common Reader*, 387.

65 "Specimens of 'Homely Ballads'", *English Woman's Journal* (March 1860), 56–59, 58.

66 Bayly, *Life and Letters*, 332.

67 Bayly, *Life and Letters*, 161.

68 Bayly, *Life and Letters*, 149.

69 "Popular Religious Literature", *North British Review* (June 1865), 413–426, 415.

70 "Lower Sherringham", *Norwich Mercury*, June 1 1878, 6.

71 *Mother's Last Words* (Philadelphia: American Sunday-School Union, 1860(?)). The American Antiquarian Society, for example, holds at least five American editions of her books.

72 Mrs. Sewell, *Mother's Last Words, and Our Father's Care* (New York: Robert Carter & Brothers, 1862).

73 Bayly, *Life and Letters*, 147.

74 "Mrs. Sewell's Poetry", *Brighton Herald*, June 7 1862, 4.

75 John Sutherland, *The Stanford Companion to Victorian Fiction* (Stanford: Stanford University Press, 1989), 566.

76 Chitty, *A Life of Anna Sewell*, 129.

77 Jane Tompkins, *Sensation Designs: The Cultural Work of American Fiction, 1790–1860* (New York: Oxford University Press, 1985), xii-xiii, xviii.

78 Bayly, *Life and Letters*, 147.

79 Bayly, *Life and Letters*, 135.

80 Bayly, *Life and Letters*, 141.

81 Trollope, "Rose of Cheriton", 253.

82 Charles Dickens, *Bleak House* (London: Bradbury & Evans, 1853), 104.

83 Stefanie Markovits, *The Victorian Verse-Novel: Aspiring to Life* (New York: Oxford University Press, 2017), 2, 7.

84 "Mrs. Sewell's Poetry", *Brighton Herald*, June 7 1862, 4.

85 "*Stories in Verse*", *London Sun*, January 21 1861, 6.

86 Bayly, *Life and Letters*, 206, 217

87 Bayly, *Life and Letters*, 236.

88 Bayly, *Life and Letters*, 271.

89 Bayly, *Life and Letters*, 281.

90 Bayly, *Life and Letters*, 288.

91 Bayly, *Life and Letters*, 173.

92 Bayly, *Life and Letters*, 327–329.

93 Bayly, *Life and Letters*, 327.

94 "Death of Mrs Sewell", *Norwich Mercury*, June 18 1884, 2.

95 Bayly, *Life and Letters*, 334.

96 Bayly, *Life and Letters*, 329.

97 Bayly, *Life and Letters*, 221.

homely
ballads
and
stories
in
verse

HOMELY BALLADS

FOR THE

WORKING MAN'S FIRESIDE.

BY MARY SEWELL.

FIFTH THOUSAND.

LONDON:

SMITH, ELDER AND CO., 65, CORNHILL.

1858.

Faith, Hope, and Charity.

A GALLANT ship went out to sea
From Scotland's rocky shore,
And with her sail'd one hundred men
To dig for golden ore.

The anchor rose, the sails were set,
And steady blew the breeze;
And merrily the vessel went
Across the tossing seas.

From morn till night her course she
  kept,
The land was still in view,
And passengers upon the deck
Oft sigh'd a long adieu.

The second day was at an end,
And night came slowly down;
But still upon the distant coast
They saw a lighted town.

Then darkness settled on the ship,
And o'er the ocean crept,
And, ere the middle of the night,
All, but the seamen, slept.

Oh! many went to sleep that night,
On whom no morn shall rise;
And many closed their eyelids then,
To waken in the skies.

And many hearts beat true and warm,
For those they ne'er would save;
And many hopes were buried then,
Beneath the green sea wave.

A heavy fog came stealing down,
And o'er the waters spread,
So thick, the steersman scarce could
  see
A dozen yards ahead.

There was a moment, and no more,
No warning cross'd the sea,—
An Indiaman, with crowded sails,
Bore down upon their lee.

No time to tack, to give her room,
No time to wake the men;
The mighty vessel ran them down,
Then bore away again.

The eddying waves closed o'er the
  wreck,
Then roll'd on as before;
And that ship's company went down,
To sail the sea no more.

A fisherman upon the beach,
At early break of day,
Observed an object on the tide,
That roll'd within the bay.

'Twas not the seaweed's heavy mass
Which clogg'd the billow's swell;
'Twas not the wood of rifted wreck,
That floated on so well.

The fisherman strode boldly in,
And, ere it reach'd the strand,
He seized upon a floating form,
And bore it to the land.

It was a child—a little girl—
Of some ten years or more,
That here the cold, remorseless wave
Was casting on the shore.

And pitiful the look he bent
On that young form so fair;
And tenderly he wiped the face,
And wrung the heavy hair.

"I'll take her home to Margaret,
And see what she can do;
If life is in the body yet,
She's sure to bring it to."

Within his dwelling on the beach
He laid the body down;
And every means the good wife used,
That she had heard, or known.

The youthful limbs were barely hid
By clothing for the night;
And heavy lay the closed lids
On eyes, that once were bright.

The soft round cheek was cold and
    blue,
That erst was like the rose
That opens in the early dew,
When morning zephyr blows.

The sweet young mouth was tightly
    closed,
As if 'twere closed in pain;
Oh! will the warm blood ever tinge
Those livid lips again?

But Margaret's patience wearied not,
She feels the warmth return,
The little heart begins to move,
The breath she can discern.

And do we say—"Thy cares forego,
And let the floweret die,
The tender bud, though blighted now,
Will blossom in the sky.

"The storms of life may beat it down,
And sin may yet prevail;
Or poverty, with cruel hand,
May crush that flower so frail.

"Oh, let it die!" but so said not
The heart of Margaret;
Her cheerful hope, like jewel bright
In simple faith was set.

Life was to her a sacred gift,
A high and priceless thing,
To which the blessed Son of God,
Did free salvation bring.

That grace came not to her in vain;
She heard the heavenly voice,
That often now within her soul,
Said, "Margaret, rejoice!"

The living stream that heal'd her heart,
Descending from above,
Left not a barren soil behind,
But rich in fruits of love.

The weeping stranger told her tale
To no unfeeling ear;
Her little brothers all were drown'd,
And both her parents dear.

And she had no relations left,
Now they were in the sea;
They all had left their pleasant homes
Upon the banks of Dee.

"Fear not, my lamb," said Margaret,
 "I will your mother be,
And you shall be as merry here
As on the banks of Dee.

"Here's Marianne, and Isabel,
And John, and little Jane;
And you shall be their sister dear,
And think 'tis home again."

The little orphan raised her lips
To kiss good Margaret's cheek;
But grief lay heavy on her heart,
And words she could not speak.

But ere a many weeks had flown,
Her sorrow died away,
And little Jessie sang as blythe
As merry birds in May.

Down to the fisher's lowly cot
The busy neighbours came
"If you take in that friendless child,
I think you'll be to blame.

"I'd send it to the Union-house,
And there I'd let her be."
Said Margaret, "The Lord has sent
That little one to me.

"I should not, of myself, have thought
A thing like this to do;
But if God laid it out for me,
Why, he will bring me through."

"You know," another kindly said,
"You have already four;
And though you're decent, honest folks,
Still you are reckon'd poor."

"And we are poor, and very poor,
I know," said Margaret;
"But God can show my husband where
To cast his fishing-net.

"For He, who made the fish, you know,
Can guide them as they swim;
The widow, and the orphan child
Hold promises from Him."

"Well, you must please yourself, of
    course;
But, in my humble thought,
You're taking on yourselves more care
Than working-people ought."

"It may be so—I know," she said,
"But still I am content;
I have a feeling in my mind
That we shall not repent.

"If your sweet darling, little Bell,
Should ever have the lot
To be shipwreck'd and cast away,
And no friend near the spot,

"Would you not bless with all your heart
The man who took her in,
And made a father's home for her
In this sad world of sin?

"Well, neighbour, that is very true,
It makes my feelings stir,
To think that such a cruel fate
Could ever come to her.

"No doubt the gentlefolks would help
If you would state the case;
She is an interesting child,
And has a pretty face."

A cloud pass'd over Margaret's brow,
But still her voice was kind—
"I'd rather not ask charity,
It always hurts my mind.

"And 'twill be time to think of that,
If we should get too poor;
I think that He will bring her bread,
Who brought her to our door."

And so the neighbours went away,
And many shook their head;
They said she was a feeling soul,
But woefully misled.

And Margaret—she sat down to read
The book that gave her light,
And, as she read, she strongly felt
That she was doing right.

In fact, it seem'd as clear to her
As noonday in the sun,
That they would ne'er repent the thing,
Which they in faith had done.

The fishing-boat went out to sea,
The fishing-boat came back,
And whichsoever way it went,
The fish were in its track.

When raging tempests roused the sea,
And sailors found their graves,
Unharm'd the little fishing-boat
Lay rocking in the waves.

For He who walk'd upon the sea,
And chose His dearest friends
From poor and lowly fishermen,
The fishing-boat defends;

No harm can ever touch the thing
Committed to His care,
Nor can a million voices drown
The voice of earnest prayer.

And He repaid the simple trust
Of faithful Margaret,
And daily taught her husband where
To cast the fishing-net.

The fishing-boat went out to sea,
The fishing-boat came back,
And whichsoever way it went,
The fish were in its track.

And when with heavy-laden nets
It reached the yellow sand,
An active little party hail'd
The fishing-boat to land.

To fill a basket or a pan
The busy children strive,
Then through the streets and in the
  squares
They cry them "all alive."

And so the years flew quickly by
Till Jessie was sixteen;
A sweeter little maiden then
You hardly could have seen.

Both Marianne and Isabel
Were married *well* and gone;
And Jessie now, with little Jane,
Did all the work alone.

"'Tis early yet," said Margaret,
"Come, set your basket down;"
For Jessie then had boil'd some
  shrimps
To carry to the town.

"'Tis on my mind, dear child," she said,
"I can't the reason give;
But something often says to me,
I have not long to live.

"Nay, Jessie, do not turn so pale,
You'll always have a friend;
I think that people need not want
Who straight on God depend.

50

"And I believe they need not beg,
If only they would try;
I'd rather want a thing myself,
Than ask for charity.

"I would not have my children beg
For all that I could see;
We've always held our heads above
That sort of poverty.

"And mind me now, it is six years,
If not a little more,
Since you were brought a senseless
  corpse
Unto this very door.

"And we have never known the day
When we have wanted bread;
Nor decent clothes to cover us,
Nor shelter for our head.

"And you are almost all grown up,
And with an honest name;
Oh, Jessie! I should die at once
If you should come to shame.

"I'm frightened now, to see the girls
That walk about the street;
Oh! God forbid a child of mine
Should look like those I meet.

"I often quake for you, my dear,
The others all are plain;
But you have got that pretty face,
That makes men look again.

"And some who're reckon'd gentlemen
I know will notice you,
And many pretty things they'll say,
They never mean for true.

"I'd rather you
should meet a bear
That's just robb'd of her young,
Than you should meet a gentleman
Who has a flattering tongue.

"Be sure they never mean you good,
'Tis only sport, or worse;
And, as you'd save yourself, don't touch
A penny from their purse."

A glow of modesty and pride
Rush'd into Jessie's cheek,
And feeling quiver'd on her lip
As she began to speak.

"Dear mother! you may trust me well,
Such thing shall never be;
No saucy gentleman I know
Shall ever speak to me.

"What business have they to insult
A girl because she's poor?
No! mother, I will never bring
Dishonour to your door.

"Beside, I've found out *this* myself,
And I believe 'tis true—
That if *you* mind what you're about,
They'll mind their business too."

"And, Jessie—John has whisper'd me
That you must be his wife,
And he's a gentleman in heart,
And loves you like his life.

"Of course 'twill be a long while first,
You both are very young;
But if you love each other well,
The time will not seem long."

"Ah, mother! John is just like you,
He is so true and good,
And steady, like his father too,
I think 'tis in the blood."

Then Margaret kiss'd the pretty face
That looked in hers, and smiled,
"Ah, little puss! I see one day
You'll be my very child.

"But, Jessie dear, still have a care,
For woman's heart is weak."
And tears rose up in Margaret's eyes,
And trickled down her cheek.

A few short months—and suddenly
There came the hand of death,—
"God bless you all, and keep you his,"
Was Margaret's latest breath.

Then did her happy ransom'd soul
Arise on joyful wing,
To dwell before her Saviour's throne,
Where blessed angels sing.

No stately hearse with nodding plumes,
Nor mutes for mourning paid,
Were seen around the humble grave,
Where Margaret was laid.

A dozen hardy fishermen,
With weatherbeaten face,
Bore that dear body tenderly
To its last resting-place.

And many join'd the weeping train
That stood around it there,
And many were the stiffled sobs
That shook the quiet air;

For she was gone, whose life had been
A constant flow of love,
And they would see her face no more
Until they met above.

Then Jessie kept the good man's
    house,
And shared his heavy grief,
Till time and resignation brought
To both of them relief.

And when two years had pass'd away
In honour of the dead,
Her lover thought the time was come,
When they might safely wed.

He was his father's partner now,
They had a busy trade;
And many times he counted up
The earnings he had made.

The old man gave the bride away,
And gave the wedding treat,
And, kissing Jessie, said, "She'll be
Another Margaret."

"Ay, that she will," said John; "she'll be
My mother to the life,
And folks will say my pretty bride
Is like my father's wife."

—

Now, parents dear, who read this tale,
Work on with love and prayer;
And children's children yet may live
To bless your faithful care.

And shut not up your charity,
Let pity have its way;
'Tis God you lend your service to,
And He will richly pay.

The fishing-boat shall go to sea,
The fishing-boat come back;
And Providence shall guide the boat,
And fish be in its track.

The Funeral Bell.

ALAS, for the village! alas, for the day!
The church bell is tolling a funeral knell,
Adam Hope from the parish is taken away,
And a sorrowful sound has the funeral bell.

Oh! toll for him—toll for him, funeral bell!
Fall sad on the heart, as you fall on the ear;
Good neighbour, good master, good christian—farewell!
Good husband, good father—in glory appear!

Oh! what will become of the destitute poor?
He was eyes to the blind, he was feet to the lame;
To the fatherless orphan he open'd his door,
And the widow's heart sung at the sound of his name.

He put down oppression, he righted the wrong,
The cause of the helpless, he made it his own;
He wrested the weak from the grasp of the strong;
His conduct was led by his conscience alone.

He hated those questions, so paltry and low—
How *much* must I give? or how *little* will do?
True charity taught him how much to bestow,
He lived for the many, and not for the few.

He delighted to show his devotion and love;
He hated pretence, as the hypocrite's mask;
His soul, full of gratitude, mounted above,
And "What shall I render?" he often would ask.

His heart was at rest; he was blessed indeed,
The love of the Poor, lay as dew on his head;
He spared of his comforts the hungry to feed,
And he, from the storehouse of heaven was fed.

Good measure, press'd down, to his bosom return'd,
Well shaken, o'erflowing, till room there was none;
Whilst brighter and brighter his light ever burn'd,
Then sunk like the glow of the evening sun,

To rise, where the faithful, apparell'd in white,
Stand round by the throne of their Saviour and King;
To work in His service with growing delight,
Whilst the waves of eternity circle and sing.

But toll for him—toll for him, funeral bell!
Fall sad on the heart, as you fall on the ear;
Good neighbour, good master, good christian—farewell!
Good husband, good father—in glory appear!

The Miller's Wife.

YOUNG Annie Smith was dairymaid
At Brookland on the hill;
The pretty farm that lies above
Old Jacob Slater's mill.

A sweeter girl than Annie Smith
Ne'er sung beside a cow;
Her cheeks were like the morn itself,
Or damask rose in blow.

Her shining hair, as black as jet,
Was fasten'd close and tight;
Her dress it fitted prettily,
Her cap was snowy white.

She was a bonny little lass
As e'er you'd look upon;
No wonder, then, she stole the heart
Of Slater's miller, John.

He went past Brookland every day,
It was the thoroughfare,
And always had a pleasant word
To say, if Anne was there.

'Twas long before she heeded much
The words he had to say;
And, if he loiter'd by the door,
She blush'd and went away.

But perseverance will prevail
Where all is right and fair,
And she became his happy bride,
His weal and woe to share.

Her mistress said she would repent,
She'd know the difference soon;
But Annie said, that "people liked
A dwelling of their own."

No doubt sweet Anne had often thought
That she would some day wed;
So put her money in the bank,
And not upon her head.

She never liked a dashing dress,
Her taste was always neat,
And now her savings help'd to make
Their little home complete.

For she had six or seven pounds,
A mine, her lover thought;
And he had laid some money by,
As every servant ought.

Between them both, with management,
With industry, and skill,
They bought sufficient furniture
Their happy home to fill.

John was the foreman at the mill,
Their cottage was close by;
It lay so handy for his work,
And stood both warm and dry.

It had a plot of ground behind,
A little piece before,
And just a sort of rustic porch
Around the pleasant door.

John made the porch, both he and Anne
Were very fond of flowers,
And work'd together happily
In many leisure hours.

The piece of ground behind the house
He cropp'd with earnest care;
You could not find a foot of earth
Without some planting there.

He left no room for weeds to grow
They could not lift a head
Amongst the rows of cabbages,
Or in the parsnip bed.

Some onions, parsley, thyme, and sage,
Quite charm'd his Annie's eye;
She thought about her soup and stew,
With potherbs savoury.

You really hardly would believe
How many things there were,
That John contrived to cultivate
In his small garden there.

Anne often laugh'd a merry laugh,
And would with triumph say—
"If people had a will to do,
They'd always find a way."

The little garden in the front
Was her especial care,
And soon was full of scented flowers,
That sweeten'd all the air.

She was a little fanciful
About the flowers she set,
And would not have a modern one
Except the mignionette.

She liked old-fashion'd flowers, she said,
That she in childhood knew;
The cabbage rose and gilliflower,
And larkspurs, pink and blue.

The honeysuckle round the porch,
The jasmine on the wall,
The rich clovepink, and ten-week stock,
And lilies, white and tall.

And many little flowers beside
She planted in between;
The hen-and-chicken daisy there
Was always to be seen.

She said 'twas like a family
About their mother's knee—
A pretty little pattern, too,
Of what it ought to be.

But let us now go in with Anne,
To see her table spread,
And there, at once, we shall perceive
A loaf of home-made bread.

John, sometimes, with a laugh would
    say,
That he could make Anne cry,
If he proposed that baker's bread
Should feed their family.

She could not bear to hear it named—
Such poor, unwholesome stuff;
A quartern loaf was eaten up
Before you had enough.

She always found it possible
To get both yeast and flour;
It only wanted management,
The will—it brought the power.

They seldom spent their pence in tea,
She said 'twas little good;
That too much tea shook women's
    nerves,
And also thinn'd the blood.

That was her notion. She and John
Had porridge thick and hot;
It was a hearty, wholesome food,
And cheaper, Annie thought.

Her John had lived in Scotland once,
Amongst the peasants there;
And sometimes all his meals were made
Upon this homely fare.

With such a breakfast, he would say,
He never wanted beer;
Yet not a workman at the mill
With him could strength compare.

His mates would often sneer and laugh,
And tempt him to "a pot;"
But he would let them laugh away,
He scorn'd to be a sot.

Tobacco he would never buy,
But they afforded meat;
And Anne was such a clever cook,
His meals were quite a treat.

When winter came, and nights were long,
They sat beside their fire;
She knitted stockings thick and strong;
He read, at her desire.

The public-house he never tried,
He hated noise and strife;
And loved so well his own fireside,
And his sweet-temper'd wife.

At church, on Sunday, they were seen—
Anne always had been there;
And now, they both together went
Up to the house of prayer.

Anne's mother always counsell'd her
To make the Lord her stay;
"'Tis sunshine with you now, my dear,
But you'll be forced to pray.

"For clouds may gather, one by one,
And you will want a friend;
If you don't know his face before,
'Twill then seem far to send."

Anne always thought her mother was
The pattern of a wife;
And now she tried to copy her
In this sweet married life.

So happily the weeks flew by,
Till just a year was o'er;
And then a little stranger came
To John the miller's door.

There was no peal of merry bells,
No cannon thunder'd loud;
But Annie she was very glad,
And John was very proud.

He said 'twas like his little wife,
So bright its black eyes shone;
But she was sure 'twas just like him—
Her own good husband, John.

But let that pass. The baby grew,
And soon could crow and pull;
It must be own'd the mother thought
Her child was wonderful!

He ran about at ten months old,
And soon could lisp her name;
And all the babies of his age
He fairly put to shame.

Oh, Anne! your mother told you true,
That clouds would gather soon;
And we must see the shade of night
Pass over Annie's noon.

There came a gentle angel down
From heaven's shining bowers,
To take the precious little one
From this cold world of ours.

Her own sweet darling pet, she thought,
It must get well again;
But fever parch'd its burning lips,
Its head was full of pain.

All night she watch'd beside its bed,
The owl went hooting by;
And, ere the early morning red,
The lark was in the sky.

She could not hear the skylark sing,
Nor see the rising sun;
Her heart was with the little one,
Whose day was nearly done.

A shade is passing o'er his cheek;
The sun begins to rise;
It shines upon the window pane,
But death has closed his eyes.

She wept there long and bitterly;
Her heart was stricken through
To see her little flower escape,
Like early morning dew.

She smooth'd his glossy ringlets down,
As smiling there he lay;
She kiss'd the little waxen cheek,
And then knelt down to pray.

And peace came back to Anne again,
Yet long it was before
She could forget the little step
That trotted round her door.

And often, on the Sabbath eve,
She went with John to see
The swelling mound of grassy turf
Beneath the churchyard tree.

She planted there the primrose pale,
And daisies pink and white,
To make her little angel's bed
Look beautiful and bright.

But soon another baby came,
And very soon another;
And now the parents saw, with pride,
A sister and a brother.

And they were fed on porridge too,
Anne firmly stood to that;
And certainly the children grew
Exceeding fair and fat.

She did not stuff their little mouths
With cakes and lumps of meat;
She said that porridge was the thing
That children ought to eat.

How many pence they saved by thrift
Was more than they could say;
But money in the Savings Bank
John weekly put away.

'Twas well he did: we do not know
When want is drawing nigh;
With Anne, it was the washing-day,
Her clothes were out to dry.

"They'll soon be dry, the wind is up,
They'll get a famous blow;"
She liked to see her linen look
As white as driven snow.

Then in she ran, and soon the soup
Was made, with right good-will;
"It is so good to-day," she said,
"He'll smell it at the mill."

She hears a groan, a shuffling tread,
And people talking low;
And to the cottage door she flew,
Like arrow from a bow.

Upon a door they bore a man,
His face was ashy pale;
It needed not that any one
Should tell poor Anne the tale.

She saw her husband's leg was broke
In working at the mill.
The doctor came and set it right,
And told him to lie still.

John's master was a careless man;
He quite forgot the case,
When he had found another hand
To take his foreman's place.

Bear up, dear hearts! though selfish men
May pass you coldly by,
You have a Friend omnipotent,
Who can your wants supply.

Fail not yourselves—He will not fail;
It is most true, indeed,
That God delighteth every day
His little ones to feed.

Don't think it is a barren form
To supplicate and pray;
There never was an humble soul,
Unpitied, sent away.

God has the world in his control,
With all its stores of gold;
He sends it forth, a flowing stream,
In ways that can't be told.

The needy poor for water seek,
Their tongue with thirst is dry;
He opens in the wilderness
A fountain for supply.

Cheer up, dear hearts! the Lord is near,
And do not be afraid-
But calmly trust His providence,
And prove what he has said.

It was the time of trouble now,
Poor Anne was sorely tried;
With wages stopp'd, and garden waste,
And food to be supplied.

And John, poor man! he could not help
Sometimes to fret and mope;
But Anne had ever cheerful words
To keep alive his hope.

It would have been an easy thing,
When she was tired out,
To slap and scold the little ones,
Who ran and scream'd about.

But she could rule her temper well,
A greater feat by far,
Than e'en to take a citadel
That's held by men of war.

She turn'd her hand to every thing,
She still was stout and strong;
Though John, he thought her rosy face
Was getting pale and long.

And she kept up her spirit well,
For she had peace within;
And well knew where to carry all
Her trouble, and her sin.

She often said, within herself,
"What shall we do to-morrow?"
But when the day was fairly come,
She did not beg nor borrow.

The quiet stream of Providence
Kept flowing on—and on;
'Twas often Anne's astonishment,
And wonderful to John,

It is so easy to forget
That God a father is,
Who loves his children, better far
Than earthly parent his.

The money in the Savings Bank
Had all been taken out;
And John upon a crutch and stick
Was hobbling about.

"'Tis no use talking now," said he,
The workhouse is our home;
'Tis long ere I shall work, you see,
And we've to nothing come."

"Oh, John!" said Anne, "though we have
   nought,
Our God is still the same;
Keep up your heart, my husband dear,
We will not come to shame."

She spoke so cheerily to him,
She saw his heart was dull;
But, as she sat alone at work,
Her own was very full.

She read the chapter through and
   through
About the widow's meal;
The little oil, the gather'd sticks,
And thought what she must feel.

"We are not brought so low as that,
Some helper still may come;
It seems to me—(I can't tell why)—
That we shall keep our home."

And so she stitch'd away again,
More briskly than before;
Until she heard her husband's crutch
Move slowly to the door.

For so it fell—that afternoon
Old Slater came along;
"Ah, John!" said he, "I'm glad to see
Your leg is getting strong.

"We want you sadly at the mill,
The men the labour shirk;
I'll give you half your wages now
To overlook the work.

"A foreman's eye about the house,
An honest workman's eye,
Is like a cat before a mouse—
It makes the idlers fly."

John thank'd his master, said he'd
   come,
And then he sought for Anne;
"Well, wife," he said, "thanks be to God,
I'm now another man!

"I think I've learn'd to trust in God—
I think I've learn'd to-day;
I really think, and do believe,
He hears a poor man pray."

He told her how he pray'd with tears,
Still fear'd he pray'd in vain;
Then, how his master came that way,
And gave him work again.

He said, "Dear Anne, you've always
   been
The comfort of my life;
What should I do without you now,
My precious little wife!

"'Twas you that kept my spirits up,
'Twas you kept bed and board;"
But Annie kiss'd his cheek, and said,
"Dear John! it was the Lord."

—

Poor women! in this world of toil
Keep up your hearts with prayer;
Still trust in God, and do your best—
You never need despair.

Abel Howard and his Family.

"I'm thinking, cook," 'twas thus a lady said
To an old servant, kneading up some bread,
"That I should like a steady girl to take,
To do the dairy work, and help to bake;
Your work is heavy, and the house is large,
And you have many duties to discharge;
I would on no account impose on you
More work than you can comfortably do;
But, really now, 'tis difficult to find
A girl brought up according to one's mind;
They are so flighty and so fond of dress,
So idle, forward, and discretionless!
There are exceptions to the rule, no doubt,
That only need some pains to find them out:
Perhaps you know a girl you would prefer,
Whose parents bear an honest character."

"I thank you, ma'am," the careful Phebe said,
And cover'd up the rising mass of bread;
"What you have said of girls is very just,
And more's the pity—that you cannot trust
One, out of twenty; if you are away
They're sure to be in mischief, or at play.
I can't tell what folks think of now-a-days,
To use their children to such shiftless ways!
It wasn't so, I know, when I was young:
I had to work betimes, and hold my tongue,
And mind my parents, and my betters too,
But that old-fashioned way is something new
To our great boys and girls, who seem to rule
As soon as they have left the village school.
But there is Mrs. Howard, down the lane,
You could not find a better girl than Jane,
She'll make a servant to your very mind!
But then her parents aren't the common kind,
As one might say: their children do not run

Before the work of teaching is begun.
I'm sure 'tis quite a pleasure now to see
Such an industrious happy family;
On Sunday morn it really is a sight
To see them all at church, so clean and bright!
The baby's quite a pattern to the rest,
Upon its mother's lap so neatly dress'd!
I've watch'd it many a time, the pretty elf,
And found the child a sermon to myself.
I think you might go far, and seek in vain,
Before you found a better girl than Jane;
So modest—cleanly—quiet as a mouse!
The girl would be a credit to the house."
"We'll try her, Phebe, and I've little doubt
You'll make a cook of her, quite out and out."

—

"John," said his master to a faithful groom
Cleaning a stall out with his stable broom;
 "You work too hard, old fellow, all the day,—
We don't grow stronger as we're growing grey;
"Tis now just forty years you've lived with me,
I do not want the last of you to see;
The place would quite be puzzled to go on
Without your honest face to look upon.
See for a lad, a strong and trusty boy,
And train him up to suit a groom's employ;
The little urchins! 'tis a puzzle now
To trust a boy to lead a horse at plough.
It is not ignorance; the boys are smart,
They know enough to make their masters start;
But school is not sufficient, that's a truth
One can't but see amongst our rising youth,
And there is certainly a fault somewhere—
I've heard myself a very infant swear;
I don't see how to mend it, but 'tis clear
We've lost a notch in manly character;
But we must have a boy, so do your best,
A good old servant shall not be oppress'd."

John listen'd silently, then bow'd his head,
Fully approving what his master said.
"I'm sure I thank you, sir, for your regard."
"Not so at all, John, 'tis your just reward
For all your faithful service night and day,
I owe you more than I can ever pay.
A faithful servant, serving as your friend,
Is such a gift as God alone can send.
But now about the boy—perhaps you know
One that will do, if you will teach him how."
"There's young Tom Howard, Abel Howard's son,
A better lad I ne'er set eyes upon.
I should not fear to trust that boy a bit
To take my place as soon as he was fit.
I often see him with his father's team;
The very horses are so fond of him.
I've mark'd it scores of times, and found it suit,
And judge a boy as he will treat a brute.
Suppose I see him speak a pony fair,
Rubbing his nose, and stroking down his hair,
Driving the sheep, and keeping back the dog,
Feeling a man although he does not flog,
Walking with patient step behind the cows,
Leaving a donkey quietly to browse;
I'd trust that boy to have a kindly heart,
And that of men, I think, the better part.
But those young rascals, with their whips and sticks,
Never contented till a donkey kicks;
Slashing the horses for a bit of fun,
Stoning a dog to make him yelp and run;
Always contriving how they can torment
Some harmless creature for their merriment—
Now, one of these—it might be reckon'd hard—
I would not have him in the stable-yard;
But young Tom Howard I should like to try,
That boy would suit us to a nicety.
So civil, so industrious, and kind!
I think he'd be entirely to your mind.
And then his bringing up has been so good—
The stock is sound, and so the younger wood;
There's not a man round here that can compare
With Abel Howard as to character.
A sober, honest, independent man;
Search round the place, and match him if you can.

And there's the mother and the girls—in short,
They fill their place as working-people ought."

"We'll try him, John, at once; I do not fear
But he will suit us well, from what I hear."

—

A clever nurseryman, with gardens fair,
And spacious houses full of all things rare,
Was going carefully his usual rounds,
And call'd to Simon working in the grounds—
"The weeds and grass are growing here apace,
This piece of ground will soon be our disgrace.
We want a hand into the garden now—
A steady boy to weed the beds, and hoe.
Most of the lads don't know the weeds from flowers,
That will not do in such a place as ours.
D'ye know a lad we could depend upon?"

"There's young George Howard, Abel's second son;
The eldest boy has got a famous place
To help the groom, who lives with Squire Chase.
But George is quite as good, for ought I see,—
They're all brought up with care and industry.
I mostly see him, as I pass at night,
At work at home to make their garden right,
And often stop to have a bit of chat;
He thinks that I can teach him this and that.
He told me, t' other night, how glad he'd be
To work in this great garden here with me.
If you thought well, I'd call in going home,
And tell him, in the morning, just to come.
It would be quite the making of the boy
To get in here for regular employ;
I'd answer for him as to character,
And that's no trifle in our garden, sir."

"That's true, indeed! a man may know the flowers,
And work all day the common round of hours;
But if his character won't bear the light,
He can't be trusted when he's out of sight.
But this George Howard seems the proper sort;
I'll try him, Simon, on your own report.

But stop a bit: you said the family
Were all brought up with care and industry.
Have they a girl, think you, would suit my wife,
To nurse a babe as precious as her life?
Not one of those low, careless girls we meet,
Who stop to stare and gossip in the street;
And leave the children in the dirt and noise,
Whilst they are prating to a lot of boys.
There are some girls, I've heard, who do delight
To nurse a baby, morning, noon, and night.
My wife wants one of these."

"Then, truly, sir,
I know of one not far from suiting her.
'Tis little Susan, sister to the boy
I just have mention'd for our own employ.
Of all the girls that I have ever seen
For nursing children, Susan is the queen.
She's just a woman as to thought and care,
But merry as a lark up in the air.
"'Tis wonderful how fond they are of her;
There's nobody like Susan any where.
I call her 'little hen'—a bit of fun—
She gives a cluck, and all the chickens run."

"Well, Simon, when her brother comes to me,
Let Susan come, and then my wife will see.
A clever workman, I have always said,
With character, will never want his bread;
Nor find his children hanging on his hands,
If he is doing what his place demands."

The Thieves' Ladder.

THE boys were skating on the pond,
And sliding on the mere,
And talking with an appetite
About their Christmas cheer.

One lad would feast on ribs of beef,
And famous hot mince-pies;
Another, with a leg of pork,
Would carry off the prize.

And such a goose as ne'er was seen
To swim upon the mere,
With sage and onions all complete,
Quite carried round a cheer!

Another lad, with sparkling eyes
And boastful manner, said,
That he should have a pudding too,
As big as father's head.

And so, with mirth and merry shout,
They follow'd on their play,
And threw the snowballs all about,
And long'd for Christmas day.

Oh! there were busy doings then,
Amongst both rich and poor;
For Christmas day brings happiness
To every body's door.

The girls were helping in the house,
With bustle and with show,
And told the boys to go away,
And not disturb them so.

And boys went whistling down the
streets,
And looking in the shops
At tempting heaps of oranges,
And piles of sugar-drops.

"Here, Willie, to the grocer's run;
Be sharp, now—there's a man,
And bring me home a pound of plums
As quickly as you can!

"Don't touch a plum—be sure you don't;
To-morrow you shall eat."
"I won't," he said, and, like a top,
Went spinning down the street.

The grocer weigh'd them in his scales,
And there was one too much;
He took it out, and all was right,
The scale was to a touch.

He wrapp'd them up in whitey-brown,
And tied them with a string,
And put the money in the till,
As 't were a common thing.

Young Willie watch'd, with greedy eyes,
As this affair went on.
The plums—they look'd so very nice!
He wouldn't take but *one*.

So going quick behind a post,
He tore the paper so
That he could take out two or three,
And nobody would know.

There was a little voice that said,
Close by, in Willie's heart,
"Don't tear the hole—don't take the plum
Don't play a thievish part!"

The little voice—it spoke in vain!
He reach'd his mother's door;
She did not see the hole he'd made,
His trouble then was o'er.

And what a trifling thing it seem'd,
To take one single plum!
A little thing we hold between
Our finger and our thumb.

And yet, upon that Christmas eve,
That period so brief,
Young Willie set his foot upon
"The ladder of the thief!"

And as he lay awake that night,
He heard his parents speak;
He heard distinctly what they said,
The blood rush'd to his cheek.

He lay and listen'd earnestly;
They might have found him out,
And he might get a flogging too,
'Twas that he thought about.

A guilty person cannot rest,
He always is in fear;
Not knowing what may happen next
To make his guilt appear.

So, when he heard his mother speak,
He rose up in his bed,
And did not lose a syllable
Of every word she said :—

"We have not any turnips, John,
I could not spare the pence;
But you can go and get us some
Through Farmer Turner's fence.

"There's nobody to see you now,
The folks are off the road;
The night looks dark and blustering,
And no one is abroad.

"It is not far—you'll soon be back—
I'll stand outside to hear;
The watchman now is off his track,
And won't be coming near."

The father he went softly out,
And down the lane he crept,
And stole some turnips from the field
Whilst honest people slept!

'Tis not the words that parents say,
It is their very deed;
Their children know the difference,
And follow where they lead.

How often, if their lives are good,
Their children's are the same;
Whilst, if they're thievish, drunken, bad,
Their children come to shame!

Now, Willie laid him down in bed,
His conscience found relief;
"I'm not the only one," he said—
"My father is a thief!

"How foolish 'twas to be afraid
About a little plum!"
He pull'd the bed-clothes o'er his head,
And dream'd of feasts to come.

On Christmas-day they had the pies,
The turnips, and the beef;
And Willie's foot was firm upon
The ladder of the thief.

And ere the snow was on the plain,
And Christmas-day came round,
And boys were sliding, once again,
Upon the frozen ground,

He, step by step, had further gone
Upon that dreadful road
That brings a man to misery,
And takes him far from God.

He cheated with his marbles first,
And then at other play;
He pilfer'd any little thing
That came within his way.

His parents did not punish him;
He went from bad to worse,
Until he grew so confident,
He stole a lady's purse.

Then he was seized, and brought before
The city magistrate;
And the police and lady came
The robbery to state.

And Willie he was proved a thief,
And nothing had to say;
So to the dreadful prison-house
He soon was led away.

In vain he cried, and pleaded hard
They would not take him there;
He would not do such things again
If they would hear his prayer.

It was too late! The prison door,
With bolt, and bar, and chain,
Was open'd to take Willie in,
And then was shut again.

He saw the handcuffs on the wall,
The fetters on the floor;
And heavy keys with iron rings
To lock the dungeon door.

He saw the little, lonely cells
Where prisoners were kept,
And all the dreary passages,
And bitterly he wept.

And through the strong-barr'd iron grate,
High up and far away,
He saw a piece of clear blue sky
Out in the blessed day.

And, "Oh!" he said, "my brothers now
Are out of school again;
And playing marbles on the path,
Or cricket on the plain.

"And here am I, shut up so close
Within this iron door;
If ever I get out again
I'll give this business o'er."

And Willie went to sleep that night
In his dark cell alone;
But often in his troubled dreams
He turn'd with heavy moan.

What sound is that at early morn
That breaks upon his ear?
A funeral bell is tolling slow,
It tolls so very near.

And in the court he sees a crowd,
So haggard and so pale,
And they are whispering fearfully
A sad and awful tale.

And all seem looking at a man
Who stands with fetters bound,
And guards and executioner
Are gather'd close around.

And he beheld that wretched man
Who trembled like a leaf;
His foot no more would stand upon
The ladder of the thief.

For he had climb'd it step by step,
Till murder closed the whole;
The hangman came to take his life,
But where would be his soul?

And still the bell went tolling on;
It toll'd so heavily
As that young man went up the stairs,
Out to the gallows-tree.

It toll'd-it toll'd-Oh, heavy sound!
It stopp'd-the deed is o'er;
And that young man upon the earth
Will now be seen no more.

Oh! parents watch your little ones,
Lest you have such a grief;
Help not their tender feet to climb
The ladder of the thief.

I have not heard young Willie's end,
I hope he learn'd that day;
But 'tis a thing most difficult
To leave a wicked way.

Yet still I know that God is good,
Most pitiful and kind;
And, if the wanderer turns to Him
In humbleness of mind,

If he will leave his former ways,
And choose a better road,
He'll find a Saviour true to help,
And pardon from his God.

The Guilty Conscience; or, Hell Begun.

Founded On Fact.

"COMRADE, listen! night is waning,
I must sail at break-of-day,
In the vessel bound for England,
Now at anchor in the bay.

"Sit and watch to-night beside me,
'Tis the last request I make;
Sit and talk away the hours
Till the light of morning break.

"I can bear my life no longer,
All I wish, is not to be;
Flames of hell can burn no stronger
Than the fire that burns in me.

"Now, the worm that never dieth
Gnaws my spirit day by day;
Eating, like a cruel canker,
All my happiness away.

"Oh! my spirit loathes the morning,
As it dreads the fall of night;
For the sunbeams seem to mock me
With their gay and gladsome light.

"And the darkness, bringing slumber
To the pure and guiltless head,
Peoples all the void around me
With the spirits of the dead.

"Should my eyelids close a moment
In the weary watch they keep,
Startled, by a scream of terror,
All my throbbing pulses leap.

"If I gaze into the darkness,
Two deep eyes are meeting mine,
Fix'd and rayless, gazing through me
With a clear unearthly shine.

"Ten long years they have pursued me
With that fix'd, unflinching stare;
Ten long years that shriek at midnight
Has awoke the startled air.

"I will tell you—'twas in Suffolk,
Ere I left my native land,
That I dyed my hand in murder—
Still, the blood is on my hand.

"When 'tis dark I always see it
Dropping down—you see it now—
Dropping, dropping, with a noiseless
Fall upon the ground below.

"See you nothing—nothing, comrade?
Look at this—this spot and stain,
On my clothes—and in my eyeballs,
Sinking inward to my brain.

"She was joyous as the dayspring,
Innocent as lamb at play;
And she loved me as her lover—
Gave her simple heart away;

"Gave her simple heart to love
Me, a demon fierce and foul!
Then I sought to shame and wrong her;
But she had an angel's soul,

"And she scorn'd me, then we quarrell'd,
I was strong, and she was weak;
By this hand the child was murder'd,—
Comrade!—did you hear that shriek?

"Oh! I heard it ring to heaven,
And my thrilling flesh doth creep;
'Tis that shriek I hear at midnight
Breaking up my fever'd sleep.

"Often round the foaming tankard,
When our messmates fill the hall,
Shouting in their drunken revels,
That shriek rings above them all.

"When the murderer was sought for,
Strong suspicion on me came;
But I had the hellish cunning
To protect myself from blame.

"Demon I was!—coward! villain!
For I schemed a crafty plan,
To affix the guilt and murder
On a harmless labouring man,

"He was brought upon his trial,
Nought avail'd that he could say;
For I stood, a lying witness,
And I swore his life away.

"The judge's sentence was to hang him,
Not the least remorse had I;
If he suffer'd for the murder,
All suspicion then would die.

"'I would see the rascal hanging!'
With indignant warmth I said;
And I gather'd with the people
When from prison he was led.

"Calm and pallid, there I saw him,
Scanning all the people o'er;
Till his eyes he fix'd upon me—
Fix'd on mine, for evermore.

"'Twas as if I'd lost my senses,
I could only stand and stare;
Some strong power of fascination
Riveted my eyeballs there.

"Till the gallows and the people,
All confused, look'd swimming round;
Then a giddy faintness seized me,
And I sunk upon the ground.

"Sense return'd, and all around me
Went on gaily as before;
But his eyes were fix'd upon me—
Fix'd on mine, for evermore.

"If I labour'd in the cornfields,
There, those steady eyes would gleam;
If I work'd amongst the woodlands,
There, the birds would mock her scream.

"Then I drank, to drown my senses,
Join'd in mirth and revelry;
Laugh'd and jested with the maddest,
So to cheat my agony.

"But it could not so be cheated—
I was like the monster Cain;
And the guiltless blood was crying,
Where it never cries in vain.

"Stay, I could not in my country,
Every eye seem'd watching me;
I enlisted for a soldier,
And was sent beyond the sea.

"For I thought the dead would never
Sail with me across the waves;
If I left my native country,
They would slumber in their graves.

"Oh! how freely on the ocean
Did I breathe and move once more;
E'en the tempest's wild commotion
Seem'd to give my spirit power.

"Every muscle grew elastic,
Life through every fibre ran;
And my spirits rose to action—
Once again I felt a man.

"Round I gazed upon the billows,
Roaring in their angry play;
Diving down in deep abysses,
Foaming up in wreaths of spray.

"O'er the vessel's bulwark leaping,
Flying upward to the sail,
Whilst the ship, in conscious power,
Ran before the steady gale.

"It was night, but scarcely darkness,
Linger'd still the glow of even;
Where the spangled moonlit waters
Stretch'd away to melt in heaven.

"'Twas so still, that e'en the seamen
Told their stories soft and low;
And the helmsman at the rudder
Lightly steer'd the silent prow.

"I stood there, and watch'd the
    moonlight,
Caring not to think or speak;
When across the trembling waters
Rung a wild and piercing shriek.

"Oh! I knew it in a moment,
She had follow'd on my track;
And my curdling flesh and spirit
Sunk upon that torture-rack.

"Words were never meant to picture
Sounds of more than earthly dread;
But that shriek would shake and rouse
    me
Though I slumber'd with the dead.

"Where is *He*? my spirit whisper'd;
Round a shuddering glance I cast;
There they were, those rayless eyeballs!
Gazing at me from the mast.

"Oft my senses seem to wander,
And I fancy 'tis a dream;
Till I start again, awaken'd
By that ne'er forgotten scream.

"Oh! I know they are the heralds
Of the everlasting years;
They will pass death's gloomy portals
To pursue my soul with fears.

"Where the worm, undying, stingeth;
Where the fires, unquenched, burn;
Where forgiveness never cometh;
Where the heart can never turn.

"Comrade—friend! the light is breaking
Slowly o'er the sullen bay;
Soon the boatswain will be piping,
And the ship get under weigh.

"Home to England I am going,
To confess my hellish lie—
To acknowledge to the murder,
Then, the murderer will die.

"I can bear my life no longer,
All I wish, is not to be;
Flames of hell can burn no stronger
Than the fire that burns in me.

"Friend, farewell! the anchor's rising,
Pray that I may be forgiven;
Oh, my comrade! hear the warning—
Cast your anchor firm in heaven."

Once again in England landed,
Every day he seem'd to grudge,
Till he stood to give his witness,
Self-accused, before the judge.

There he gave the proof they needed
To convict him of the crime;
Help'd them out in every question—
Show'd them both the place and time;

All the mystery and obstruction
Clear'd away by force of truth;
Like a plaintiff seeking favour,
Not a culprit fearing wrath.

All was said—the case was perfect—
Evidence as clear as day;
Not another link was wanted,
Wherefore, then, the verdict stay?

On that plain, once more, are gather'd,
Round about a gallows high,
Crowds of people, mutely gazing
On a man condemn'd to die.

Not a whisper broke the silence,
Not a murmur shook the air;
Wherefore looks the man around him
On the crowd assembled there?

Does a face steal from the distance,
Through the long-departed years?
Does the voice of maiden pleading
Thrill upon his dying ears?

That we know not—he departed—
God in heaven knows the rest;
Human beings err in judgment,
Leave to Him the guilty breast.

But, before with crime we trifle,
And the Almighty justice dare,
Think—how could we bear the anguish
Of eternal, black despair!

The Poor Little Boy.

I SAW just now a little boy
Go limping down a narrow street;
His clothes were wet and ragged too,
He had no shoes upon his feet.

His feet were red and blue with cold,
He look'd at me so sad and grave;
And as he pass'd he seem'd to say,
Oh! what a happy home you have!

His hair was rough, his cheeks were
    pale,—
I wonder where his home can be;
And if he has a mother there
To take him kindly on her knee.

I wonder if he has a bed,
And where he went this stormy day;
If he has milk, and meat, and bread,
And books to read and toys for play.

I've read of little orphan boys
Who had no home but in the street;
And begg'd about from door to door
For bits of broken bread and meat.

Who slept on straw, alone and sad,
With hunger pinch'd and full of pain;
Oh! I do wish that little boy
Would come along the street again.

I'd take him gently by the hand,
And speak as mother speaks to me;
So sweetly kind, poor little boy!
I wonder where his home can be.

I should not like such clothes to wear,
To limp along with naked feet;
I should not like such tangled hair,
Nor home in that dark dirty street.

How many pleasant things I have!
I never thought of that before;
I will not keep them all myself,
But give some of them to the poor.

Like Jesus Christ—who could not bear
That we should not to heaven come;
He wish'd so much that we should
    share
The pleasures of his glorious home.

If I can act like Jesus Christ,
I know I shall be always right;
If I could find that little boy,
I'd give him all my tea to-night.

The Common.

ON a wide and open common,
Where untended cattle stray—
Where the broom, with golden blossom,
Scents the breezes far away;
Where the asphodel and heather
Mingle in the dark morass,
With the snowy silken feather
Of the waving cotton-grass.

Where the white flower of Parnassus,
And the sundew's glistening eye,
Grow beside the lordly bulrush,
And the sedge-grass waving high;
Where the shy and wily plover
Hides with care her lowly nest;
And the wild-bees hum and hover
Lightly o'er the flowers at rest.

Where the pathways all are narrow,
Track'd by sheep at shepherd's call,
Highways to the rabbits' burrow,
Little paths for creatures small,
Twisting, turning, in and out,
Under heather, bush, and brake,
Zigzag windings cross'd about,
Like the speckles on a snake.

Here, remote from town or village,
On the common, bare and wild,
In a solitary cottage
Lived a widow with her child;
Old and crazy was the dwelling,
Patch'd and marr'd with streak and stain,
And the moss-grown thatch was telling
Tales of winter storm and rain.

Travellers on the distant highway,
Passing to the market-town,
Pointed out a lofty fir-tree,
Which for ages there had grown
Ever green through spring and winter,
Roughly bark'd, and rudely bent,
Stretching out its arms of shelter
O'er the ruin'd tenement.

Ever whispering, sobbing, sighing,
In a language little known;
Sometimes like an army flying,
Sometimes like a passing groan,
Roaring with the winter gale,
Falling as the tempest fell;
Like a mourner's lowly wail,
Or the ocean's angry swell.

Here the widow lived from childhood—
She had grown beneath its shade,
And she thought its music sweeter
Than the sweetest serenade;
And she marvell'd when a stranger
Thought she must be lonesome there;
All the creatures on the common
Were like neighbours unto her.

When her Willie's work was ended,
And the day was nearly done,
They would roam about the common,
Looking at the setting sun;
Looking at the clouds afar,
And the falling shades of night;
At the glow-worm's little star,
And the stars in heaven's height.

They would stand and breathe the perfume
Floating on the balmy air;
Thinking how the poor in cities
Would enjoy a dwelling there.
They would listen to the silence
Till the tears were in their eyes;
And their hearts, with lowly reverence,
Sought their Father in the skies.

"Oh, my Willie!" said the mother,
"What a happy home have we;
Thankful peace, and sweet contentment
Dwell with us beneath our tree.
In the city, there are quarrels,
Swearing, stealing, care, and want,
Drunken husbands, wretched women,
Children disobedient.

"When the mother rises early,
In her close and dismal room,
She sees nothing of the glory
Gilding all our yellow broom;
She knows nothing of the sweetness
In the air at early dawn;
She has not her spirit brighten'd
By the music of the morn.

"I would rather hear the skylark,
And the lapwing's lonely cry,
Than the grandest music playing
To a noble company.
I would rather see the moonlight,
And the stars all looking down,
Than the flaring gas, and lamplight
Of the black and noisy town.

"All things here are well contented,
All are rich, and none are poor;
Every creature, uncomplaining,
Takes its food at heaven's door.
All are busy, all are cheerful,
Minding laws they never break;
And their hearts are never careful,
Whatsoe'er they undertake.

"Heard you, now, the mother calling
To her lambkin far away?
Did that little creature ever
Think that it would disobey?
Did the rabbits' merry party,
Frisking on the dewy heath,
Ever slight their mother's caution,
When she bade them hide beneath?

"Did we ever find a nestling,
And the parent birds were flown?
Did we ever know the wild-duck
Left to rear her young alone?
Oh, my Willie! men may, heedless,
Pass them by, with scornful eyes;
God has placed them here, to teach us,
That we also may be wise.

"He, who made them is our Father,
All their sense by Him is given;
And he minds the little sparrow,
Even from his throne in heaven.
'Tis a hateful sin to crush them,
Or to harm in any way;
Cruel men are wicked, Willie,
Let the world say what it may.

"He's a coward—trust him never—
Who will cause a needless smart;
'Tis the great and manly spirit
That will own the tender heart.
Let us love God's harmless creatures.
Oh! what love to us is given;
We shall never know its fulness
Till we meet our Lord in heaven."

The Working Woman's Appeal.

AMONGST the hard and cutting things
Poor women have to feel,
When poverty is serving out
Their lean and hungry meal,
Is the unthinking ignorance
Of some we call genteel.

I would not wish to name the thing,
To give the least offence;
But folks like these appear to me
To lose a certain sense,
And quite forget that, just like theirs,
Are working-people's pence.

Our shilling seems to them so big,
It surely must be able
To furnish luxuries, as well
As comforts, for our table;
And what ten shillings ought to do,
That, really, is a fable!

When I was young, and did not think
How fast the money ran,
But spent my wages as they came,
Without a thought or plan,
I was the upper housemaid to
The young Squire Goldiman.

They kept a famous table then,
And never thought to spare—
They always had fine company
And hospitable fare;
And nothing was for them too good,
Magnificent, or rare.

'Tis not for me to give a guess;
I could not guess at all,
How much was spent in luxury
At that old manor hall—
But I should think a thousand pounds
Would never cover all.

And so they went on, year by year:
They used the servants well,
Though many tales of shameful waste
'Tis certain I could tell;
The mistress never came to see,
She only rang the bell.

And then the lady's-maid went in,
So dressy and so gay;
Or nurse-maid, with the children, came
To bid mamma good-day;
Or stately-looking housekeeper
Her orders took away.

The servants' hall, without control,
Without advice or care,
Was not the very best of schools
A woman to prepare
To marry in her proper rank,
With only poor man's fare.

I lived at Squire Goldiman's
Three years, and something more,
And, when I left the fine old hall,
My heart felt rather sore;
But, thinking of a married life,
I got my trouble o'er.

My mistress told the servant John,
Who told me in a trice,
That she had wish'd to see me first,
To give me some advice,
Before I left my service there,
To face a world of vice.

She hoped I never should forget
The mercies I had there,
The reading of the Bible,
And the use of daily prayer;
And the service on the Sabbath-day,
With all the servants there.

She hoped I should be serious,
And have my spirit bent
To use my talents faithfully,
As they were only lent,
And never, on the least pretext,
To yield to discontent.

"You say your husband's wages are
Ten shillings, if not more;
Well, if you're not extravagant,
You'll not be very poor;
But you must always strive to keep
A little sum in store."

And so I left the Manor Hall
To try my luck in life—
It seemed to me a charming thing
To be a married wife—
It is since then I've learn'd about
The struggle and the strife.

The house in which I went to live
Was in a narrow street;
I tried to do my very best
To have it always neat—
But, I had lived at Goldiman's,
Where all was so complete.

Oh! then I never thought at all
How much it cost for tea;
For, always in the servants' hall
We had the best Bohea,
And put in sugar to our taste,
A handsome quantity.

We always had good beer to drink
Within the servants' hall,
The butler and the lady's-maid
Would never touch it *small*;
And as to drinking water—*that*
They would not drink at all.

Of course, there never was a thought
Of any want of meat;
We always had as much of that
As ever we could eat,
And sometimes made a pretty fuss,
And said it was not sweet.

Of course, within the servants' hall
We had a famous fire;
We never thought about the coals—
Our master was the buyer;
And so we piled it merrily,
Just to our hearts' desire.

And as to light, we never thought
Of such a thing to spare;
We let the candle stand to burn,
Or let it stand to flare—
No matter if 'twere used or not,
By any body there.

Oh, deary me! the soap we used
At Squire Goldiman's!
The suds flow'd over all the tubs,
And over all the pans—
To think of saving soap at all,
Was not amongst our plans.

It need not be a mystery, then,
If any one would try
To calculate the wants of e'en
The poorest family,
That, in my alter'd circumstance,
I now and then should sigh.

I know it may, and has been said,
I'd but myself to blame;
I might have lived a single life,
And not have changed my name
Well—I may have my thoughts of that,
My betters do the same.

Besides, I've heard when gentlemen
Have lost a fine estate,
And bore the loss right manfully,
That people call'd *them* great—
Whoever cheer'd with word like that
A working woman's fate?

Yet we are great as well as they,
I know it, and will speak,
Although we're only working folks,
And women poor and weak;
And though at times we cannot check
The tears upon our cheek.

I know it needs a noble heart,
A spirit true and just,
To want a hundred little things,
Yet never go on trust;
And keep a hope alive within,
And never let it rust.

I know it needs a strength of love,
With nought of selfishness,
To eke the little victuals out,
That all may have a mess,
And hardly touch a bit yourself,
Though faint with weariness.

I know it needs a courage stout,
A right and ready will,
To twist and turn the clothes about,
And darn, and darn them still;
Not knowing where to get a bit
Another hole to fill.

I know it needs the patience
That a martyr may require,
To wash without a copper,
With a pot upon the fire;
The chimney smoke all driving down,
And smuts as black as mire.

Then, not to have a garden!
Not the smallest of the small,
Where one could stretch a line across
To meet your neighbour's wall;
But forced to dry before the fire,
In smoke, and steam, and all.

And then, when you are fit to drop,
Your spirits almost beat,
The children squalling on the floor,
The baby got to fret;
Your husband coming in, perhaps
With clothes all wringing wet.

And next may follow hasty words,
As if you'd been in bed,
When what you want is tenderness,
And praises in the stead;
Oh! it well may break a woman's heart,
And nearly craze her head.

I was in this condition once,
When Mistress Goldiman
Came in her carriage just to see
Her humble servant, Anne;
My word! I cannot tell you how
My blood both leapt and ran.

Her face was like an apple-bloom,
Her eyes like bits of sky;
Her shotten silk of pink and green,
She lifted daintily;
And held her head up like a queen,
So mighty grand and high.

Her little bonnet, made of lace,
Displayed her golden hair;
The flowers look'd all so natural,
They might have blossom'd there.
Oh, deary me! she could not sit
Upon my smutty chair.

She only knew of cottages
That poets write about;
Where work is pleasant exercise
Both in the house and out,
And children all have curling hair
Like cherubim, no doubt.

Mine never could come up to that,
However much I tried,
And on a washing-day, of course,
The tub, one could not hide;—
We had no lean-to at the back,
Nor any room beside.

She cast a freezing look around,
Reproach was in her tone;
She lectured me on many things
She said I should have done;
And many other things, she said,
I should have let alone.

She hoped the children went to school,
And always kept to church;
She should herself inquiry make
Of honest Mr. Birch;
And then she look'd as though she'd
    brought
A warrant for a search.

She felt herself quite mortified
To find me in this way,
She could not understand the things.
That working people say;
She could not sympathize at all,
And so she went away.

And I, who really do believe
That women, weak and poor,
Who, with ten shillings in the week,
Keep debts outside the door,
Are high and noble-hearted, then,
Felt spiritless and sore.

It is not always one can laugh,
And turn it into joke,
When people teach you how to draw,
Who never tried the yoke;
But think they have a right to scold
Us, stupid labouring folk.

The worst revenge that I would take,
The only one I'd seek,
Would be, that Mistress Goldiman
Should manage here a week;
And after that experience,
I'd like to hear her speak.

But still I often blame myself,
When I reflect again,
How wastefully we used the things
Of Squire Goldiman;
I wish I had a quarter now,
Of what I wasted then.

As I get opportunity,
I'll speak to girls in place,
And tell them what a shame it is,
And what a great disgrace
But, deary me! the servants now,
Won't hearken to your case.

Mrs. Godliman.

"WHEN I was just about fifteen,
And seeking for a place;
My constitution rather weak,
And not a pretty face,
(Though of an honest family,
Whose name had no disgrace;)

"I heard at young Squire Godliman's
There was a chance for me;
So I put on my Sunday clothes,
And quickly went to see;
My mother she walk'd all the way,
To bear me company.

"I felt so flutter'd in myself
For fear I should not speak,
That all the blood rush'd from my heart
To burn upon my cheek;
And then I turn'd so faint again,
I might have walk'd a week.

"But when I'd fairly pull'd the bell,
And heard the ringing sound,
I really thought I should have sunk
Upon the very ground;
My heart beat quick against my side,
My head felt swimming round.

"A pleasant-looking servant-maid
Came quickly to the door;
I told her what I came about,
As well as I had power—
'Well, sit down here and rest,' she said,
'Till parlour lunch is o'er.'

"I sat down by the kitchen fire,
And could do nought but stare
At all the quantity of things
The cook had ranged up there;
And all as neat and nice as wax,
So orderly, and fair.

"But soon there came another maid,
I thought they call'd her Grace;
A kind and cheerful voice she had,
And such a happy face!
'And so you wish to try,' she said,
'The under housemaid's place?

"'Well, come along with me, my dear,
Mistress will see you now;'
And I went with her through the hall,
I cannot tell you how;
But every step I felt my face
Still hot and hotter grow.

"When she had shown me in the room,
She gently closed the door,
And it was Mrs. Godliman,
Whom then I stood before;
But when I saw her lovely face,
I never trembled more.

"It was a mystery to me then,
And now, it is not clear,
That in a moment I should lose
All fluttering and fear;
I must have thought that she would look
Suspicious or severe.

"I've heard folks say—(I'm sure I hope
That they may be forgiven)—
That not a feature of her face
Was beautiful or even;
If they weren't beautiful for earth,
I'm sure they were for heaven.

"She spoke as if herself was made
Of common flesh and blood;
And though she such a lady was,
My feelings understood,
And trusted me, that I should be,
Both honest, true, and good.

"I felt the power of goodness come
As she sat talking there;
She seem'd to make all goodness look
So beautiful and fair;
I really felt to hate the things
She said she could not bear.

"'You are in mourning, child,' she said;
'Whom have you lost, my dear?
I've lost a little darling child—
We've both had grief to bear.'
I felt that moment I could give
My life away for her.

"I'd lost my father, that was why
I must a service take,
And we had had distress enough
Our very hearts to break!
But she seem'd more to take to me,
E'en for my trouble's sake.

"'You are not strong,' she said again,
'It may have been from want!
When sickness came, and poverty,
Your comforts were but scant;
A little better living here
Will alter that complaint.'

"And she engaged me then and there,
She said she'd no mistrust
I should abuse her confidence,
Or violate my trust;
And, after she had spoken so,
I would have perish'd first.

"It was ten years I lived with her,—
She died upon my breast;
If ever saint was fit to dwell
In God's eternal rest,
It was my angel mistress then,
Who join'd the good, and blest.

"Oh! such a mourning as that was!
The very light of day
We seem'd to bury in the earth
With that dear lady's clay;
Tears, fell like rain about the grave,
And also far away.

"I often wish I could recall
The very words she said;
So full of wisdom and of love,
They seem'd like daily bread;
And many a weak and weary soul
With comfort they have fed.

"But, then, 'twas not her words alone,
It was her actions spoke;
I've seen the stout rebellious will
Before her sweetness broke;
And anger seem'd to melt away
Like snow, upon a brook.

"The ladies never look'd at her
For fashions in the place;
She never set the fashion there,
In any thing but grace—
But how could all the fashions mend
That dear and lovely face?

"The servants seem'd to catch her
  taste,
And dress'd in neat attire;
Poor finery ran all to waste,
With no one to admire—
I've really seen a young girl cast
Her flowers in the fire.

"The wheel of life ran smoothly on,
As if 'twere daily oil'd;
She was the oil that kept it smooth,
And all the friction foil'd,
That in so many families
Has peace and beauty spoil'd.

"Amongst the poor she was adored,
Yet not for money's worth;
Her presence seem'd to make their
  homes
A heaven upon earth—
For sweet encouragement she gave,
And hopes of heavenly birth.

"She never took the teacher's place,
Nor made herself more wise;
But praised their struggles and success,
And gave her sympathies,
Until they felt within themselves
Capacity to rise.

"And so, a fine ambition grew
To be what she approved,
And thus she drew them happily
To Jesus, whom she loved;
And she had more humility
Than any she reproved.

"Ah, well! she has behind her left
A path into the sky,
That shines with love and holiness,
And purest charity;
And we must follow in that path
If we would mount as high.

"I do remember once, I saw
Those soft and loving eyes
Flash out with indignation
And sorrowful surprise—
I would not for the world have had
Them fix'd on me that wise.

"It happen'd thus—I know it well—
'Twas on a Christmas-day,
When all the house was full of friends,
And every body gay,—
An orphan boy who came to beg,
Was huff'd, and sent away.

"She always held that Christmas-day
Was made for happiness;
For showering bounties on the poor,
Or any in distress—
That 'twas a day that preach'd to all
To cease from selfishness.

"The man who sent the child away,
Had quickly off to pack,
Through drifting snow, and pelting
  sleet,
To fetch the young one back,
If haply he should have the luck
To follow on his track.

"A parson, or archbishop, might
Have learn'd from her that day
To take a text on charity,
And also what to say—
To fix a lesson on the mind
That would not pass away.

"She set the shivering urchin down
Before the kitchen fire,
She cut him beef, and pudding too,
As if he'd been the squire;
Then shod his feet, and clothed him
  well
With all he could require.

"She did it with such tenderness
As if she'd been his mother!
As if some time she'd had herself
A little starving brother—
Ah, lack-a-day! when shall we see
Her likeness in another?

"And then so meek she turn'd to us,
Who all were standing by;
"Twas not our worth,' she said, 'that
  brought
Our Saviour from the sky;
It was our hopeless misery,
Our helpless poverty.

"He did not stop to ask our sin,
Our station, or our name;
He saw that we were perishing,
And from His glory came;
And let us, in our humble way,
All try to do the same.'

"That sermon never was forgot
Within the servants' hall;
The man who sent the child away
Was most upset of all—
I saw the tears run down his face,
And on his coat-sleeve fall.

"Well, well—her works will follow her
Above this setting sun,
And many will come forth to tell
The good that she has done;
And yet she was not very old—
She was but forty-one."

A Religious Woman.

'TWAS early morn in the early spring,
But Peggy was moving about,
Preparing to leave her dwelling all right,
As she had engaged to be out.

The table was spread for her simple meal,
The kettle sung loud and high;
But, as she look'd over the window-blind,
She said, with a thoughtful sigh—

"There's Martha Low's husband is just gone past,
And left her alone—poor heart!
I cannot think what that woman will do
If nobody takes her part.

"No doubt she has worn and worried him out,
And none of her family come;
She never has taken much trouble, I doubt,
To make them a happy home.

"And a mischievous neighbour she is, indeed,
That I can never deny;
For many a mean ungenerous thing
I've suffer'd in days gone by.

"But what is the good of thinking of that,
Now she is so weak and low?
She has it paid back in trouble enough,
That I should not like, I know.

"Poor soul! she has no one to make her bed,
Nor to give her a bit nor sup;
Nor to kindle her fire, nor lend her a hand,
If she would be getting up.

"I am sure 'tis enough to make her complain,
To have such a wretched home;
I could not endure it, I know, myself,
To live in a dirty room."

The tea it was hot in the bright teapot,
And, oh! it was smelling so good,
And holding it up in her hand awhile,
'Twas thus she reasoning stood—

"There's no use in thinking of times gone by,
But try to forgive and forget;
Please God she recover this illness now,
She may be neighbourly yet.

But whether or not—what's that to me?
My duty is all the same;
If I pay her back in her surly ways,
Why, I shall be much to blame."

So Peggy, she took down one of the cups
That stood on the cupboard shelf,
And wiping the dust with her apron, said,
"'Tis tea I should like myself."

The beautiful tea! and she pour'd it out,
And sugar was not forgot;
Then toasting a slice of her home-made bread,
She butter'd it nice and hot.

She peep'd from the window, and down the street,
Nobody was going by,
So, slipping away to her neighbour's door,
She open'd it silently.

And, oh! what a desolate room it was!
All comfort had left the place;
The poor woman lay as white as a sheet,
With a frown upon her face.

The cinders were cold in the rusty grate,
As if they had never burn'd;
The poker and tongs had fallen about,
The fender was overturn'd.

And pewter pots on the table stood,
In circles of porter stain;
And tobacco-ashes, and broken pipes,
For days might there have lain.

And ragged old bits of carpet and mat
Were kick'd up here and there;
A medicine bottle and broken mug
Were standing upon a chair.

The chamber was close, and the sheets were black,
The bed was tumbled and toss'd,
And look'd as if never a neighbour's foot
Had over the threshold cross'd.

It look'd as if pity and peace had flown
From the comfortless place away,
And left the woman to suffer alone,
Still weaker from day to day.

Good Peggy, she cast a pitying eye
On Martha's sorrowful case;
And, moving about with a quiet step,
She tidied the dirty place.

She kindled a fire, she swept the hearth,
And made an orderly shelf;
And thought, as she laid the carpeting straight,
I hate a muddle myself.

The woman observed her neighbour at work,
But never a word she said;
But sullenly turn'd her body about,
And sullenly turn'd her head.

But Peggy was not in the least dismay'd,
'Twas pity that fill'd her heart;
And all her concern was how to perform
A generous neighbour's part.

She drew up the table close to the bed,
She set the tea thereon;
And then it was time, by the early chime,
For Peggy herself to be gone.

She nodded to Martha, and closed the door,
But never a smile had she;
Yet, not for that did she grudge her time,
Nor yet the toast and tea.

"It wasn't for thanks that I went," she said,
As she set her pot on the hob;
"It was for no manner of good to myself
That I did the little job.

"And yet, in some way, I feel as if I
Had had a reward in view;
My breakfast is just as welcome again,
Now Martha has got some too.

"Those were pretty words my Emily learnt
One day at the Sunday school,
About loving your neighbour as well as yourself—
They said 'twas the Golden Rule."

Now Peggy, that day, would wash at the Hall,
With two or three women beside;
And, rubbing or rincing, the chatter went on,
A constantly flowing tide.

"Mistress Peggy," said one, as she rung out the clothes,
Just tinged in delicate blue,
"Your neighbour has said some scandalous things
About your husband and you."

"I know it," said Peggy, "but never mind that,
The truth she may some day learn;
There's no use in playing at tit for tat,
Nor evil for evil return."

"Well, I never heard such a woman as you!
There's nothing that she would not say
To hinder your getting a good day's work,
Or to slander your name away."

"I know it," said Peggy; "I know it, poor soul!
Her malice she does not hide;
But we've enough victuals to eat, thank God!
And a little to spare beside."

It never was part of Peggy Hall's plan
To gossip to every one;
For even her left hand never could tell
The good which the right had done.

"They say, her husband is always in drink,
And makes her dwelling a sty;
And then her family never come near—
That's what she has earn'd, says I.

"She always was scolding and storm'd about,
No comfort they ever knew;
And now she is left to shift for herself—
I say, she has got her due."

"You may be right," said Peggy, and took
Some soap from off the shelf;
"But sure, Mrs. Sharp, you never would like
To be in that state yourself."

"Why, no, to be sure, that's certainly true,
But mine is a different case;
I do all I can for my neighbours, I know,
And keep up a cheerful face."

Now, Peggy had never been given to preach,
She wasn't a woman of words;
So went with the linen away to the bleach,
And hung it up on the cords.

She pegg'd up the sheets on the curving lines,
And look'd to the clouds and wind,
When thoughts of her neighbour's dirty old sheet
Came flashing across her mind.

"Poor Martha!" she said, and she heaved a sigh,
"I'll try it to-night, I will—
Clean linen is one of the pleasantest things
When people are sick and ill.

"I'll carry the sheet that I always keep
In case of a sudden need,
And put it on there instead of the one
That's laying upon her bed.

"I'll wash out her own in the early morn,
And hang it up out of view;
And, if it is dry when my work is done,
I'll wash out the other, too."

And so, on these neighbourly thoughts intent,
She rubb'd and she rinsed away,
Till the copper was dry, and the tubs put by,
And they finish'd the washing-day.

And Peggy is now on her homeward path,—
Her step has a joyful spring;
The love of her God is filling her heart,
She's half inclined to sing.

O pitiful love! and charity kind!
Ye are the sweetest flowers
That ever were strewn, by God's own hand,
To gladden this world of ours.

Her finger is now on her neighbour's latch,
Her heart is up to God;
The tea and the toast had vanish'd away,
And Martha, she gives a nod.

And that was the most that happen'd that night,
But Peggy, she got her ways;
"She's easier now in her bed, poor soul!"
That pleased her more than praise.

You could not describe, if you tried your best,
The clever devices she had;
But woman's quick wit is never at fault
When she would make others glad.

It was not a day, it was not a week,
Nor months, you well may say,
That Peggy's long-suffering had to endure—
Bad tempers don't change in a day.

But Peggy could feel, and she could forgive,
And ever was slow to blame;
"Poor soul! if I had a temper like hers,
I'm sure I should be the same.

"Thank God, that he has bestow'd upon me
A temper not apt to fire;
But I have no warrant to boast about that,
For I am no better than her.

"But she will come round, I fancy myself,
I'm certain almost she will;
One cannot expect good temper to grow,
Whilst a woman is weak and ill."

And thus she went on for many a day,
And strove with all her might,
To bear with her neighbour's fretful ways,
Who never took things right.

"'Tis not for the value of thanks, at all,"
She said to herself apart;
"But 'tis for the sake of her precious soul,
Please God would change her heart."

She was not content with a powerless wish—
But pray'd that her God would take
Compassion upon that ignorant soul.
For the merciful Saviour's sake.

And Time flew by, on those wonderful wings
That never turn back again;
And some he bore to their final rest,
And some he heal'd of pain.

And spring had pass'd by, and summer had flown,
It was on a Sabbath eve,
And Martha sat then by her open door,
For that she could now achieve.

The bells rung out for the evening prayer,
And people throng'd the street;
"I wish I could join once more," she said,
"My prayers with those who meet.

"Oh! how I wish I could sing in the church
The hymns that once I knew,
And join again in the solemn praise,
And in the confession too.

"I used to consider religion a plague,
Or only a false pretence;
And if people preach'd a sermon to me,
I used to take great offence.

"But now, I am sure, 'tis a beautiful thing,
And not a pretence at all;
If all the religious people were like
My neighbour, good Peggy Hall.

"I used to believe it was only for talk,
(That certainly is a fact;)
But dear Peggy Hall never talk'd at all—
With her it was all an act.

"And if she had not been an angel quite
She would not have borne with me;
For a more dissatisfied, heathenish wretch
I know there never could be.

"I could not endure to see her come in
With that sweet pitiful face;
I wish'd she would leave me to perish alone,
And never come nigh my place.

"I knew how shamefully I had contrived
To blacken her spotless name;
And then to be help'd at every turn,
I hardly could bear the shame.

"If patience could fail or be wearied out,
Hers certainly would have flown;
But my sharp words never anger'd her more
Than if she had been a stone.

"She only appear'd more tenderly kind,
And fear'd I was not so well;
She seem'd to me just fit for the sky,
And I seem'd fit for hell,

"And when she sat down and read me a psalm,
Her voice was so full of love;
I knew she would go to the blessed God,
And sing with the saints above.

"Oh, yes! and she will, if the Bible is true,
And that I never can doubt;
For she is the woman that's doing the things
That others are talking about.

"God bless her! I say, for a better friend
 On earth there never did live;
And may she never come short of the help
That she is so ready to give."

The Young English Gentleman.

WE have the King in royal state,
The Bishop in his stall,
The Peer within his castle gate,
The Duke in princely hall.

We have the Squire of high degree,
The Poet of renown;
The Admiral who rules the sea,
The Judge in flowing gown.

But I have seen another man,
A man who pleased me more—
A little English Gentleman
Within a cottage door.

His step was light, his eyes were bright,
He was but twelve years old;
But he had strength that put to flight
The braggart and the bold.

His soul was full of honour true,
His heart with kindness warm;
His form was strong and active, too,
And ready was his arm.

He made his mother's heart to sing:
It was his great delight
To please her well in every thing,
And help her morn and night.

If she were ill he loved her more,
He watch'd her weary look;
He lit the fire, he swept the floor,
He did his best to cook.

So gentle were his words and ways,
His habits were so clean;
He was an English Gentleman
As true as e'er was seen.

He scorn'd to teaze a little boy,
He scorn'd to cheat at play;
He scorn'd his knowledge to employ
To lead the weak astray.

If he was going any where,
And saw a child oppress'd,
He took its part with all his heart,
And got its wrongs redress'd.

He did not stand to gape and stare
At ladies in the street;
But raised his cap respectfully,
And gave them honour meet.

He listen'd when an aged man
His words of wisdom spoke;
He never laugh'd behind his back,
Nor turn'd him into joke.

He would not stoop to tell a lie,
He would not swear at all;
Nor jostle past you in the street,
Nor drive you 'gainst a wall.

He would not roughly shut a door
Or gate before your face;
To be uncouth to rich or poor
He reckon'd a disgrace.

If he were standing in the street,
Or stopp'd with boys at play,
And heard them wicked words repeat,
He left and went away.

He would not learn their vulgar ways,
Nor imitate their plan;
He heeded not their blame or praise
He was a gentleman.

He ne'er was seen to teaze a cat,
Nor set a dog to fight,
Nor beat down insects with his hat
That was not his delight.

But he would sometimes share his meal
With poorer boys than he;
He had a noble heart to feel
And do a charity.

If we had gentlemen like these
Amongst the rich and poor,
We need not fear what enemies
Would land upon our shore.

If Britons all were resolute
To be both good and true,
Our country would be prosperous,
With work for all to do.

There would not be the poor man then,
Without his food and fire;
There would not be the wealthy man,
Without his heart's desire.

For God would bless our country,
And guide it with his hand,
And give us great prosperity,
And plenty in our land.

Let every youthful Briton, then,
Exert both heart and hand
To be a Christian Gentleman,
The glory of our land.

The Primrose Gatherers.

COME! Mary and Jane, and Johnny and Joe,
Let us all to the copse in the high wood go;
The primroses now are in blossom I know,
And the pretty anemones white as the snow.

Now, take hold of hands as we run down the lane,
And just in the middle we'll put little Jane;
She's smaller than we are, and isn't so strong,
But, safe in the middle, we'll skip her along.

Don't you smell something sweet here? I'm sure that I can;
There used to be violets grow in this lane.
Oh! here I have one, how it cover'd its head,
But I spied it out in its snug little bed.

Look! now there are plenty, all blue in the grass,
We'll each make a bunch just to put in a glass;
I'll make one for mother, she thinks them so sweet,
And, Jane, you can make one for little Rose Fleet.

Ah, poor little Rose! the doctor has said
In a very few months that she will be dead;
So take her, dear Jenny, a nice bunch of flowers,
They'll be pretty to look at in wearisome hours.

See! there's a fine butterfly, yellow as gold,
They never come out when 'tis rainy and cold;
They would spoil all their beautiful colours, they say,
And so they keep house till a sunshiny day.

Let us sit down and listen! I never did hear
Such a number of voices, all singing so clear;
There's the thrush and the blackbird—I like them the best,
Except, in the winter, the little redbreast.

And there's Mr. Cuckoo—he's always the same—
He never seems tired of telling his name;
And there is the skylark, high up in the skies,
I cannot look at him—it dazzles my eyes.

And there goes the rook, with his fine glossy coat,
For ever repeating his rookery note;
I could sit here and listen the whole summer long—
Every bush in the thicket is merry with song.

Ah! what have you got, Johnny Jones? let us see—
A little bird dropp'd from its nest in the tree!
How it shivers and flutters, and opens its beak!
And looks all about it, as if it would speak!

It wants to be put in its warm nest again—
Do climb the tree, Johnny, and try if you can.
Ah! you've got it safe there; now, quick, run away—
It was a good thing that we came here to-day.

It soon would have died at the foot of the tree;
How merry and happy its mother will be!
But here are the primroses—oh! look, how gay;
Now gather, and gather, and gather away.

Boy Going to Service.

"You've got a service now, John,
To-morrow you'll be gone;
So listen to your mother, child,
Whilst here we sit alone.

"We've brought you up so far, John,
And you've been good and true;
And we've been always proud to say
There was no boy like you.

"Your father, all the country round,
Has had an honest name;
And I, although I would not boast,
Have always had the same.

"Now, Johnny, mind your master,
Whatever he may say;
A servant's duty always is
To listen and obey.

"If you are trusted with his goods,
Oh, Johnny! have a care;
The goods are his—he trusted you—
To touch them never dare.

"They may be great, they may be small,
But still, the smallest bring;
He that will take a pin, they say,
Will take a bigger thing.

"Don't stop to play at marbles, dear,
Nor loiter in the street;
Your time is all your master's now,
To waste it is to cheat.

"But let him trust you, like a man,
You'd like to hear him say—

'Johnny will do his duty well
Though I may be away.'

"And never tell a lie, my boy,
Whatever may befall;
But tell the truth out manfully—
My Johnny, tell it all.

"It may bring trouble at the first,
But always bear the blame;
'Tis better to have punishment
Than thoughts of sin and shame.

"And there is God in heaven, John,
Who sees you every day;
Don't be ashamed, but go to Him,
And every morning pray.

"He knows what you may have to bear,
And what temptations meet;
And you can speak to Him in prayer,
At home, or in the street.

"He'll be your friend, my little boy,
A better friend than I;
For there is nothing hard to Him,
And he is always nigh.

"And don't think 'tis a trouble, John,
To tell Him if you're sad;
For He is very pitiful,
And soon can make you glad.

"And He has been your parents' friend
Till now we both are grey;
He will be yours, my dearest child,
I'll ask him every day."

The Drunkard's Wife.

"OH, Edward! do not laugh, I pray,
To see that drunken man;
I'll tell you what I've seen to-day,
And then you hardly can.

"Our servant Jane learnt in the town—
I cannot tell you how—
That some one had been starved to
  death
In little Wapping Row.

"And so I stored my basket well,
And went out there to see,
And found it was the truth indeed—
A dreadful history.

"I pass'd through many dismal courts,
Through lanes and alleys low,
Before I found the wretched house
I sought in Wapping Row.

"High up a dark and winding stair,
From floor to floor I went,
And heard sometimes a woman swear,
Or beaten child lament.

"Upon the topmost flight I found
A close and wretched room;
Alas! that any human soul
Should call such place a home.

"No fire was burning in the grate,
The walls were damp and bare,
The window panes were stuff'd with
  rags,
No furniture was there.

"But in a corner, dark and chill,
Some dirty straw was spread,
And there a little ghastly child
Was lying stiff and dead.

"But still there was a moaning sound,
As if from one in pain;
But many times I spoke before
An answer came again.

"At length a woman slowly moved,
Roused from unquiet rest;
And, wailing with a feeble cry,
A babe clung to her breast.

"'Twas long before she was revived
Sufficiently to speak;
But then began to tell her tale
In words so faint and weak—

"I fear'd that I should lose them all;
But as she went along,
Her hollow cheek grew fever flush'd—
Her words came quick and strong,

"As though she wish'd, but once again,
Now death was drawing near,
To pour out all her misery
Into a woman's ear.

"'I was,' she said, 'a farmer's bride,
With love and peace content;
I was his heart's delight and pride,
Fair, young, and innocent.

"'He was an honest, sober man,
I loved him as my life;
And never—I may say it now—
Was more devoted wife.

"'Our house stood in a bed of flowers—
I think I see it now,
With all the roses clustering thick
Around the window bow.

"'It was a little Paradise,
And full of happiness;
For God's good angels guarded us,
And we had no distress.

"'But when my little child was born,
My cup ran o'er with joy;
The days were never long enough
For all my sweet employ.

"'Her prattling tongue, her pretty ways,
Were always new delight;
And she grew up so strong and well,
And was so quick and bright.

"'And yet she had a tender heart,
The least reproof could move;
And, oh! she look'd so earnestly,
Till certain of my love.

"'And when she flung her little arms
Close fondling round my neck,
My foolish heart broke down with joy,
Sweet tears I could not check.

"'Then came a shadow o'er my life-
My husband took to drink;
And lower down, and lower still,
My heart began to sink.

"'Still lower down, and lower down,
We left our pleasant home;
And, sinking still from worse to worse,
To this poor place we've come

"'Our little comforts, one by one,
Were sold away for drink;
The pawnshop has our furniture—
My husband would not think.

"'At last they took away our bed,
Regardless of my tears;
They brought a warrant of distress,
To seize for rent arrears.

"'The father's heart was flinty stone;
He valued us no more
Than this damp bed of filthy straw,
That lies upon the floor.

"'I work'd till all my strength was gone,
Till this poor boy was born;
Since then we've pined from day to day,
More famish'd and forlorn.

"'But soon 'twill end; beneath the sod,
My little girl and I
Shall find a place of peaceful rest
From all our misery.

"'Oh, lady! did you ever watch
A rose fade day by day,
Till all its grace and loveliness
Were gone and pass'd away?

"'So did I watch my little flower
With anguish and despair;
The silken curls that used to shine
Around her face so fair,

"'Were matted now, and soil'd with
    dirt—
No soap nor fire had we;
But, oh! her cheeks, so deadly pale!
Look! lady, you may see.'

"'And then she groan'd a heavy groan,
And, with a ghastly stare,
She pointed to the little corpse
That lay so quiet there.

"'I could not hold her little head,
As there she moaning lay;
We had no light—'twas in the dark
Her sweet soul pass'd away.

"'Oh! I had seen the crimson flush
Upon her hollow cheek,
And fever lighting up her eye,
But 'twas no use to speak.

"'Her father never thought of her,
Poor helpless innocent!
But often down that dismal stair
Her trembling feet were sent,

"'On, through the foul and filthy haunts
Of misery and sin,
Into the drunkards' palaces,
To get her father gin.

"'The piercing cold, and fog so raw,
Struck to her little heart;
Her shivering limbs and chattering
    teeth
Oft made the people start.

"'Her hollow cough would sound at night
Along the lonely street;
But no one ask'd her where she went,
Nor track'd her naked feet.'

"Again the woman heaved a groan,
And, with a ghastly stare,
She look'd upon the little corpse
That lay so quiet there.

"Her sunken eyes she feebly raised,
Then faintly bow'd her head;
A struggling sigh escaped her lips—
I saw that she was dead.

"Her wretched, lonely, broken heart
At last had found its rest;
But, wailing still, the baby lay,
Close clinging to her breast."

The Young Nurse Girl.

"I'VE watch'd you many years, Katie,
Since you were quite a child;
And seen you daily growing up
Industrious and mild.

"I've seen you nurse your mother's child
With tenderness and care;
And noticed your obedience
And reverence for her.

"On this account, I choose you now
To nurse my little boy;
And hope you will be happy, child,
And love your new employ.

"Come with me to the quiet room
Where baby lies asleep;
I'll lift the little coverlid,
That you may take a peep.

"Look at his softly closing eyes,
His glowing cheek so bright;
No tears of grief have wetted them,
Nor sickness made them white.

"Look at his rosy, open mouth,
That never spoke a word;
He never knew the meaning yet
Of any thing he heard.

"Look at his little helpless feet,
That cannot stand nor run,
Nor skip about, nor leap for joy,
Nor frolic in the sun.

"He's like the closely folded bud
Upon a sweet rose-tree,
That only shows a tiny glimpse
Of what it is to be.

"Bring me that little rose-tree, Kate,
That's blowing on the stand;
I'll show you buds and flowers there,
To make you understand.

"You know how many tender leaves
Are closely hidden here;
What sweet perfume, what colours
  bright,
Will day by day appear.

"It needs the warm and pleasant sun,
The soft and gentle air,
To make this pretty bud unfold
With all its leaves so fair.

"How beautiful this full-blown flower!
How brilliant is the hue!
How perfect each transparent leaf,
As if this moment new!

"But soon it will begin to fade,
And fainter every day
Its colour and its scent will be,
Till all has pass'd away.

"Now set down that, my child, and we
Will talk of this sweet flower,
Which every day will open more,
And alter every hour.

"And it will never pass away,
'Tis made by God to shine,
With holy angels, in the sky,
Immortal and divine.

"'Tis made to dwell where all is good,
And pure, and bright, and true;
And little Kate I hope will live
In that bright country, too.

"A baby's mind is like a book
Where nothing has been writ,
Where every page is fair and white,
No soil upon them yet.

"But every day will now turn o'er
One of those leaves so white;
And every thing, both seen and heard,
A secret hand will write.

"If one should say a naughty word,
The unseen hand would write
That naughty word upon the leaf,
That little leaf so white.

"If one should do a wicked thing,
In earnest or in play,
An ugly picture would remain
We could not take away.

"A frowning look, an angry voice,
Would all be printed there;
And stain those leaves so delicate,
So innocent and fair.

"And day by day, and day by day,
Dark pictures thus would grow;
And words unkind, and angry too,
The little boy would know.

"And he would recollect them all,
And soon himself would try
To say those naughty words again,
Or even tell a lie.

"For children like to imitate
What others do and say;
They'll even try to swear and steal,
And soon will learn the way.

"If baby learn'd such naughty words,
Such wicked ways from you,
Oh! think how sorry you would be!
What would you, Katie, do?

"Suppose you write upon your slate
Words from an evil mind,
And then repent, and wash them out,
No marks are left behind.

"But never from the human soul
Can you remove the trace;
The thing you write on that to-day,
You never can efface.

"A man may live a hundred years,
And roam the world about;
But all the way, and all the time,
May never blot it out.

"But, see! the little boy's awake,
We'll talk to him and play;
The unseen hand shall print a smile
Upon the leaf to-day.

"We'll speak to him with soothing words,
And make him very glad;
It is a thing most pitiful
To see an infant sad.

"And never slap or shake him, Kate,
Nor speak with peevish tone;
Don't snatch him roughly by the hand,
Nor let him cry alone;

"For if you do, the little leaf
Will all be written o'er
With tales of sorrow and distress,
That will come out no more.

"And never tell him foolish tales—
Don't let him hear you say,
The beggar man will come for him,
And take him quite away.

"For he will think you speak the truth,
And will expect to see
Some frightful creature stealing in,
To snatch him from your knee.

"No tongue can tell what horrid fears
Will fill his little heart;
He'll be afraid to go to bed,
The night will make him start.

"I charge you, Katie, never try
To make him good by fright;
For dreadful, dreadful pictures then,
The unseen hand would write.

"And he would think of them and
  scream,
And turn both cold and pale,
And lose his playful joy of heart,
From your sad, lying tale.

"But speak the words of truth and love,
And ever bear in mind,
That, as the little 'twig is bent,
The tree will be inclined.'

"God loves to see a little child
Grow stronger every day;
He loves to see its happiness,
And smiles upon its play.

"And He will notice all you do,
And write it in his book;
He'll notice every gentle word,
And every patient look.

"But if you teach him naughty words,
And naughty habits, too;
And he grows up a wicked man!
Oh! what would Katie do?"

The Bad Manager.

"OH, Fanny! my dear, what a beautiful pie!
I declare that I never did see
A crust so delicious—and risen so high!
And baked, as they say, to a T.

"It makes me feel hungry to see it, I own,
And really it flavours the street;
That boy smack'd his lips, he would like to have one—
Who would not enjoy such a treat?

"I cannot think how your good mother affords
To feed you on victuals like this;
My father has just the same wages as yours,
But doesn't give mother all his.

"You see sister Susan is so fond of dress,
(She's older than me by three years;)
She will have her way, and I leave you to guess
That sometimes we've little but tears.

"'Twas only last week that she quite set her heart
On a wreath of red roses and green,
To wear round her head like the ladies, you know;
She said she would look like a queen.

"She's pretty, they say, I don't see it myself—
I think she looks foolish and vain;
Be that as it may, she's no comfort to us—
I'd rather by far she were plain.

"She determined to go to the dance t'other night,
In the room at the 'Hatchet and Wood;'
She came home at midnight, and father was cross,
And said she would come to no good.

"And so, you see, mother gets worried and plagued
For money by night and by day,
And says, just for peace and for quietness sake,
That Susan shall have her own way.

"But I can assure you, if you will believe,
We often have nothing to eat;
And there's little Charley, the doctor has said,
That he should have plenty of meat.

"But we are in debt to the butcher, I know,
And the baker will trust us no more,
And the landlord has call'd for his rent many times,
And says he'll soon show us the door.

"Then that beautiful shawl, that my mother would buy
Last winter to go to the play;
The people won't wait any longer, you see,
But say they'll compel her to pay.

"So father gets angry, as you may suppose,
And isn't to blame, that I see;
For supper at night, he has often no more
Than bread, with a poor cup of tea.

"So he takes up his hat, and flings out of the house,
Like an angry and quarrelsome man,
And says, if he cannot find comfort at home,
He'll go to a place where he can.

"And when he comes knocking late into the night,
We tremble to open the door.
I'm sorry for father, it isn't his fault,
He always was sober before.

"If mother and Susan would keep the house neat,
Nor let such extravagance come,
We'd have a nice pie, just the print of your own,
And father would keep to his home.

"But why should I keep you out here in the street,
Whilst I have my troubles to tell?
If you'll let me, Fanny, I'll come to your house,
To learn how you manage so well."

Sixty Years Ago.

LOOK back to England sixty years ago!
The schoolboy then, is now a man in years;
The village beauty has a wrinkled brow,
A tottering step, and furrows for her tears.

The gravestones, then so white, are broken down,
Grown o'er with creeping moss and lichens grey;
And the green hillock hardly can be shown
Where the young infant by its mother lay.

Yet let us turn to those old times again,
And take a parting look before they fade;
A little while, and those who acted then
Will only live in footprints they have made.

The flying "train" was then a hidden thing;
The gas-lit city but a fairy dream;
And gold fields—common now as flowers in spring—
And boiling water moving ships by steam—

Such things as these, but sixty years ago,
Had been a fable for a wise man's scorn;
For people always have been very slow
To think that wiser people might be born.

But, though they knew not these, and would have thought
The man a fool, a madman, or a liar,
Who dare affirm a message might be brought
By sea and land upon a slender wire;

Yet they had knowledge that we ill can spare,
And thrifty ways we should not lay aside;
Our science has not yet outwitted care,
Nor learning shown the ignorance of pride.

The great mill cities had not risen then,
To draw the labourer from the country air;
He work'd the corn-land, and he drain'd the fen,
With hardy vigour and on frugal fare.

Then village sires lived on to see their sons
Settled beside them on the self-same farms;
Great emigrations had not then begun—
Their little properties had many charms.

They fed their cows upon the common land,
Their goslings nibbled where we drive the plough;
The Acts of Parliament were scarcely plann'd
Which make enclosures round those commons now.

A spinning-wheel was seen at every door,
And knitting-needles were in every hand;
Good knitted stockings were a precious store,
And busy housewives had a great demand.

Then, every little lass could milk a cow,
And print the butter with her mother's pat;
Could heat the great brick oven to a glow,
And fill with snowy curd the brimming vat.

A cup of tea was then for ladies' drink,
For working people it was far too dear;
How little did those thrifty housewives think
'Twould soon be common as their home-brew'd beer!

The village maid with modesty was dress'd,
"A lilac cotton" bounded her desires;
And flower'd kerchief, folded on her breast,
With all the grace simplicity requires.

No flaunting finery was then display'd,
The prudent mothers then discouraged show;
You might have known the mistress from her maid,
In those old times, some sixty years ago.

And girls had then a modest pride to keep
A blameless character untouch'd by shame;
And parents then would break their hearts and weep,
If their young daughter lost her maiden fame.

'Tis not so now-with gossip, dress, and play,
And great neglect upon the mothers' part,
Sweet modesty is flying far away,
And England mourns it with a bleeding heart.

Where are the future mothers of the free
And noble sons of Britons' favour'd land?
Not those bold, dressy creatures that we see—
With flippant tongue, loose life, and lazy hand.

Shame on you, mothers! is it come to this,
You care so little for your daughters' shame?
You see her plunging in a vile abyss,
And call dishonour by an easy name.

Look to it, mothers! 'tis a fearful thing
To have the charge of souls that never die;
In that great day of solemn reckoning,
Where will the wanton and the careless fly?

Where will the souls committed to your care,
Stand in the judgment on that awful day?
Now is the time for diligence and prayer,
To walk before them in the narrow way.

'Tis not enough to talk, to scold, to beat,
The living lesson they will take from you;
Their quick discernment you will never cheat,
They heed not what you say—but what you do.

Oh, English matrons! guide and guard the young,
Still take the lead in purity of life;
All round the world your praises have been sung,
And the sweet virtues of an English wife.

We have gone backward, let us turn again,
And do our duty with a cheerful brow;
Let women be good helpmates to the men,
Improving still on sixty years ago.

THE END.

STORIES IN VERSE

FOR .THE

STREET AND LANE:

BEING THE

Second Series

OF

"HOMELY BALLADS FOR THE WORKING MAN'S FIRESIDE."

BY MRS. SEWELL.

LONDON:

SMITH, ELDER AND CO., 65, CORNHILL.

M.DCCC.LXI.

The Chaffinch's Nest.

ADOWN a green lane, seldom travelled by man,
A bright little brook in its cool current ran;
For many long years it had trickled that way,
And never had loitered by night or by day;
By starlight and sunlight it glided along,
And sung to its neighbours the very same song;
And when the deep dark over all of them fell,
It still had the same pleasant story to tell;
But whence it had come, or the words that it said,
Were thoughts that ne'er puzzled a passenger's head;
Though still where the little brook trickled along,
The flowers grew bright, and the rushes grew strong.

A noble elm-tree, that was stately and tall,
Looked down on its neighbours and sheltered them all,
Its delicate leaves were yet tender and new,
The brown spreading branches were visible through,
 But never a bit of the stem could be seen,
'Twas covered so thick with the bright ivy green.
The ivy ran straight, and it grappled him fast,
It flung its arms round him, and lovingly clasped,
That one might have fancied the ivy and tree
Were true-hearted friends, that would always agree;
And many a cosy and snug little bower
They formed as a refuge from tempest and shower,
Where any small creature, that travelled that way,
Found shelter and lodging, with nothing to pay;
And thus they grew on, in the green shady lane,
Whilst deep in their shadow the rivulet ran.

One beautiful morn, in the fine month of May,
Two sweet little birds were seen flying that way;
They'd business on hand, it was easy to see,
As they lighted among the small twigs of the tree;
They hopped about here, and they peeped about there,
Considering every corner with care;

When, twittering gaily, they both seemed to say,
"We've settled the matter"—and then flew away.

In a very few minutes—it could not be ten—
They both had come back to the elm-tree again,
'Twere vain to conjecture what burden they bore,
As both disappeared in the leaves as before.
They just had agreed to be husband and wife,
To settle for comfort, and never for strife,
To build a small dwelling, and carefully rear
A family safe from destruction and fear.

They had not a pattern, a rule, nor a line,
Nor compass to set them a circle so fine,
They neither had gimlet, nor hammer, nor saws,
But only their beak and their dexterous claws;
But sensible workmen, 'tis said, as a rule,
Will hardly find fault with the commonest tool,
And these little workpeople never had thought
That new-fashioned implements need to be bought;
So away they were flying, away and away,
To fetch and to carry the whole of the day,
And then in a branch of the sheltering tree,
They both were as busy as busy could be.
At close of the day, when the shadows grew dim,
And each little chaffinch had warbled its hymn,
No robbers to fear, and no money to keep,
They perched themselves easy, and then fell asleep,
And all the night long a light westerly breeze
Was humming a tune in the rustling trees;
But soon as the morning's first roseate ray
Had sent them a sign of the new coming day,
They washed in the streamlet, and when they were trim,
They sang in the elm-tree a sweet morning hymn,
Which people might hear, if they would but arise,
When little birds first tune their notes to the skies.

This done, they went forth in the fresh dewy morn,
To pick off the wool from the scrubby old thorn;
They knew where the sheep had been taking its rest,
And thought of a tuft for their own little nest;
And where in the meadow the horses had lain,
They gathered some hairs that had dropped from the mane;
The duck by the water sat pluming her breast,

Some feathers were left for the chaffinch's nest;
And whether they gathered wool, feather, or hair,
They knew how to make the best use of it there.
The cobweb hung out with its dew-spangled line,
They rolled up the thread as a fine ball of twine,
And mosses, and lichens, green, yellow, and brown,
Well answered the purpose of soft eider down;
They carried them all to the sheltering tree,
And there were as busy as busy could be.

And oh! what a spirit they had in their work,
From earliest dawn till the evening dark,
It only seemed pastime and pleasure to be,
So gaily they worked in the shade of the tree;
But when the soft walls were beginning to rise,
The hen-bird bethought her to measure the size,
She elbowed about her, and puffed out her breast,
To settle completely the round of the nest,
And when she was certain the circle was true,
She said with a twitter, "My dear, it will do,"—
The ivy leaves hung as a green folding door,
And now the small architects' labour is o'er.

Next day came a joy too delightful to tell,
One should be a chaffinch, to write of it well,—
A smooth little egg was observed in the nest,
Laid soft in the warmth of the mother bird's breast;
The colour was whitish, and authors have said,
The spots and the streaks should be purplish red;
On this point the chaffinches fully agree,—
A lovelier object they never did see.
Another egg came, then another was laid,
And great was the joy in the green ivy shade,
For when they had added another or two,
The number was right, as they perfectly knew.
And then the hen-bird, without further delay,
Sat close on the eggs through the whole of the day,
Do you think she grew weary in sitting so long?
Her husband amused her by singing a song,
And out of the joy of his heart warbled he,
Perched up on the twig of a neighbouring tree.
Perhaps he was singing about the small things
That soon would be nestling under her wings;
Perhaps he was planning, along with his wife,

The future concerns of their innocent life;
To train up their children to love and obey,
And not let them quarrel, nor get their own way;
He might be protesting how faithful he'd be,
And watch night and day, as she sat in the tree;
Whatever it was, they had plenty to say,
To make conversation the whole of the day;
He whistled his loudest, and plumed up his crest,
Whilst she answered low from the snug little nest;
And when she was hungry, and wanted fresh air,
He sat on the eggs with a fatherly care;
They'd one common object, this husband and wife,
Their home and their eggs were the joy of their life.
And so they sat on them, by night and by day,
For more than a week in the sweet month of May.
The mother then whispered her partner so dear,
She thought that their young ones would shortly appear,
Nor could he prevail on her even to go
To sip a cool draught at the streamlet below.

She hears a faint tap—and another—and then—
Oh! who can imagine the joy of the hen!
She hears a low chirp—and with pleasure elate,
She tells the glad news to her listening mate,
And soon he'll be off to select the right food,
Long known as the best for a chaffinch's brood,
But first pipes a ditty, rejoicing and clear,
That all their good neighbours the tidings may hear.

Ah! what is that noise that is coming along?
The chaffinch has suddenly stopped in his song:
The mother's heart beats in her poor little breast,
And throbs hard against the warm sides of her nest.

Loud shouting and laughing come near, and more near,
And beating on bushes, they anxiously hear,
And ere they can fancy what next there may be,
Some boys have come up to the foot of the tree:
They beat on the ivy—the mother-bird flies—
"Oh! there's an old chaffinch," a little boy cries;
"They've built in that ivy, as sure as a gun.
I'll climb up and get it—now isn't that fun?"
And up went the boy with his hands and his knees,
And soon the poor chaffinch's treasure he sees.

"Ho! ho! I have got it—young birds, I declare.
Now lend me a hand, lads, for I must take care."
Then down he came sliding, till firm he could stand,
The poor little chaffinch's nest in his hand;
And away go the boys, with a laugh and a shout,
Still beating the hedges and bushes about.
But hardly the robbers had quitted the lane,
Ere both the birds flew to the elm-tree again.

And oh! what a havoc and ruin they see;
The branches were broken away from the tree,
And the green folding-doors, that so easily swung,
Were torn from their places, and heavily hung;
And their own little nest, that was hid in the green,
They looked all about—it was not to be seen.
The mother-bird uttered a piteous cry,
And dropped on the ground, as unable to fly;
She ruffled her feathers, and drooped down her wings;
There's no one to pity you, poor little things!
Her mate hides beneath the low branch of a tree,
But no word of comfort to give her has he.

Again and again they return to the place,
No sign of their own little home can they trace,
Except a small bit, that was left here and there,
Of the moss or the lichen, the wool or the hair;
Yet still they fly round it, and anxiously call,
But the boys are away to their home at the hall,
Telling one to another, with boasting and glee,
How they saw the old chaffinch fly out of the tree;
And the nest of small birds, with a piteous cry,
Deprived of their mother's warmth, shiver and die.

Widow Haye; or, The Gossiping Neighbours.

THERE was a small town, without any renown,
Or place in our national story,
Where members of Parliament never came down,
Nor mayoralty gave it a glory;

Where wheel of a cotton-mill never had whirled,
Nor tourist passed through to the Highlands;
Nor railway approached it;—'twas out of the world,
As much as the "Friendly Islands."

But save the great stir and the struggle of life,
'Twas like other towns in the nation;
Ill-nature, and envy, and gossip, and strife,
Were found there without importation.

The people were, mostly, a specimen fair
Of those we oft designate brothers;
Good neighbours, and very bad neighbours, were there,
Who envied the welfare of others.

And sorrow had found for herself a retreat,
And joy had her season of pleasure,
And poverty suffered, with little to eat,
And vanity squandered her treasure.

In one of the dwellings just out of the town
(In the suburb, they'd say of a city),
A widow had settled in penury down,
And she is the theme of our ditty.

Long time she had mourned, in disconsolate grief,
The friend God had given and taken;
No sympathy soothed, or afforded relief—
A widow, poor, sad, and forsaken.

At length it passed by, as the sweet showers of rain
That fall when the winter is over,
When the turtle comes back to the valley again,
And the honey-bee hums in the clover.

Her eyes, that so long on the pavement were bent
In sorrow and weeping dejection,
Looked cheerfully up, with a smile of content,
As if under the Royal protection.

She murmured of hardship and trouble no more,
Or that poverty soon would assail her,
But spoke as a person possessing a store,
With a banker who never would fail her.

And though she still wrought with a diligent hand,
Her labour seemed constantly lighter;
If oppression were practised, or injury planned,
She knew of a Friend who would right her.

Her neighbours they wondered, and gossiped, and laughed,
They'd neither a doubt, nor a question,
But luck had come to her, by favour or craft;
They read it in every action.

Some jeeringly said, she would marry again,
And some had begun to suspect her,
And one woman hinted, a very rich man
Would soon be the widow's protector.

But a sharp little neighbour, who happened to come,
Gave quite a new view of the matter,
Which carried unwilling conviction to some,
And spoiled all the mischievous chatter.

One night, as she passed, it came into her mind
(The room being light with a candle)
To peep through a little round hole in the blind,
To learn what she could of the scandal.

"And what do you think that I saw in the place?"
"Ah! what?" said the neighbours—"a lover?"
"No—the widow sat there with the tears on her face,
And the Bible lay open before her.

"On her trouble-worn features, so placid and pale,
Was a look of such sweet resignation,
That led me at once to discredit the tale
As slander and sheer defamation.

"But much more than that, if you like, I could tell,
And of Peter, as well as his mother;
One instance there is I know perfectly well,
'Twas kindness he showed to my brother."

—

MRS. PERRY'S STORY.

"You know that last spring-time John injured his leg,
'Twas a terrible fracture, and healed very slow;
He's too independent to borrow or beg,
But a family can't live on nothing, you know.

"With his garden, he always had managed right well,
For he mostly had luck with his fruit and his crops,
And plenty of customers, when he could sell;—
But what can be done when the labourer stops?

"I was sitting beside him, and talking it o'er,
And his heart was so full that the tears could not stay,
When I heard a light step, and a tap at the door,
And there, with his pleasant face, stood Peter Haye.

"Said he, 'Mrs. Perry, I've just come from plough,
And it entered my mind, as I came down the lane,
The garden down here would be going back now,
Till your brother got out to his labour again.

"'An hour or so, now, after work every night,
Or one in the morning sometimes I could spare,
And nothing would give me a greater delight
Than to rid him of some of his trouble and care.'

"'Ah! Peter,' said I, 'but you know he can't pay'—
'Now hold there!' said he, ' You don't mean to offend;
Don't take me for such an old miser, I pray,
I'll come here to help like a neighbour or friend.

"'So give me the spade, and the dibble, and hoe,
I'll ask him myself how the work should be done;
The potatoes he'll want to be getting in now,
To have them in market the middle of June.'

"'Twould have done your hearts good, as I'm sure it did mine,
To see what I call such nobility shown,
And I can assure you, in rain or in shine,
He has worked in that garden, as if 'twere his own.

"The crops are all thriving, as if they were pleased
To reward such a heart with a plentiful store;
And even poor John, now his spirit is eased,
Is getting on faster a deal than before."

The neighbours agreed that 'twas pretty indeed,
They hoped all the others would turn out as well,
"'Tis likely they will, from a sample I've seen:
I'll tell you about it," said Margaret Bell.

—

MARGARET BELL'S STORY.

"Widow Haye's little daughters, Jemima and Jane,
Attend the same school with my Betsy, you know;
She's the very worst tom-boy that ever was seen,
And always is getting in trouble, somehow.

"The two little Hayes looked as nice as a print,
A thousand times better than if they'd been fine;
I felt rather jealous, I'm sorry to hint,
Her children behaved so much better than mine.

They took hold of hands, and they tripped off to school,
So daintily stepping, to keep their shoes neat,
When off went my Betsy, as wild as a fool,
And threw little Jane in the dirt of the street.

"I laughed, I must own, though I'm sure 'twas not right,
I thought how the widow would grumble at noon,
For the little round tippet, so pretty and white,
Had a mud-coloured pattern all over it soon.

"I slipped on my bonnet, and went down the street,
I wanted to see how the matter would end,
And there was my Betsy, her frock with a slit
That would take a good seamstress a half hour to mend.

"I thought to myself, you shall pay for this sport,
Miss Betsy, with loss of your dinner to-day;
They none of them saw me—my temper was short,
And I waited impatient, my lady to pay.

"She was later than common, and red as a coal,—
No sign of a slit could I anywhere spy;
At last I said, 'Betsy, who darned up the hole
That you tore in your frock, Miss, this morning?' says I.

"She looked quite astonished, and said, 'It was Jane;
She's the best tempered girl that I ever did see;
I toppled her down in the gutter again,
And yet she has mended this great hole for me.

"'I never will act in this way any more,
I don't think I ever did feel so ashamed;
Look here 'twas a terrible place that I tore,
And she darned it because she knew I should be blamed.'

"'And was that her reason?—now, Bessy be plain—
Don't you think she had any reward in her view?'
'Oh! no—for Jemima just whispered to Jane,
'Return good for evil, dear—pray, Jenny do.'"

"To tell the truth, neighbours, I hardly could speak,
I felt so confounded, it really was pain;
And Betsy stood there, with the tears on her cheek,
Declaring she'd never tease Jenny again."

The neighbours agreed that was pretty, indeed;
They hoped little Joseph would settle to work;
But one of them, shaking her head, was afraid
That Joseph would turn out a terrible Turk.

But Margaret Bell took the story again,
She could not help saying she liked little Joe;
The boy had a spirit just fit for a man,
That she saw a sign of some evenings ago.

She was coming herself from the farm on the "Rise,"
Quite laden with baskets, and weary and warm,
When Joseph ran up, with his merry black eyes,
And lifted a great basket off from her arm.

"We walked on, you know, till we came to the pond,
And there were some boys with a frog and a string—
It was shocking to see how they could be so fond
Of teasing the harmless and innocent thing.

"He put down the basket as quick as the light,
He looked like a lion, and fiercely he spoke;
The boys only mocked him: he scolded outright,
They laughed at his passion, and turned him to joke.

"A moment he stood to consider his foe,
Then dived in his pocket his marbles to find:
'Here, these shall be yours if you let the frog go,
And the marbles, I hope, will be more to your mind.'

"The bargain was struck, and the string was untied,
I saw the frog plunge in the water below;
He took up the basket and trudged by my side,
His eyes flashing bright and his cheeks in a glow.

"Thinks I to myself then, 'you never will see
The poor and the feeble oppressed by the proud—
You'll stand up, my lad, by what's noble and free,
And not be led on by a clamouring crowd."

Then the neighbours agreed that 'twas pretty indeed;
They wished their own children were like Joseph Haye;
And, so being all on this matter agreed,
Were just turning homeward, and bidding good day;

But ere they had parted from Widow Haye's door,
Came out an old neighbour, well known in the Row
Contented and thankful, though sightless and poor,
And his few scattered hairs were as white as the snow.

"You have just come in time, Father Faithful," said one;
"We want your opinion, you must not say nay;
We've had a long gossip and good bit of fun,
About the fine luck of your friend Widow Haye.

"She looks so contented, so thriving, and well,
We fancy she's going to marry once more—
That something has happened 'tis easy to tell,
She's not the same woman we've known her before."

"Good neighbours," he answered, "you're wrong and you're right,
She has a good husband, the Lord up on high;
Her fatherless children He feeds with delight,
And His merciful ear is awake to her cry.

"He brought her to Jesus to rest in His love,
Who bears all her care and her sorrow away;
She has a kind Saviour her sins to remove,
And she trusts in His promises every day.

"When sitting beside her, I feel God is near;
No gossip, good neighbours, nor slandering words;
But the voice of content, and the spirit of prayer,
Bears witness that she is a child of the Lord's.

"His blessing is on her, and never will cease;
His love is her shield, and her shelter alway;
Like a lamb in His fold she reposes in peace,
He guards her by night, and He guides her by day.

"Dear friends, hear the words of a simple old man,
Love God, the good Father, and Jesus your friend;
Then, love all your neighbours as well as you can,
For Love is the thing that will last to the end."

Miriam.

THE funeral bell swung sad and slow
One Autumn afternoon;
A drizzling mist began to fall,
And sparrows chirping on the wall,
Foretold rain coming soon.

The mournful sound kept circling round,
The air was full of woe,
When falling on the silent street
A distant tread of pacing feet,
Came solemnly and slow.

Two friendly neighbours heard the bell,
And stood beside their door,
And presently there came in view
A little train of two and two,
A coffin went before.

That feeblest form of grief was there—
A Workhouse funeral;
When friends too poor to show regret,
Leave strangers' hands to pay the debt
Of decent burial.

Some aged paupers formed the train,
And by the hand they led
(Along the damp and narrow street,
And guiding their unconscious feet)
The children of the dead.

A smiling boy of three years old,
Looked round with happy face,
As glad to find himself once more
Outside the gloomy Workhouse door,
His latest dwelling-place.

The second was a little girl
Too young her loss to know;
She only thought 'twas very sad,
Now they were all in mourning clad,
And walked along so slow.

The eldest girl was eight years old,
A shrinking tender flower,
Ne'er brightened by the joyous sun;
Dark clouds rolled o'er it one by one,
And saddened every hour.

The boundless wealth of childhood's
   mirth
Was never her's to know;
The sharer in her tender years
Of all her mother's grief and tears,
She only knew of woe.

And when that mother's wasted hand
Dropped lifeless on the bed,
And when she spoke to her no more,
When that dear face was covered o'er,
She wished she too were dead.

And now in that small company
She takes the foremost place,
And vainly with her 'kerchief small
She strives to check the tears that fall
Fast down her sad young face.

The heavy bell went tolling on,
It smote upon her ear,
And curdled all the creeping blood,
As by her mother's grave she stood,
In agony and fear.

The burial service has been read,
The clerk has said, "Amen,"
A child's convulsive sob is heard
To mingle with that solemn word,
And then is hushed again.

Fast falls the chill autumnal rain,
As back with hastening feet,
The neighbours watch the workhouse
    train,
And friendless orphans pass again
Along the narrow street.

"Poor Miriam!" said Mary Howe,
And drew a heavy sigh,
"How little any of us know;
Who would have thought she'd come
    so low,
Who once looked up so high."

"You knew her well?" said Mrs. Head;
"Pray what has brought her down?"—
"Oh! yes; I knew her from a child,
When every face upon her smiled,
And no one had a frown.

"But if you'd like to hear her tale,
Come in, and bring your work;
It is a melancholy case;
But many such are taking place,
Almost without remark."

—

"As I was saying, Mrs. Head,
I've known her all my life,
At school, in service, and at last,
When she became a wife.

"Our homes were never far apart,
And when we were at school
We grew fast friends, and always said
Our love should never cool.

"Our characters were not alike;
I was sedate and plain,
And she was like the wild-briar rose,
That glows in summer rain.

"I see her, as she used to laugh,
And shake her curling hair,
And dance along, as though her feet
Were treading on the air.

"She was a wild and winning girl,
She always got her way;
Though people might protest and scold,
They never said her nay.

"She knew her power, and used it, too,
She laughed if she were schooled;
If she had been a young princess,
My word! she would have ruled.

"And yet her nature was as frank,
And free as mountain air;
The clouds that gathered on her brow,
Could never tarry there.

"Oh! what she might have been, with
    care—
But that is gone and past;
The training, that her childhood missed,
She sorely gained at last.

"You've heard of old Squire Harkaway,
Who lived at Ferney Chase,
Both she and I were servants there,
'Twas Miriam's second place.

"I was engaged as laundry-maid,
And she was housemaid then;
A large establishment was kept,
Of maids, as well as men.

"The family was very gay,
The world was all in all,
Amusement was the only thing
That pleased at Ferney Hall.

"My lady liked to see her maids
'Well dressed,' as she would say;
For Miriam that was quite enough,
Her thoughts all ran that way.

"I've heard it said, that e'en the Poor
Are sometimes born with grace;
It was a natural gift in her,
And she'd a lovely face.

"She knew of course that she was fair,
That need be no surprise;
Admiring looks oft told her *that*,
Beside, she used her eyes.

"And when she dressed, and looked her
   best,
And shook her glossy curls,
I've often thought her prettier
Than ladies dressed in pearls.

"The company all took to her,
And made her presents, too,
Of clothing they had cast aside,
Though just as good as new.

"It was a pity; gifts like these
May often prove a curse;
For girls once dressed in ladies'
   clothes,
Don't fancy what are worse.

"I saw this growing love for dress,
And how it fed her pride;
I cautioned her, and when she laughed,
I often could have cried.

"I loved her, as you love a child,
She weighed upon my mind;
I never hold with those who say
That all true love is blind.

"I had a fear about the end,
And sometimes told her so.
'My dear,' she'd say, 'you can't expect
That I should dress like you.'

"And then she'd pull a prudish face,
And straighten down her dress,
Or toss her head, and fling away,
With childish carelessness.

"The servant men all courted her,
Of that you may be sure;
And she would laugh and flirt with them,
But kept her heart secure,

"Until, as I remember well,
The Squire went up to town,
And brought with him, on his return,
A fine new footman down.

"My mind distrusted him at once,
Despite his polished air;
He'd mince and smile with us young
   girls,
With men he'd drink and swear.

"I never was a favourite,
I hated all his ways,
And often spoke my mind, to check
His foolish, fulsome praise.

"'Twas different with Miriam;
She thought the man sincere,
And to his wily, flattering tongue
Soon gave a ready ear.

"She thought him quite a gentleman,
As coming fresh from town;
He brought to our old country place
Some fine new fashions down.

"We used to call her Miriam,
But 'twas 'Miss Miriam' now,
And when he spoke to her, he smirked,
And made a genteel bow.

"They met about their work sometimes,
She was not there to blame,
If I had had her work to do,
It must have been the same.

"But she was forward, light, and free,
And sought his company,
And I should say, she courted him,
And gave him liberty.

"She'd steal away to take a walk,
And thus her work neglect,
And stand outside the door to talk,
With little self-respect.

"She liked his fine affected ways,
His foolish talk and mirth;
I never heard him say a thing
That I thought any worth.

"But this was clear, he won her heart;
She wished to be a bride,
And reckoned little what might hang
To that sweet name beside.

"My warnings were of no avail,
She turned them into fun;
'My dear,' she said, 'I could not wed
Your sober sweetheart, John.

"'I'll twist Fred round my thumb, you'll
    see,
When I am once his wife;
I don't see, Mary, why he may
Not worship me for life.

"'You'll have your John, and I'll have
    Fred,
And when the knot is tied,
I think, my dear, the folks will say
That I'm the blithest bride.'

"'Twas no use talking, I could see,
He had her in his power;
You'll judge yourself, with such a man,
There came a darker hour.

"And that bright face, that used to look
So innocent and clear,
Shrunk from your gaze, and turned away,
With sickening guilt and fear.

"She sought her ruin; I don't say
That he was most to blame;
She should have prized herself too high
To lose her virtuous name.

"She was dismissed with great
    contempt;
The man was kept on still;
I never thought it right and just,
But 'twas the Squire's will.

"He said the man should wed the girl,
If not, he'd lose his place:
He would not have his family
Mixed up with such disgrace.

"And so they married,—one poor room
Was all that she could get;
She never laid her wages by,
And he was deep in debt."

"Poor thing! she was unfortunate,
I'm sure," said Mrs. Head.
"Pray, neighbour, do not use that word,
It never should be said:

"'Twas not misfortune—it was sin,
That carries in its train
The loss of woman's loveliness,
And leaves a lasting stain.

"No woman is the same again;
She cannot claim respect,
And often from her husband gets
Hard words, or cold neglect.

"I did not see her from that time,
Till my own wedding day;
And then the pathway to the church
By her poor dwelling lay.

"I never shall forget her look;
She just came to the door,—
So changed, I scarcely could have known
The face I loved before.

"She took my hand in both her own,
And heavily she sighed;
'Mary!' she said, the folks may see
Who is the blithest bride.'

"She tried to smile—but oh! so wan
And haggard was her cheek;
I only squeezed her hand again,
I had no voice to speak.

"When I got settled here with John,
And all my comforts round,
Bought with the money we had saved,
Just five-and-twenty pound;

"I often thought of Miriam,
So altered and forlorn;
And went to call, the very day
Her little girl was born.

"When first she saw me coming in,
She raised her head and smiled;
Then laid her poor cheek on my hand,
And sobbed just like a child.

"She raised the sheet, to show her babe—
The little Miriam:
But oh! 'twas not a mother's joy
There was a look of shame.

"She did not name her husband then—
'I blame myself,' she said;
'The misery I suffer now
I've brought it on my head.

"'I might have been so different,
Had I been warned by you;
But I have made my burden now,
And I must bear it through.'

"She never said so much again,
She kept herself apart,
As if to hide from everyone
The anguish of her heart.

"No neighbour ever heard her speak
Of him with any slight;
Though some are sure they've heard her
        scream,
When he came home at night.

"He was a wild and wicked man,
He'd bet and drink and curse;
But for her comforts always had
A mean, or empty purse."

"How was it that he kept his place?"
"Well, that I cannot tell—
He waited on the company,
And cleaned the plate so well.

"She lost all pride about herself—
Grief broke her spirit down;
I've even seen her go about
With tatters in her gown.

"She had no heart for anything—
She started wrong in life,
And found no blessing in her path,
But ever toil and strife.

"So years passed on; at last I heard
That he had run away:
'Twas rumoured he had stolen plate—
That may be, as it may.

"I told my John I could not rest
Till I should know her state;
Her youngest was but three months old,
And she'd been ill of late.

"It was a bitter blowing day,
The sleet was driving fast,
And John was wishful I should stay
Until the storm was past.

"But something in me drove me on;
And when I feel just so,
I think there's something to be done,
And I resolved to go.

"He would not let me walk alone,
He said 'twas slippery:
You smile, and think that my good man
Makes quite a child of me.

"I almost trembled at the door
Of that deserted home;
She had the infant in her arms,
And walked about the room.

"She moved with that determined step,
As if she'd do and dare
All that a woman can and will,
When driven to despair.

"The little children, blue with cold,
Were shivering by the grate,
Where it was plain enough to see
No fire had been of late.

"She looked upon the little babe
That laid upon her arm;
She looked upon the little girls,—
But still her face was calm.

"It wasn't natural—she seemed
Insensible to pain,
And much I feared that it might turn
To frenzy on the brain.

"I tried my best to comfort her,
But what was there to say?—
I seemed but speaking to the wind—
Until my heart gave way.

"I wept the tears ran down my cheeks,
She seemed to watch them fall—
At last she said, 'these tears of yours
Do me more good than all.'

"And then she talked more like herself,
Of what she meant to do,
And I could see her mind was bent
To strive and struggle through.

"I said, 'perhaps some small relief,
The Parish Board may grant.'
She tossed her head in her old way—
"No, I had rather want.'

"'I spoke of *him*—she quickly said,
'I've but myself to blame;
I chose my lot, and I must bear
My punishment and shame.'

"But to cut short my dismal tale—
She worked like any slave,
And ne'er gave in, though one might see
Her hastening to the grave.

"Out in the fields in fog and rain,
At early dawn and late;
But sparely fed, and thinly clad,
She almost dared her fate.

"And little Miriam was left,
So patient and so mild,
To nurse the babe and mind the house—
She never was a child.

"I've often slipped in as I passed,
To take a piece of cake,
And many a time to see her there
Has made my own heart ache.

"No one can sin, and they alone
The consequences bear;
And parents' crimes are sure to fall
On those they hold most dear.

"It could not last; about three years
I think she persevered,
And then, poor thing, was forced to yield
To what she scorned and feared.

"She waited till the very last,
And when starvation came,
The child went to the Overseer,
Some parish help to claim.

"They gave an order for the 'House,'
And then of course she went;
Her independent soul at last,
Was forced to give consent.

"But once I saw her after this,
She sank so very fast,
And then 'twas evident to me
That she was near her last.

"She raised herself upon her bed:
It seemed a great relief
To open out her heart to one
Who understood her grief.

"Her talk was of her little dears
That she must leave behind;
And many things she charged me with
That weighed upon her mind.

"E'en to the last she blamed herself,
And laid no fault elsewhere;
'Do watch my little girls,' she said,
And bid them both beware.

"'When my poor Miriam's old enough,
Then tell her of my fall;
And, Mary, do not spare the truth,
But let her know it all.

"'Tell her how bitterly I rued
The loss of maiden fame;
And how the troubles of my life
From that beginning came.

"'And tell her, when I thus was sunk
In shame and poverty,
I had no comfort in my soul,
No blessing from on high.

"'And now, I go in prime of life,
Mary—I know not where—
And leave my helpless little ones
Without a mother's care.'

"A dreadful coughing fit came on,
She uttered no more then,
And my old friend, poor Miriam!
I never saw again.

"My dear, good John has promised me
To bring up Miriam,
That we may teach her how to shun
Her mother's sin and shame.

"John never liked her—men, you know,
See through such girls as these;
And sensible, right-minded men
They hardly ever please.

"But, as he says, 'tis not for us
To take the judgment-seat;
But, like our Saviour, strive to turn
The sinner's wandering feet."

"Well, you will have your recompense,
I'm sure," said Mrs. Head,
"And may the Lord in heaven bless
The children of the dead."

"Amen," said Mary, and she raised
Her eyes in silent prayer,
That these poor orphans might be kept
Beneath God's tender care.

The Boy and the Rooks.

"OH, dear! oh, dear! how hoarse I am,
I do declare it is a shame!
These rooks are here before 'tis light,
And I've to shout from morn till night.
I can't think why such birds were made,
I only wish they all were dead;
'Tis no use giving them a chase,
They light upon a another place."

Poor little Will! The day was hot;
At sunrise he had left his cot,
And cross and weary now was he,
As down he sat beneath a tree.
He nodded, then he rubbed his eyes,
He yawned again, and tried to rise;
But watch no more, his eyes will keep;
Beneath the tree he falls asleep.
But, in his dreams, the rooks still fly
In numbers, darkening the sky,
Alighting on the sheaves of corn,
As if in very spite and scorn.
Anon, he hears them lightly tread
Amongst the boughs above his head,
Hopping about with clamorous croak,
And joining in an angry talk.
At length they ceased, and from them
  spoke
An old, experienced, sober rook,
To whom the others bowed with awe;
And when he paused, they answered
  "Caw!"

"For many years," he said, "I've seen
The ways of these ungrateful men;
Through my long life I've watched the
  elves,

And think them far beneath ourselves.
But most in this—they are so mean;
These men will only think of men:
I do not wish to boast—but you
Are well aware the fact is true;
Because we know the starlings say
They can't alone secure their prey;
They're welcome, in our company,
To take whatever they can see.
If we were like these stingy men,
Those birds would hunt the fields in
  vain;
For we have might upon our side
To scatter them both far and wide:
But we agree with them to feed,
And give assistance, if they need.
How is't with man, I ask you now?
Pray what example does he show?
Has he not broken mercy's law?"—
And here the rooks responded "Caw!"
"I ask you, where had been this wheat,
So plentiful! so ripe and sweet!
Had we not followed when the plough
Turned up the earth so deep and slow,
With courage true, and eye intent,
And all our resolution bent,
To clear the ground of worms and slugs,
And multitudes of insect plagues?
And when again the seed was sown,
If we had not to aid them flown,
Those chafer grubs, and many more,
Would here have left a meagre store!
But we—who helped, and asked no pay,
Though toiling with them all the day—
Are treated now as enemies;
Forgotten all our services,

And hunted out by that poor child,
Whose howling nearly makes me wild.
Beside this base ingratitude,
We have the loss of needful food,
Which 'tis our right to share with man,
Because it is in heaven's plan.

And here—so strangely dreams are
    mixed,
Old Rook, he seemed to quote a text,
Which filled the boy with secret awe,
As all the others answered "Caw!"

"You know, my friends, how oft we've sat
Upon the trees in deep debate,
That we might wisely comprehend
Our wants and duties, means and end;
And, not through ignorance or fear,
Yield up the claims of children dear;
And we've by one consent agreed,
And in the rookery decreed,
By every wise expedient,
The plans of men to circumvent.
And thus, before the morning breeze
Has wakened up the sleeping trees,
We're sailing through the silent grey
That clothes the sky till break of day:
Before the smoke curls from the thatch,
Or labourer lifts the cottage latch,
We're on our way to take the store
We planned to take the night before.
But soon a troop of people come
To drive us from our "harvest home:"
Such is not the Creator's law.
Again the rooks responded "Caw!"

"Nor is that all, nor worst by far,—
They take away our character!
That every honest creature should
Hold dearer than his daily food.
They call us 'Thieves!'—'tis false, I say,
We're not so much of thieves as they;
They steal from all the things that live,
And very little do they give!

This field we helped to cultivate,
And worked at early dawn and late;
And now, when all is ripe, 'tis fair
That we should take our little share.
'Thieves!' do they say? We break no law."
The rooks with clamour answered, "Caw!"

"You know quite well," the bird resumed,
"Our law:—
        "If any have presumed
To steal a stick from neighbour's nest,
Instead of seeking, like the rest,
And working, willingly and free,
Like all the honest family,—
You know how then, by one consent,
We all inflict the punishment;
That they may learn such ways to dread,
We pull their house about their head.
We ought not, friends, to bear the shame
Of thief upon our ancient name;
We are not thieves; we know 'tis fair
That those who work should have a
    share."

With that, all rising from the bough,
They lighted on the field below.
The rooks in loud approval spoke,
And with the noise young Willy woke.
And many a day he pondered through
The things he'd heard, so strange and
    new;
And when he drove them from the wheat,
He almost thought they called him
    "Cheat!"
But this, it may be safely said,
He no more wished they all were dead.
Indeed, the text he learned to say,
From which the rook had preached that
    day,
When perched upon the old oak stem,—
"My Heavenly Father feedeth them."

The Lady's Dilemma.

"My son is going suddenly to countries far away,
And I must have his shirts cut out, and made without delay,
And get a set of stockings darned, and look to all his clothes,
That everything may be complete and nice before he goes.
Maria, come here instantly, and tell me if you know
Of any needle-women here I could engage to sew;
There's not a single day to spare, and therefore you may tell,
That I will pay them handsomely, if they will do it well."
"Why, ma'am, I've heard repeatedly, that not a woman here
Can make a shirt, with work that's fit for gentlemen to wear;
I'm sure I don't know where to ask, with any hope to find
A person who can do the work according to your mind."
"It can't be quite so bad as that; but bring my bonnet down,
And I will go myself and make inquiry in the town."

The lady stopped before a house, and there upon a line,
Were children's garments hanging out, trimmed round with crochet fine.
"Maria was not right, I see, I thought she could not tell;
For people who do crochet-work, of course can sew as well."
She stood before the open door, and quickly she espied.
Some children's bonnets gaily trimmed with bows and flowers beside;
But lying on the table there, and hanging on the chairs,
Were many other articles that wanted great repairs;
The husband's shirt was cobbled up, his stocking heels were out,
And, with a flounced and dirty gown, were lying tossed about.
The lady turned her quickly round, just saying with a sigh,
"If husbands drink and women beg, I see the reason why."
The next house looked more promising, for there were daughters four,
The eldest might be seventeen, the youngest ten, or more.
"Oh! here's a nest of workwomen," the lady thought and smiled.
"And can you make a shirt?" she said unto the youngest child.
"No, ma'am," replied the little girl; "but I can crochet do;
And sisters they do broderie, and can knit borders too."
"But all your elder girls can work, I'm sure," the lady said.
The mother looked uneasily, and rather shook her head.
"Well, ma'am, they can't do work that's fine—they've little time to sew;

135

At school there are so many things to learn beside, you know."
"But needle-work should surely take the very foremost place;
To fail in that must ever be a woman's great disgrace."
"Yes, ma'am, indeed that's very true, 'tis what I've always thought,
And I can't see the worth of all my children have been taught.
I've always kept my girls to school, to do a mother's part,
And sure enough there's many things which they can say by heart;
They've lessons in the grammar rules, and history, and spheres,
And such a power of learned words, I'm fit to stop my ears;
But still I'm never quite content about this education,
For now the girls are too genteel to fill a humble station;
They get too proud for servants' work, but few will learn to cook,
And at a place of *all-work* now they're quite too grand to look.
The ladies' object is not *this*, I'm certain, in the schools,
Which makes me think there may be something wrong about the rules.
By my experience, I should say a poor man's child should read,
Make out a bill, and write and spell, and sew right well indeed;
Should darn and stitch, work button-holes, and make and mend, you see;
But as to crochet, that may go to Jericho for me.
Of course the maps and other things are useful in their place;
But *then* to fail in needlework, that is a sore disgrace."
The mother cast an anxious eye upon her eldest there,
Who wished a lady's-maid to be, or else a milliner.
A flush passed quickly o'er her cheek, a cloud was on her brow;
"Young girls," she said, "were hard to keep from bad companions now."

The lady still pursued the search, and found where'er she went,
The power to make a *finished* shirt a rare accomplishment.
At last she tried another house that she had heard about,
And here she found a "hand," indeed, a sempstress, out and out;
But when she told her pressing need, she learned with great dismay,
That needlework had been bespoke for many a coming day.
"I can assure you, madam, I refuse it with regret,
But many hands would fail to do the work that I could get.
Now ladies do not work themselves, and poor folks do not learn,
I find it is not difficult my livelihood to earn.
I often wonder how it is, that such a thing could grow,
That only *fancy* needlework should be in fashion now;
Of course the gentry please themselves, but for a humble station,
I think that needlework stands first, in woman's education;
To make the most of everything, and in the neatest way,
And earn an honest shilling too, against a rainy day."

The lady left the sempstress there with many a sage reflection,
To try the school submitted to the Government inspection;
The hum of youthful voices, and the glance of eager eyes,
Gave hopeful expectation still, that they were growing wise;
Her heart swelled with emotion, her eyes were filled with tears,
To see these young ones gathering in a store for after years,
To fit them for the toils and cares of working women's lives,
As skilful household servants, or as thrifty workmen's wives.

The school was all in classes then, of children great and small,
The eldest stood before a map that hung against the wall;
All eyes were fixed intently, as the pointer flew about,
And darted here and darted there, to point the places out;
And one might almost smile to see the lady's great surprise,
When children small repeated all the principalities,
The duchies and the provinces, Danubian and French,
In words almost as accurate as those we gain from Trench.

They told where all the rivers rise that feed the Mississippi,
And where the famous sage was born, the husband of Xantippe.
They posted then to Paraguay, and touched at the Brazils,
Nor stopped, till quite confounded, on the Neilgherry hills.
The lady said, "This surely is an almost useless task."
"The Inspector's coming shortly, Ma'am-we don't know what he'll ask.
And in the maps especially we wish them to excel;
Lest when he makes report of us, we should not stand so well
As other schools, and thus incur discouragement and blame,
And bring a slur, it may be, on the governess's name."
The lady felt the reasoning, and turned her to a class,
That round a pupil-teacher had arranged itself to parse.
She listened with astonishment, to hear grammarians young,
Anatomize the very roots of our fine English tongue;
They marshalled all the parts of speech, and with no hesitation,
Of every kind of verb they showed mood, tense, and conjugation,
The lady felt her ignorance, and was afraid to show
To those triumphant, eager eyes, how little ladies know;
So passed to where another class was then in full display,
And here again she almost felt inclined to run away.
Such miracles in rule of three! such mental calculation!
Whilst billions and quintillions ran in easy numeration.
But now at last she called to mind the thing for which she came,
And straight went to the governess, her business there to name.
Could she have half a dozen shirts made by the children there?
About her shirt work, she must say, she was particular.

The mistress looked along the forms, and scanned her workers o'er;
But one might read upon her face, that she had not the power.
"We've very few good workers now—our time is very full—
So many other things have been put foremost in the school—
And little interest is felt about the sewing too,
Compared with many other things the children have to do.
The learned gentlemen who come, with college education,
Of course consider needlework beneath their observation.
But as we gain a grant of books, and money for the schools,
The whole committee think it best to carry out their rules.

I wish that ladies *competent* were made inspectors too,
To give importance to the things that women ought to do;
We should not then be posed to find young people who could sew;
'Tis nothing but encouragement, that children want, you know.
And were my own opinion asked, I certainly should say,
The time that's spent on needlework, is never thrown away;
But 'tis with that, as other things, in order to excel,
There must be time, and practice too, before they do it well."

The lady looked at all the work, and sadly shook her head,
She plainly saw that at the school, her shirts could not be made.
She went away—what next she did, I need not now relate;
But I have heard it, as a fact, that from that very date,
She reconciled her mind to what she had opposed before;
That we must have machines to sew, now hands can sew no more.

The Drunkards.

Now drunken Tom went posting on,
Went posting to the pot-house door;
Twas Saturday, his work was done;
His comrade, Ned, was there before.

"Come in, come in," to Tom, he said,
"Now let us have a pot of drink;
You've been so plaguey long, old lad,
I fancied you'd begun to slink;

"I fancied you'd begun to think,
To take to *water*, and to *sign*;
What, Tom! says I, afraid to drink!
And turn us off like Peter Pine!

"But here you are—now sit you down;
There's plenty of 'em in the tap;
There's Simon Sour begun to frown,
And heavy Jack begun to nap;

"There's Billy Pitcher on the bench,
I saw his wife, as I came in;
She's very fond of him, poor wench;
But he don't care for her a pin."

"I've had a row," said Tom, "just now;
I met my missis by the way;
She thought to catch me, any how,
Before I paid the tin away.

"Now, that's a plan won't suit my turn,
And so I told her pretty plain;
I packed her home to wash and darn,
And not hunt after me again."

"Tom, you're the lad," his comrade said,
"You are a brick, upon my life;
You'll never by the nose be led,
Nor yet be mastered by your wife.

"Who do you think I just now met,
But that old turncoat, Peter Pine?
I told him I would make a bet
He'd never get old Tom to sign."

"I sign!" said Tom, "you'll not catch me
At any foolery like that,—
I sign the pledge? ha! ha!—he! he!
Here's to the 'Jolly Brewer's Vat!'"

They drank, they swore, they danced,
   they sung,
They quarrelled, fought, shook hands,
   and laughed,
About the room the dancers flung,
And deeper still the drinkers quaffed.

Unseen, the Devil watched them there,
To stir up every foul desire,
To help their drunken lips to swear,
To set their evil hearts on fire.

Confused and fierce the uproar grew;
Tom dared his comrade to a fight;
Away their guardian angels flew,
And left them as the Devil's right.

Wild rose the yell of closing fight,
The combatants like demons strove;
Bill Pitcher clapped with all his might,
"Now, Ned, my lad, your mettle prove."

"Take that—and die," said Ned, and flung
His reeling mate upon the floor,—
With loud hurrahs the pothouse rung,
Which drunken Tom would hear no more.

The man was killed. The jury met,
And Ned upon his trial stood:
"The man, his death in fighting met,
And Ned, was guilty of his blood."

Tom's widow never shed a tear;
His comrades said he was a fool,
Who always got too full of beer,
And then his temper could not rule.

But where is Tom?—Before a court
Where God is judge, who knows the
     whole,
Who waiteth not for man's report,
But gives a verdict on the soul.

Before that high and holy throne,
How conscience stung him none can tell;
He dared not face the Righteous One—
Self-doomed, his spirit sunk to Hell,

To dwell where devils haunt the place
With cruel mockery and jeer;
Where never sight of happy face
His everlasting grief might cheer.

To recollect, he might have been
An angel in the world of light,
Redeemed from sorrow, pain, and sin,
And filled with ever new delight.

And Billy Pitcher—where is he?
He saw Ned strike the fatal blow;
He saw his vain attempt to flee;
He saw him off to prison go.

And he stole out, a sobered man,
Aghast with fear, and cold with dread;
And hardly knowing where he ran,
He took the path that homeward led.

That drunken yell of dying pain
Kept ringing in his haunted ear;
He stopped and listened, ran again,
With horror dumb, and guilty fear.

The gusty wind, in fitful moans,
Went wailing through the rushing trees;
His flesh was creeping on his bones,
His very life-blood seemed to freeze.

Dull, murky clouds flew wildly fast,
The moon just seen, then pitchy night;
A shrouded form is gliding past—
A shriek appals him with affright.

Twas but a screech-owl, hooting shrill
Its dreary and foreboding cry,—
The moonlight glanced upon a mill,
Its ghostly form uprising high.

He stumbled on with headlong speed,
The wild briar switched across his face;
The startled birds whirred o'er his head,
Affrighted from their roosting-place.

At last, beneath the parting gloom,
He saw his cottage, dull and dim;
No cheerful ray bade welcome home,
No loving face looked forth for him.

A squalid form unclosed the door,
Why did she shrink and tremble so?
Oh, hardest lot! oh, poorest poor!
Her husband's greeting is a blow.

But not to-night—he stumbled in,
And not a single word he said,
But with a vacant ghastly grin,
He flung himself upon the bed.

The little ones, afraid to hear
Their mother's cries, their father's blows,
Crept down the bed in trembling fear,
And hid themselves beneath the clothes.

In troubled sleep the night passed on;
The wretched wife, too, sank to rest,
Till startled by a frightful groan,
That shook her husband's heaving breast.

He did not wake, but muttered o'er
Disjointed words; then, with a cry,
Sprung out upon the cottage floor,
And stared about with glaring eye.

But still he spoke not: at the dawn.
He left his house, and slunk away,
With haggard look and step forlorn,
As though he loathed the light of day.

He sat him down upon a bank,
The lark was singing in the skies,
Straining its little throat to thank
The unknown author of its joys.

A linnet's nest was in a bush,
He listless marked their busy cares
To feed their young—the constant gush
Of love from faithful hearts like theirs.

He sat and watched, till o'er his soul
A gentle thrill of nature crept,
And softer feelings kindly stole,
Until he bowed his head and wept.

He wept, that hard and selfish man,
Such tears as gave his heart relief;
Fast down his rugged cheeks they ran,
Yet were not wholly tears of grief.

Oh, heavenly pity, love divine!
Omnipotent, unsearchable—
Above our thoughts Thy counsels shine,
We only know Thou doest well.

Poor prodigal, He looks on thee!
Before thy God and Saviour bow;
Like wool thy scarlet sins may be,
Like snow upon the mountain's brow.

"Repent and live: why will ye die?"
The door is open—tarry not;
To Him who died for sinners fly,
And all your sins shall be forgot.

Poor Will! he pondered o'er his life,
His mad career of hardened crime;
He thought of his neglected wife,
Whose days he darkened in their prime.

He thought about his little ones,
Who never climbed their father's knee;
He thought of Ned, the dead man's
    groans,
And what he yet himself might be.

He thought about his youthful days,
When he was innocent and good,
About his mother's pious ways,
And how she prayed for him to God.

His memory brought clearly back
The steps by which he'd hurried on,
A frightful path of sin, as black
As ever faced the mid-day sun.

Amazed, and sore perplexed he stood,
The sweat streamed off his rugged brow;
Like midnight wanderer in a wood,
More hopeless still his prospects grow.

The day wore on, he marked it not,
He felt not that his cheeks were wet;
He saw himself a drunken sot
Bound fast within the devil's net.

He groaned beneath his heavy load;
At last, a bitter cry there came,—
"Be merciful to me, O God!
For I, a wretched sinner am."

The soul has dealings with its God
In such an hour, we may not write,
When all His grace is shed abroad,
And darkness melts in floods of light.

Thus, even now, that mercy came,
And righteous retribution slept,
The man could trust a Saviour's name,
And like a little child he wept.

And through his soul there ran a sense
Of hope, and faith, and sin forgiven;
A healing glow of penitence,
With power to lift his heart to heaven.

At length the slanting western ray
Streamed glancing through the leafy
  trees;
The birds sang forth on every spray,
And softly sighed the evening breeze.

And all around, the peaceful earth,
Glimmering in purpled sunshine lay,—
He felt the sweet harmonious mirth,
The grateful hymn of closing day.

Homeward he turned—he thought of
  Jane,—
Meek victim of his vicious course;
And bitterly, with stinging pain,
Came inward shame and deep remorse.

His children saw him drawing nigh,
Their playful mirth at once they check;
The little one began to cry,
And clung around its mother's neck.

He met her with a timid gaze,—
His heart was full, he could not speak,
But with a look of early days
He pressed a kiss upon her cheek.

Oh, faithful woman! gentle dove,—
Her pent-up heart she could not check,
But, with a bursting cry of love,
She flung her arms about his neck.

"Dear William! love me once again;—
Oh! heal your Jenny's broken heart;
Forget this horrid dream—and then,
With love all new, our lives shall start."

"I'll try, indeed I will, my love;
Forgive me, Jenny, if you can;
As God is true, in heaven above,
I'll try to be a better man."

As winter streams that long have lain
In icy fetters darkly bound,
When spring returns, leap forth again,
And fill the vale with song and sound;

So did their spring-time now return,
And love dissolved the icy chain,
And smothered hopes began to burn,
And Jenny was herself again.

The children stole in one by one,
And sidled round with downcast eyes;
The baby clapped its hands for fun,
And stared about with laughing eyes.

The father took them on his knees,
And gave each little cheek a kiss.
Poor Jane the sight with rapture sees;
Oh! when was Sabbath eve like this?

Himself—he now began to fear;
He felt he stood on peril's edge,
And whispered in his Jenny's ear,
"I'm going, wife, to sign the pledge."

He signed it, and he kept it, too,
And more than that, he fled from sin;
The Saviour's love he held in view,
And so his strength increased within.

With wages good his work was paid;
He served his earthly master well;
But oh! his heavenly Master made
His heart more rich than words can tell.

A Sad Story

"OH, mother! I see Mr. Sharp—
He's coming up this way;
He's coming for the rent, I know—
He said he would not stay,
But put an execution in
If 'twas not paid to-day."

"Well, Mary, child! don't tremble so,
For I have paid the rent;
When you were fast asleep last night
I to the Pawn-shop went,
And left my woollen shawl behind,
And they've the money lent.

"I've said, I never would go there;
But then, what must be, must:
Your father says he can't get work
To earn the barest crust;
And, seeing we've no chance to pay,
I dare not go on trust.

"I could not let them take our bed
Whilst Jane is lying there;
She has not many days, poor child!—
I'm sure it is my prayer,
That God would take her to Himself,
Away from all our care."

"I think I'll go again, mother,
To Mrs. Cramp, and see
If she will give her anything,
However small it be,
To tempt her just to eat a bit—
She can but scold at me.

"We've lived so long near Mrs. Cramp,
She knows you are no cheat,
Nor like the common beggar-folks
That go about the street,
And boldly ask for charity
From any one they meet."

"No, Mary, child, 'twill be no use,
For people do not think,
Whilst every day they have themselves
Enough to eat and drink,
That people starve about their homes,
Who still from begging shrink.

"No doubt it is an easy thing
To reckon us a mass,
And say, imposture and deceit
Are common to the class;
And that it is on principle
Our misery they pass.

"I'm sure I hate to beg myself,
I'd rather work to death;
But what you would, and what you can,
Is not like drawing breath:
You may be forced to do a thing,
And hold it far beneath;

"I felt it far beneath myself
That woollen shawl to pawn;
I hold the plan, and always did—
And always shall—in scorn;
But what to do, I know no more
Than infant just new born.

"You can't make work, I wish you could—
I hope that by and by
Our work will look a little up,
And bread not be so high;
If not—we have but two things left—
The workhouse, or to die.

"It passes me to understand
Why things should go this way;
Why some folks' life is chained to work,
And some do nought but play—
But 'tis a riddle I suppose
Will all be clear some day.

They talk of great advantages
That working folks have now,
And wonderful improvements too,
They're quite prepared to show;
Well—if 'tis in the dwelling-house—
I should be glad to know.

"I'm sure, when I remember now,
The house where I was born,
When through the old oak-trees I've
    watched
The earliest flush of dawn,
I never thought that life could be
So utterly forlorn.

"Our rooms were large, and rather low;
We did not care for that;
There was the chimney corner, where
My mother always sat;
But here, they are so cramped and
    small
You could not swing a cat.

"I hate these gloomy papered walls,
They eat up all the light;
They're not so wholesome, any way,
As when they're clean and white;
And if they do put papers up
They might be clean and bright.

"We've had the fever, now three times,
Within this dwelling here—
They say, infection has been left,
And we should get it clear;
'Tis in the paper, I've no doubt,
If 'tis left anywhere.

"Tell us to clear it!—What's the use?—
Why just look in the street!
The horrid standing puddles,
And the filthy smells you meet,—
And landlords not at all concerned
To make the drains complete.

"I think that landlords should be forced
To make good sound repairs;
Just see that leakage in the roof
That we have got upstairs.
I know it's just the death of Jane,
With that bad cough of hers.

"The room is always damp and cold,
It strikes one to the heart,
But when I've asked to have it stopped,
He says that we can start;
That if folks are dissatisfied,
They'd better far depart.

"He knows 'twould cost us many pence
To move our things away;
And so he calculates on *that*
To force us on to stay—
And let the dripping wet come in
On every rainy day.

"Then, in such wretched holes as these
To preach of modesty!
When we are forced to sleep as thick
As pigs within a sty;
When they have room, poor folks don't
    lack
A sense of decency.

"Oh! what a little thing would make
A toil-worn woman glad!—
But all the round of day and night,
Is only sad, and sad;
Shut out of light, and air, and room;
And pay and victuals bad.

"I've been a fool, I know sometimes,
For really I could stop
And cry my heart away before
An ironmonger's shop,
And wish a little cooking stove,
Would from the heavens drop.

"I've heard there are advertisements,
About them in the 'bus,'
And every paper tells of some
Fresh novelty or fuss;
Oh! why will nobody contrive
A cooking stove for us?

"One might begin to see a chance
Of management once more,
Which seems to me a banished thing
From many people's door;
We have not things to manage with,
And so—we've lost the power.

"The everlasting cup of tea,
And loaf of baker's bread;
Without the least variety,
The family is fed;—
You cannot make your husband guess
What he may find instead.

"I've sometimes thought, and
    sometimes dreamt
About a little range,
And through me ran a thrill of joy,
A happy sort of change;—
I saw the smoking home-baked bread,
All smelling sweet and strange;

"I thought of puddings made of rice,
To fill the children well,
Just sweetened up with treacle too,
To make it taste and smell;
And baked potatoes!—nice and hot!—
Too good almost to tell.

"I've thought, if there should be a
    chance,
To get a bit of meat,
How nicely I could bake it then,
And have it so complete!
And always have the water hot,
To wash, and keep us neat.

"Yes, then I'd manage with a hope,
And prize my little pelf;
They would not find our bread, I know,
Come off the baker's shelf;
For I would buy good household flour,
And bake it for myself.

"It almost goes as far again—
Of course, if not cut *new*;
A hundred little odds and ends,
I've thought to bake and stew,
And get a better nourishment,
With pleasant changes too.

"But that's a dream—an oven here,
With copper and a fire,
So bake and boil, and dry at once
Your very heart's desire!
You might as well ask for the moon,
Or think that you could buy her!

"I can't think what will come to us!
I really cannot tell!
I'm sometimes frightened at myself,
My feelings will rebel;
And then I'm fit to think that earth
Is half as bad as hell.

"If any one had said to me,
 About six years ago,
That I should talk of Jenny's death,
And not a tear would flow,—
I should have said—'A mother's heart!
You cannot feel, or know.'

"But so it is—poor little dear!—
The horrid thoughts I have,—
That when the first distress is past,
And she is in her grave,
That we shall then be better off,
And some expenses save.

"I hardly think it is myself,
When I go on this way;
I feel so lost, and wretched, too,
I cannot read or pray;—
There's nothing but a miracle
Would help, as you may say.

"I dreamt last night—the whole night
    through—
About a funeral,
And I walked foremost in the train,
And nearly touched the pall,
And there were many mourners there,
The clergyman and all.

"We stood around an open grave,
Beneath a spreading tree;
A pleasant sound the branches made,
All waving light and free;
The service and the tolling bell
Seemed music unto me.

"I knew it was my mother's grave,
That we were standing by,
And all were dressed in handsome black,
And so were you and I,
Whilst she, dear soul! was sleeping there
Amongst her family.

"A little robin sat and sang
So sweetly o'er the dead;
And far above, a lonely rook,
Went sailing overhead,
Calling aloud from time to time
The friends, who onward sped.

"It was so still, that you could hear
The insects in the air,
And sunshine flickered through the
    leaves,
Just stealing here and there;
And all came in so peacefully,
To join the solemn prayer.

"I saw the sexton take his spade,
And heard the fresh earth fall;—
Then, suddenly, I stood beside
 A dirty churchyard wall,
And there a wretched coffin stood,
Without a bit of pall.

"It was a little coffin, too,
Just big enough for Jane;
It was a pauper's funeral,
I saw that very plain;
The people talked and pushed about,
As if there were no pain.

"The service, that was hurried through,
You could not catch the words;
And then, they let the coffin down
With two old dirty cords;
And filled the grave a little bit,
And took away the boards.

"The yellow fog was thick and raw,
You could not see the sky;
And no one had a mourning dress,
And no one stopped to cry;
A woman and a girl stood there,—
And that was you and I."

"Oh, mother! pray don't go on so,
You make me quite afraid!
Do you forget the beggar-man
Who every day was laid
Before the cruel rich man's gate,
For only crumbs of bread?

"But when at last they came to die,
The rich man and the other,
The beggar went to Abraham,
As if he were his brother:
Then he was richest of the two,
And that for ever, mother!

"We are as badly off, I think,
As Lazarus could be;
And if we bear our troubles well,
And patiently as he,
We, too, may rest with Abraham,
And all the blessed see."

"Don't talk so, child—I'm not like him:
I hope there'll come the day
When I shall read the Bible, too,
And go to church and pray;—
I wonder if our troubles here
Do take our sins away."

"I dreamt a dream last night, mother,
I thought that I was dead,
And I was laid upon the floor,
Because you'd sold the bed,
And you were kneeling by my side,
And gently held my head.

"Your face seemed then to fade away,
These walls grew thin as air,
And light broke in on every side,
So beautiful and fair,
I never saw the sunshine look
So dazzling anywhere.

"I heard you cry, 'Oh, Mary! stay;'
Your voice died on my ear,
But suddenly the air was filled
With music, far and near,—
Sweet, lovely sounds, that sunk away,
Then rose up high and clear.

"I cannot tell you how I went,
My spirit seemed to fly,
I left the earth behind, and flew
Right upward to the sky;
And I was singing as I went
I was so full of joy.

"I heard the angels' wings around,
And brighter grew the light;
They seemed to watch and welcome
    me,
And guide my spirit right,
Until I reached a lovely place,
Where all was glowing white.

"I can't describe it—'twas too bright
For any living eye;
But if poor Jane, and all of us,
Might go there when we die,
I would not care, nor fret again,
About our poverty.

"I saw ten thousand faces there,
All beaming like the sun,
Such blessed joy and happiness
On all their faces shone,
And when they sang, their voices
    seemed
To mingle all in one.

"And there I saw the Saviour stand,
My very heart did melt—
Ah! mother, I can never tell
How happy then I felt,
When He looked down and smiled on
    me,
As at his feet I knelt.

"I woke up then, for Jane began,
Her dreadful cough and cry;
But though I woke, I saw that face,
And shall do, till I die:
I long to take dear Jenny's place,
And to my Saviour fly.

"Oh! how I wish that you could dream
My dream a little while,
And see that shining company
Rejoicing in his smile;
I think 'twould give you heart to bear
Our poverty and toil."

"Well child, perhaps it might be so,
If I had less to bear;
But now I'm almost worn to death,
And driven to despair:
'Twould be hypocrisy in me
To talk of God and prayer."

"Oh! mother, don't you recollect
The words which Christ addressed
To weary, heavy-laden souls,
With care and sin distressed:
He said if they would come to Him,
That He would give them rest.

"Do let us try to bear our lot,
However hard it be,
And take our troubles all to Him,
Who looked so kind at me;
And think how pleasant rest will be
Throughout Eternity."

"Why, Mary child, you've learned to
      preach,
Just like a minister
Go, tell poor Jane your pretty dream;
Perhaps 'twill comfort her;
And I will go and try to raise,
A little spark of fire."

The London Attic.
Another Story.

FAST fades the year, and Christmas
  time
Has travelled round again;
The naked trees are shivering
Upon the barren plain.

The birds are mute, the bees are still,
Their pleasant mirth is done;
There's not a fly, to hum or buzz
Beneath December's sun.

But men and boys are shouting there,
And beat the bushes round,
And huntsmen in their scarlet coats
Are riding o'er the ground.

And they will ride, and laugh, and shout,
As long as they can see;
Then hasten home to blazing fires,
And jovial company.

But we will leave the Christmas sports,
And all the Christmas fare,
To watch a lady, in a court
Of London town so fair.

Take care! take care! the place is dark,
That narrow stair is steep—
And broken, too, and dangerous—
She'll scarce her footing keep.

But up she goes—she's at the door,
And trembles now with fear;
She'd better far go back again—
The dwelling looks so queer.

One cannot tell what people dwell
In such abodes as these;
The worst of thieves, or murderers,
Might shelter here with ease.

But there she stops—she fears to knock,
Yet will not go away;
For she has heard the folks will starve
If left another day.

She stands, and listens for a while—
The door is just ajar—
And dimly now she can observe
A boy and woman there.

The woman's voice is sweet and low,
Her face is very pale;
But there's a calm upon her brow,
That tells a thoughtful tale.

What have they in that dismal place?
The room looks very bare;
There's something like a wretched bed,
And children sleeping there.

And what beside? there is no fire;
And this is Christmas eve!
And not a sign of any food,
That she can yet perceive.

The woman's light is burning low;
She lays her work aside;
And still keeps talking to the boy,
Who listens at her side.

"I do not yet despair my child,
We've been as low before,
And God has not forgot His way
Unto the widow's door.

"We have no food, nor work to do,
We've neither light nor fire;
But still, my heart says God is true,
Though man may be a liar.

"I've proved Him oft, through year and
    year,
That He will not forsake—
Will not forsake me utterly,
Though sore my heart may ache.

"He feeds the ravens when they call;
He clothes the lilies fine;
And he has numbered every hair
Upon your head and mine.

 "I say it, James, with sense of sin,
And yet with humble trust,
That we have tried to do His will,
And sought His kingdom first.

"I do not claim, as our desert,
That God should give us bread;
But He has promised that He will,
And there my faith is stayed.

"Your father on the day he died,
In deep and earnest prayer
Gave up his helpless family
To God's almighty care.

"He knew the world was rough and wild,
And all its ways uneven;
He knew we should have weary feet
Before we got to heaven.

"His prayer was heard, and heeded too,
And registered on high;
I've always felt that he was heard,
Through all our poverty.

"What but the grace of God has kept
Our hands and hearts from sin,
When day and night we've wanted
    bread,
And nothing coming in?

"Oh, Jemmy, lad! it was the Lord
Who kept you in the street
From joining in with wicked boys,
Or stealing food to eat.

"Oh! many a time, and many, child,
My heart has trembled through,
Lest hunger, and temptation sore,
Should be too strong for you.

"But you are my sweet comfort, James,
My good, my honest son!
And we will trust our Father still,
And say, 'Thy will be done.'

"I once had hoped on Christmas-day
That you might have a treat,
But now, I fear, the little ones
Will cry for bread to eat.

"The Lord can send it, if He will;
We cannot beg, or steal;
He knows we've tried in vain for work,
And now have not a meal.

"'Twas on this evening, Jemmy dear!
Our Saviour came to earth;
A lowly manger was His bed,
And poor men hailed His birth.

"And now He'll not forget the poor,
In poverty's dark hour;
He died to save us from our sins,
And lives to give us power.

"'Tis hard, I know, 'tis very hard,
To bear these things in mind,
When all the world, and every thing,
Looks hopeless and unkind.

"But 'tis in worst extremity,
The Saviour draweth nigh;
We'll tell Him, once again, my child,
Of all our poverty."

She knelt beside the flickering light,
Upon that naked floor,
And lifted up her voice to God,
His mercy to implore.

And angels bowed their heads to hear—
It was a solemn sight
To see those lonely pleaders there,
In that dark attic height,—

Speaking to Him who guides the stars,
Who makes the welkin ring,
And "taketh up the islands
As a very little thing;"

Pleading with Him as children plead
Who know their parent's heart—
Not with a wordy eloquence,
Nor speeches framed with art;

But in a language clear and full,
And simple and sincere,
As if they knew that every word
Would reach their Father's ear.

And thankful praise ascended, too,
For mercies even then;
And Jemmy, with his youthful voice,
Responded his "Amen."

And when they both had risen up
From off that hallowed floor,
The lady, with a swelling heart,
Tapped gently at the door.

We need not tell what then befel,
But this can truly say,
That their's was not an empty board
Upon that Christmas day.

Because the God of Providence
Is watching everywhere,
And sending forth His ministers
To answer faithful prayer.

The Green Hillside.

THE sheep are browsing on the hill,
The shepherd boy all day,
Has no one but his faithful dog
To hear what he would say.

But yet, he has companions here
Who many tales could tell,
If he had wit to question them,
And mark their answers well.

"Just let us ask the little bee,
That makes that pleasant hum,
How first it found the mountain thyme
So far away from home?"

The bee raised up its knowing head,
And poised upon its wing,
And as it hummed, methought it said,
"When first a little thing,

"I knew where all the flowers grew
As well as I do now;
I knew the way to build a cell,
And no one taught me how.

I found the pattern in my heart,
And printed in my mind,
I could not make the least mistake
If I had been inclined.

"I never sting, unless provoked,
Unless compelled to stay,—
My work is all of consequence."
With that it flew away.

"Now down upon the ground, my boy,
And see if you can find
Who made this sheet of gossamer,
That's floating in the wind.

"You see it spread o'er all the hill,
And shining in the sun,
Some skilful workman surely has
This wondrous labour done."

"I see a little tiny thing,
Scarce bigger than a pin,
But that can never have the power
A web like this to spin!"

"We'll ask it,—'Did you make this web,
Small thing, who look so weak?'
Upon the web its foot it set,
And seemed inclined to speak.

We laid our heads close to the ground,
The tiny voice to hear;
And then methought there came a
    sound,
Clear ringing in my ear:—

"The webs you think so wonderful
We make with great content;
We are a numerous family,
But work with one consent.

"We all have made a slender web,
To fasten in this way,
Lest we should lose the little flies
Sent to us day by day.

"We spread them in the twilight hour,
When stars begin to wink,
And thus we get the mountain dew,
The purest kind of drink.

"We don't keep always on the ground,
Because we have the power
To rise up lightly in the sky,
Above your steeple tower.

"If you were on the pinnacle,
And looked around you there,
You'd see a fleet of silken sails,
All floating in the air.

"Sometimes the giant foot of man
Our slender work will tear;
But knowing how to make the web,
We also can repair.

"I made a web the very day
When first I saw the sky;
No one instructed me;" it stopped—
For then a little fly

Came skimming lightly o'er the grass,
It fell my face before;
I saw the little cobweb shake,
And then, I saw no more;

But down we sat upon the turf,
And looked around the skies,
And talked of God, whose wisdom made
These little creatures wise.

And we resolved another day
To come, whate'er betide,
To hear the little teachers talk,
Upon the green hillside.

The Traveller and the Farmer.

"THERE's a snug little farm in the valley below,
Lying up to the road, by the overshot mill,
And stretching, I fancy, as far as the brow,
That shelters the beech-wood, on Honeydown Hill.

"I've travelled this road twice before in my life,
And have pulled up my horse to observe and admire;
But this time, I thought, as I said to my wife,
The name of the farmer I'd stop to inquire.

"Your farm, sir, I see borders close upon *that*,
Of course you can tell me the gentleman's name;
But if you have leisure for traveller's chat,
I may learn *why* that farmer puts others to shame."

"You are heartily welcome, sir, 'light from your horse,
And make no apology, pray sir, I beg;
And whilst we are having a little discourse,
My groom shall attend to your capital nag."

"Oh! you have an eye for good horses, my friend,
A better than that never took to the road;
He's good wind and limb, you can't alter to mend;
He's one that may warrant a man to be proud.

"But not to intrude on your time very long,
For I see that your reapers are slashing away,
To whom do those glorious wheat-fields belong,
And the barley-fields there, that compelled me to stay?

"I ride through the country, and see pretty much,
And know many farmers who stand very high;
But still I must say that I never saw such
A farmer as this man appears to my eye.

"Sir, the farm is a garden!—he knows the right way
To cajole mother earth, to afford him a prize."
"Well, that is what I and my neighbours all say;
But he maintains this, sir—it comes from the skies.

"He's a comical fish, as you'll find in you'll find in your time,
But a farmer to beat him you'll not find at all;
His crops, as you say, and his stock are all prime;
But a saint or fanatic old Peter we call."

"Oh! that is the genus! Well, what does he do?
Saints arn't very common 'mongst farmers, I've heard;
But let him be Gentile, or let him be Jew,
He knows how to manage a farm and a herd."

"Well! what does he do? Now I'm sure you will laugh,
Though I cannot but say I'm afraid he'll go mad;
And value his barley no more than his chaff;
He's a teetotal fool, sir, or something as bad."

"Well! that is a subject I quite let alone;
For a drunkard I reckon much worse than a brute;
But 'tis not through water such crops have been grown,
I'd drink it myself, sir, if that were the fruit."

"'Tis not as you say, and, of course, cannot be;
But he beats us quite hollow, and, year after year,
We can't take a sample to market, not we,
That can in the least with his samples compare.

"We farm much alike, but he still keeps ahead;
His sheep now are sound, sir, while mine have the rot;
I lost many lambs, while he hadn't one dead,
And his bullocks are always a capital lot.

"I tell him he's lucky! He says, 'No such thing;
He takes but the means that are put in his power;'
So he prays for a season to sow and to spring,
And asks for the sunshine, the rain, and the shower.

"'Tis childish to hear him, how often he prays!
As if all his praying the weather had made!
But he really has faith in these credulous ways,
And the Bible, he says, put it into his head.

"He has proverbs and texts that he strings by the score,
About covenants under an old standing lease,
Where special regard is bestowed on the poor,
And their treatment connects with the farmer's increase.

"There's one way he has—and it isn't quite fair—
He gives higher wages than we have agreed;
He says there's enough for himself, and to spare,
And 'tis right that the folks should have plenty of feed.

"Well! of course he gets all the respectable hands;
He employs, I should think, twice as many as I;
But it answers, he says, on his arable lands,
And he likes them about him, and under his eye.

"And they like it, too, sir; he's foolishly good,
His men are all spoiled for a farmer elsewhere;
There's no end of lending, and helping, and food,
And mending their dwellings, and mending their fare.

My little girl read about Boaz and Ruth;
Old Peter might well for the likeness have sat,
With his people about him—his children forsooth—
Well, it kept in my memory days after that.

"I expect the old man likes to copy those ways;
You would not believe, what the gleaners will find;
There's gleaning and gleaming for days upon days,
All the wheat in the corners he leaves it behind.

"I should not much wonder, if he'd been a Jew—
For Peter, you see, is a Testament name—
And it's written, they say—but I hope 'tis not true—
That some day they'll put all the Gentiles to shame."

"Hold! hold! for I think you have got from your text;
I should call him a Christian, quite sound to the bone,
And whether the Gentile or Jew flourish next,
Old Peter the saint is a Christian alone."

"Incendiary fires he would not much dread,
If I've a right guess of his people at all ?"
"Oh, bless your heart! no—every hair of his head
They would catch it, and kiss it, before it should fall."

"Well then, I must say that his plans answer best;
He's a blessing to others, as well as himself,
His barns are all full, and his mind is at rest,
And his riches increase, though he scatters his pelf.

"When I turn a farmer, I'll come to his school,
For I hate all oppression, and grinding, and strife;
And I think that the Bible will do as a rule
For a farmer to work by, and order his life.

"But further intrusion I'm sure would be wrong,
Whilst your reapers are gallantly work away;
So I'll ponder our talk as I'm riding along,
And I heartily thank you, and wish you good day."

The Little Schismatics; or, Irreligion.

THREE little girls were walking home from school,
Engaged, it seemed, in very warm debate,
And though I do not listen as a rule,
I heard the converse, which I now relate.

The eldest of them might be twelve years old,
The youngest ten—she might be near eleven,
But felt herself quite competent to hold
Discourse on Doctrine, and the things of Heaven.

For there had been, what people call a "split,"
A cruel jar, which rends a church in two,
And brings forth many things, alike unfit
For Christian men to sanction or to do.

It often rises from a simple cause,
In which religion has no real part,—
A love of rule may be—or splitting straws,—
Or narrow views of God's paternal heart.

And friendly neighbours who had chanted praise,
And walked together in communion sweet,
Will then another little chapel raise,
And pass each other in the public street.

And listening children these contentions hear,
And think religion is a thing of strife,
To talk and boast about, and domineer,
And not the balm that sweetens human life.

And so these children tossed their bags about,
All speaking loud, the other's voice to drown,
Then drew up short, to crush an honest doubt,
Or pin a little adversary down.

The robin redbreast hopped upon their path,
And watched them keenly, with his bright black eye,
Then picked a worm to pieces, as in wrath,
Meaning, we thought, to warn them on the sly.

The butterflies were dancing in the sun,
Chasing each other in their loving play;
The well-grown lambs, so full of freak and fun,
Were starting races on the upland way.

The ants all toiled together on the ground;
With pleasant greetings, on their busy road:
The bees hummed gaily, flitting round and round,
To gather wax and honey for their load.

The nightingale was singing in the oak;
The blackbird whistled from the apple-tree;
The skylark from the clouds his music shook,
Not two alike—and yet they all agree.

The poplar and the elm stood side by side,
The weeping willow grew beneath their shade;
The little brawling brook went tumbling wide,
But joined the stream that rippled through the glade.

Bright flowers together nestled on the bank;
The foxglove rose above, with no pretence;
There was no squabble there, for rule or rank,
And all were lovely in their difference.

The little girls who strayed along the path,
Did not perceive these lessons, all so good;
But as the robin picked the worm,—in wrath
They mangled things they little understood.

FANNY FLIP.
"My father and the deacon got to words,
They both were angry, as they well could be,
My mother said, 'twas well they had not swords,
It might not then have ended peaceably.

My father—he took Mr. Sawyer's part,
The deacon—he was quite the other way,
And he declared the minister should start,
My father said, the minister should stay."

MARY BROWN.
"Well, Fanny Flip, then come to church with me,
You chapel folks do always quarrel so,
I never see our clergy disagree,
And church is more genteel, of course you know."

FANNY FLIP.
"Well—are you High Church then—or are you *Low*
For all *low* doctrine we esteem as nought;
We call ourselves High Calvinists, you know,
We're very different from the common sort."

MARY BROWN.
"We are *The Church*, and we shall go to heaven,
If we're baptized, and always go on right,
Our sins are washed away, and we're forgiven;
'Twas said so in the sermon t'other night."

FANNY FLIP.
"Pray, what's the good your infant sprinkling does?
Are Christian people manufactured so?
Without immersion, 'tis an idle fuss,
And who knows where your sprinkled babes will go?

"My father says that infants go to hell
Before they even know they have a soul,
That reprobation lights on them, as well
As wicked people who have lied and stole."

"Well—that I don't believe," said Jessie Young,
"Or why should Jesus little children call?"
"No, you don't know—you'd better hold your tongue,
You Independents aren't baptized at all."

JESSIE YOUNG.
"Oh! Fanny Flip, how can you be so rude?
We call ourselves baptized as well as you;
We have our way, that we think quite as good,
And hold it to be scriptural and true.

"Baptized or not, I never will believe
That Jesus meant that babies should be lost;
My mother says 'tis shocking to conceive,
She thinks they're all among the heavenly host."

FANNY FLIP.
"Yes, you are ignorant, but we are right,
And that we'll stick to, for we know it well;"
"You're wrong," said Mary Brown, "for Mr. Blight
Said, where Dissenters went he could not tell."

"I shall not speak to you, Miss Mary Brown,"
"Nor I to you, Miss Fanny Flip—you'll see—
We'd better part at once, and walk alone,
It's no use talking if we can't agree."

It would have come to this; but very near,
A gentlewoman followed on their track;
They talked so loud, that any one could hear,
And were too eager to be looking back.

"Stop, little girls!" she said, "and rest awhile;
You all look heated on this pleasant day,
There's room to sit upon this meadow stile,
And we can talk, and pass the time away.

"I've read this morning of a robbery
That very nearly into murder ran;
But that a traveller, passing by the way,
Came just in time to save the wretched man.

"It seems that he was going to a town;
His business there, the writer has not said;
When cruel robbers came and knocked him down,
Took all he had, and left him there for dead.

"Alone and bleeding on the ground he lay—
At last, poor man! he saw a priest draw nigh,
One of the sect with whom he used to pray,
A man renowned for rigid piety,—

"Who kept his Church's law with strictest zeal—
In forms and festivals was quite at home;
'Twas said, his heart was not much given to feel,
But still the man was glad to see him come.

"He did not doubt in him a friend to find,
To bind his wounds, and give a little ease,
Who would at least be pitiful and kind,
And like a minister, speak words of peace.

"But would you think it? When the priest came by,
And saw him lying in that doleful case,
He crossed the road with cold averted eye,
Spoke not a word, but went a quicker pace."

"Oh! what a shame," the little girls replied,
"How could he leave the poor man on the road!"
"The priest, my dear, was full of self and pride,
And so despised his neighbour, and his God.

"The hours passed on, the sun looked fiercely down;
Still from his wounds the crimson life-blood flowed,
All hope of succour from his mind had gone,
When he perceived a traveller on the road.

Oh, joyful sight! this man was reckoned good;
An office-bearer in a church he knew:
Oh! he would come and staunch the flowing blood,
And be a friend, and sweet companion too.

"He could not speak, the power of speech had fled;
But up he looked with mute imploring gaze:
The traveller paused—then on his way he sped,
He would not stop the dying man to raise."

"Oh! what a shame," the little girls reply,
"For good men should be always very kind."
"They should, my dears, and so should you and I
Do good to others with a willing mind.

"The night was drawing on; the sun was set;
The cold wind blew upon his stiffened limb;
His naked body with the dew was wet;
And not a soul had come to pity him.

"His heart was heavy in his aching breast;
How could his brethren so unfeeling be?
How could they see a creature so distressed
Without a touch of love or sympathy?

"He closed his eyes, and waited now for death;—
What sound is that which strikes upon his ear?
His blood runs chill, he holds his failing breath;—
The tramp of feet is quickly drawing near.

"He starts—he looks—then turns his head away;
'Oh, worse than death! that such my fate should be!
That man's a wicked heretic, they say;
And I may die ere he will care for me.'

"It is not so; there's kindness in his eye;
A generous pity fills his manly heart;
He leaves his mule, he lifts him tenderly,
And pours in oil to heal the wounded part.

"With wine he cheers—oh, hospitable feast!
He shields his body from the cold night air,
Then gently puts him on his trusty beast,
And leads him on with all a brother's care.

"He brought him to a comfortable inn;
He fed and lodged him at his own expense;
He did not think what he might lose or win,
He felt that kindness has its recompense.

"And on the morrow, when he went away,
He paid his money cheerfully and free,
And to the host he said, 'My friend, I pray
That you will nurse this stranger here for me.

"'Don't let him want; the charges I will pay;
Whate'er you spend, put down to my account;
I shall be back again some future day,
And then will settle for the whole amount.'"

"Oh! what a tender-hearted man was he,"
Exclaimed the girls; "and what a noble mind!"
"Yes, my dear children, in that man we see
A copy left for us and all mankind.

"He did not stop to ask of sect or name,
He did not think how he had been baptized;
His heart responded to a sufferer's claim,
And, like our Lord, he blessed and sympathized.

"My little friends, 'tis not the name we bear—
Church, or Dissent—Immersion, or such things,
That make Religion—'tis the earnest care
To be like Christ, the glorious King of kings.'

"God loves us all, whatever name we take,
If Christ's dear name be still before them all:
He condescends to many a poor mistake,
And always hears a humble sinner's call.

"He gave His Son that we might learn to love;
And He loved us that we might love again.
Dear little children, try this love to prove,
And then my story will not be in vain.

"And do not judge or quarrel, and despise,
For God will judge us all some future day;
But view each other with indulgent eyes,
And walk as kind companions by the way."

The children rose;—they felt their friend was right,
And, gently thanking her, they bade good-bye.
Oh! that all Christian people would unite
To love as brethren of one family!

Marriage As It May Be.

It was a quiet Sunday afternoon,
About the middle of the month of June,
The very pattern for a summer's day,
The very weather for the corn and hay.

A Sabbath feeling spread itself around,
A calm delight that spoke without a sound,
A soft o'erflowing tenderness of joy,
A sweet conspiracy against annoy.

The horses knew it was the day of rest;
The sheep and cows they knew it, or they guessed;
No farm boy shouted; village bells rung clear
From all the steeples round, both far and near;

And little parties strayed across the meads,
Over the brooklet, with its waving reeds,
Slow pacing onward to the shady mound,
From whence there came the solemn church bells' sound

Yes, cattle knew, and settled down in peace;
The horse rolled over, snorting at his ease,
Or with his working friends stood nose to nose,
In quiet converse, or in mute repose.

But now, the church has closed its ancient door,
The service in the meeting-house is o'er:
In country places it is still the way
To hold the worship in the light of day.

And thus it was: the evening prayer was done
Some hours before the setting of the sun,
Leaving at leisure many happy folk,
To rest in social groups from labour's yoke.

The farmers lingered round the porch and gate,
Talking of crops, the weather, and the State;
They all could rule, they all had got *the* plan,
And every farmer was a Solomon.

Young village maids, in all their Sunday best,
Looked sharp to see how other girls were drest;
And notes were made in many a giddy pate
Of shapes and colours, blue, and green, and slate.

With some there was a deeper spring of joy,
Which ran and rippled through the week's employ,
And sweetened even scolding, toil, and pain,—
It was the meeting in the "Lover's Lane."

On Sunday eve they'd have a pleasant walk;
On Sunday eve they'd have a happy talk,
And fix, if possible, the wedding-day;
If not, they'd know the reason for delay.

And many pairs from church and chapel door
Strayed through the meadows or across the moor,
Building bright castles of a future home,
Where pain and poverty should never come.

Stray on, young hearts, the Sabbath-day may be
The day most fit for vows of constancy;
For marriage is a blest and holy thing,
Round which the purest joys of life may spring.

But see, 'tis holy—see, 'tis good and true;
Let not your lover be deceived in you;
Your pretty face will quickly cease to charm,
If you are sullen, or your temper warm.

If you are wasteful, idle, flippant, gay,
A wise man's love will surely steal away;
If you disgrace yourself still lower yet,
Be sure of this—he never will forget.

The fairest dress in which a bride is decked,
Is virtuous love and perfect self-respect;
If clothed in these, the very humblest dress
Can never hide her real loveliness.

If these be wanting—if disgrace and shame
Should blot her character, or blight her name,
With silks and lace she may be covered o'er,
But she herself is beautiful no more.

Keep yourself spotless; see the man you love
Has qualities your reason can approve;
Do not be dazzled with his chain or pin,
His handsome clothes,—but mark the man within.

If he's unsteady, fond of company,
Without regard to strict integrity,
You may be married, but you will be sad;
A man like this can make no woman glad.

He will not be your helpmate on the road;
He'll spend in drink, what should be spent in food;
Your little comforts he will turn to joke,
And puff away your happiness in smoke.

He'll treat his mates amidst a drunken roar,
And leave you lonely, penniless, and poor;
Half starved and ragged, wishing, with a sigh,
That you could once again that knot untie.

The very man you now so much admire
May go still further, and may sink still lower;
Till you—the girl he promised to adore—
He drives with blows and curses from his door.

Oh, have a care! It is not children's play,
To be begun and ended in a day;
"For better or for worse," it is your life
To spend in toil, and wretchedness, and strife,

Hopeless and heartless, sad, and full of fear,
Your haggard cheek oft moistened by a tear,
Watching at night till he shall stagger home,
Trembling to hear his footsteps as they come,

Waking at dawn, afraid to face the day,
Having no credit, and no means to pay,
Ashamed of him, who should have been your trust,
And finding love is turning to disgust.

Your little children, careful ere their time,
Growing familiar with the face of crime;
Stunted in growth, without the youthful glee
That bounds and frolics round the parent's knee.

Is this a fancy picture of the brain?
No, gentle maiden, this is all too plain;
'Tis common in our land; and you may be
As wretched as the picture that you see.

'Twill not be luck, nor fortune, nor your fate;
Your lot, dealt out by hell or heaven's hate,
Which you could not avoid—it will be this,
You chose an evil man, and chose amiss.

And as the buds of evil grow and shoot,
What was the bud, will blossom into fruit;
A bitter fruit! that you must taste with pain;
The marriage tie will ne'er untie again—

Till death shall cut it; then, for evermore,
You two may sever at your cottage door;
One may in heavenly joys forget her pains,
Or both may groan in everlasting chains.

But now choose wisely; and your wedded life
Need be no tale of drunkenness and strife,
But a sweet history of faithful love,
Admired by man, and blessed by God above.

The Bad Servant.

"So! Rachel's going to leave her place
I hear!" said Mrs. Moore
Unto her neighbour, Mrs. Green,
Who just came to the door.

"I have not heard the reason why,—
My Alice would not tell,
She's very happy in the place,
And likes her mistress well.

"But do come in, and rest a bit,
You look quite jaded out;
And I should really like to hear
How it has come about.

"There's not a mistress anywhere
That bears a better name,
If girls will be obedient,
And keep themselves from blame.

"I know she is particular,
And won't let things pass by;
And girls have lost their service there
By telling her a lie."

"That's just the thing," said Mrs. Green,
"And hard it is, I say,
For such a little thing as *that*
To turn a girl away.

"I'll tell you how it came to pass,
And you'll agree with me,
That for a little fib or two,
So strict she need not be.

"Rachel had things to put away,
And quite by accident,
A glass fell on the floor, and broke,
Without the least intent.

"The foolish child picked up the bits,
And hid them in a hole;
She did not like to mention it,
Poor silly little soul!

"But as bad luck would have the thing,
Into that very place,
The mistress chanced to cast her eyes,
And this brings on disgrace.

"For Rachel, she went on to say,
She did not put them there;
But afterwards she turned so pale,
The truth was pretty clear.

"The mistress saw, but did not scold:
She gave her good advice:
It was the first offence, she said,
She would not bear it twice.

"And, certainly, she kept her word,
For yesterday, at noon,
The child had luncheon to take in,
With tea-cups, and a spoon.

"I can't tell how it happened quite,
But going through the hall
She tripped her foot, one tea-cup fell,
And broke against the wall.

"Miss Margaret was standing there,
And Rachel was afraid
The child would go and tell Mamma
The mischief she had made.

"And so she said, 'Miss Margaret,
If you won't tell of me,
I'll give you some nice currant cakes,
And sugar for your tea.

"'But you must eat them on the sly,
For fear Mamma should see,
So come with me, I'll hide you up,
And then I'll get the key.'

"And then she got the store-room key,
That Rachel never takes,
And opened the tin canister,
And gave the child the cakes.

"It happened in the afternoon
Some unexpected friends
Called in to take a cup of tea,
And so, the Mistress sends

"Your daughter Alice, Mrs. Moore,
To bring the cakes to her;
And when she brought her only five,
It really made her stare;

"Because it seems she was aware
That there were many more;
So then she sent for Rachel in,
And bid her shut the door.

"And speaking very steadily,
And looking straight at her,
Said, Rachel, did you take the cakes
Out of the canister?'

"The child protested and declared,
As sure as she was born,
She did not know, and could not tell
'Where could the cakes be gone!'

"Then Alice, and the children all,
Were sent for, one by one,
And each was questioned privately,
If she the thing had done.

"When little Margaret's turn was come,
She blushed, and then denied;
But when her mother questioned her,
She told the truth, and cried.

"So then the mistress sent for me,
To come without delay:
She said a thief, and liar, too,
With her should never stay.

"And if she got another place,
She must not come to her,
For she felt bound to tell the truth
About her character.

"And more than that, she said to me,
Which I took somewhat hard,
I must have brought her badly up,
And this was my reward.

"She said, 'A mother may be known
By what her children do:'
And then she said some handsome things
Of Alice and of you.

"Your children differ, I suppose,
They're good, or else pretend;
My children always told a lie,
If it would serve their end.

"I'm sure I've scolded them enough,
And beat them black and blue;
It never seemed to do them good,
I wonder what you do."

"'Tis difficult," said Mrs. Moore,
"To say, what I have done;
For I have watched my children's hearts,
Before their feet could run.

"I know you never can deceive
A child's observing eye;
They're quick enough to notice it,
If you should tell a lie.

"I don't think beating would prevent
Their doing just the same;
They dread, no doubt, the punishment,
But don't regard the shame.

"I praise my children more for truth,
Than any cleverness;
I like to see them quick and bright;
But truth, is heaven's grace.

"And truth and love will last, I know,
When cleverness will fade;
Our children are ashamed of lies,
Whilst yours are but afraid.

"I would not say that pride is good;
But still a proud disdain
Of lying, is a better thing
Than slavish fear of pain.

"I hope that as my children grow,
They'll choose the better road,
And follow on to know the way
That leads us all to God.

"I can assure you, Mrs. Green,
I often wake at night,
And pray that He would strengthen me,
To walk before them right.

"I think, if ever my neglect
Should make them go astray,
What would my bitter feelings be
Upon the Judgment Day.

"But, then, for sweet encouragement,
I think what joy 'twill be
To rest in heaven safe at last,
With all my family.

"And so with hope, and fearing, too,
I go on day by day,
And often get a lifting up,
When heartily I pray.

"There are so many evil ways
To tempt young people now,
And if you let them get a root,
You can't tell how they grow.

"It is with thankfulness I say,
We never speak in vain;
Our children pay respect to us,
And don't reply again.

"Now, many people spoil a child,
And then they punish it,
Or else deceive it with a lie,—
What honour can they get?

"We try to make a happy home,
As well as make them good,
And that's a point, I always think,
Should be well understood.

"If you would like some early day,
To send your Rachel here,
I'd speak to her, just like a friend,
A mother—can't despair.

"This bitter lesson, well improved
May last for many a day."
"Thank you," said Mrs. Green—"I will;"
And then she went away.

A Ghost Story.

THE winter night had settled down
Upon a stormy day,
And drifted banks of frozen snow
O'er all the country lay.

And darker as the darkness grew,
So fiercer grew the blast;
But striving on through storm and snow,
A weary horseman passed.

He'd ridden all the livelong day,
And with his jaded beast
Looked anxiously along the road
To spy a place of rest.

At last he saw a lonely inn
A little way before;
The swinging sign creaked drearily
As he stopped at the door.

Inside the house a roaring fire
A friendly welcome cast,
And savoury supper, smoking hot,
Paid well for peril past.

Three other men, arrived before,
Sat in the cheerful light;
And they were playing cards, to cheat
The dulness of the night.

But heavy grew the traveller's eyes,
And to the host, he said,
"I'm drowsy with my ride to-day,
You'll show me to my bed."

The host looked down, and then looked
  up,
Then coughed—and coughed again,
"Our beds, good Sir, are all engaged
By these three gentlemen."

"No bed for me?—why then, in sooth,
A luckless wight am I,
You don't suppose to turn me out,
In snow-drifts here to lie!"

The landlord coughed full three times
  more,
And then he spoke again—
"I'm sorry, Sir, they're all engaged
By these three gentlemen."

Unto his wife he sidelong cast
A sly and stealthy look;
The traveller saw the signal pass,
And angrily he spoke.

"You're cheating me, I plainly see,"
And crimson grew his cheek;
The woman to her husband looked,
But neither chose to speak.

Then uprose one of those three men,
And answered for the host—
"There is another chamber, Sir,
If you can face a ghost.

"A bed there is—full warm I trow,
A-top the winding stair,
But something has an ugly way
Of waking sleepers there.

"When winds blow high, and wild clouds
   fly,
Due westward from the sea,
A voice cries then, once and again,
'Sha-a-ve me! sha-a-ve me!'

"But if your life be free from sin,
Your heart and conscience light,
The haunted room you need not fear,
Nor yet the evil sprite."

Then out spoke that young traveller,
"I fear no ghost, nor sprite;
Lead up the stair, my hostess fair,
Brave gentlemen—Good night!"

The hostess, she grew deadly pale,
And trembled on the stair,
The chambermaid waxed bold, and
   said—
"Good Sir, don't venture there."

"You foolish girl! make up the bed,
And do not shake for me;
This merry ghost I hope to find
Right pleasant company."

The bed was made, he locked the door,
From friend and foe to keep,
Then said his prayers, jumped into bed,
And turned him round to sleep.

"Brave heart he has—no coward he,"
The three men jointly say;
The cup goes freely round the board,
And higher goes the play.

But ever and anon they pause,
As driving squalls go by,
Declaring they should like to hear
The spectre's doleful cry.

And ever and anon they pause,
And listen with alarm,
To hear the bellowing of the wind,
The raging of the storm.

The hours pass on, the fire burns low,
The sparks die out and fall;
The candle in the socket burns,
And flickers on the wall.

But still the players play their game—
'Tis on the stroke of one,
When, just outside, is faintly heard
A low and hollow moan.

And all at once, the oaken door
Steals back without a sound—
A feather's weight might then have
   struck
Those three men to the ground.

Aghast they stood with staring eyes,
And hardly drew a breath,
But shook in every joint, as though
They saw the form of Death.

For *there* it stood, a figure tall,
All in a winding sheet,
That trailed its length upon the floor,
And wrapped about its feet.

The face—if face it were, was black—
Most hideous to see,
And with a cry, that curdled them,
It said "Sha-a-ve me!"

On, to the table straight it came,
As if to join the men,
Then with a doleful, quavering voice,
It cried "Sha-a-ve me!" again.

Oh! little recked the gamesters then,
Of what the ghost might find;
Quick through the door they madly
  dashed,
And left their cash behind.

And softly, slowly round the board,
"Sha-a-ve me! sha-a-ve me!"
It gathered all the money up,
"Sha-a-ve me! sha-a-ve me!"
And ne'er, I ween, again was seen
By that brave company.

—

But where is that young traveller,
Who laid him down in bed,
All in the lonesome, haunted room,
To rest his weary head?

Kind sleep that night had taken flight,
And time moved on but slow,
As wide awake he lay and heard
The gamesters' talk below.

He heard the battling of the blast,
That drove the sleety rain
With sudden squalls that shook the
  room,
And lashed the window pane.

The chimneys rocked before the storm,
The sign creaked drearily,
When through them all there stole a
  voice—
"Sha-a-ve me! sha-a-ve me!"

He started up—his heart beat loud,
Smit with a moment's fear;
But still he laughed, despite himself,
This quaint appeal to hear.

"Come, I'm your man, Sir Ghost," said
  he,
"I'll shave you passing well,
If you'll be pleased to certify
The place where you may dwell."

"Sha-a-ve me! sha-a-ve me!" the Ghost
  replied
More eagerly again;
"Oh! oh! said he, you dwell, I see,
Close by the window pane."

And then forthwith he sprung from bed,
And to the casement went,
The Ghost resuming with the blast
Its tremulous lament.

The casement opened on a spring
That held it in the wind,
And there, close by, a vine-tree branch
Had grown and intertwined.

And when the wind, with sudden swell,
Swayed every leafy thing,
The knotted branch moved to and fro,
And grated on the spring.

And thus the creaking sound was made,
So tremulously drear,
That filled the minds of simple folk
With superstitious fear.

The traveller got his pocket knife,
And then, without remorse,
Cut through the branch, and down it fell,
Henceforth a speechless corse.

"Now, I will have *my* fun," thought he,
And from the bed he took
A long white sheet, and robed himself
As in a flowing cloak.

And lest his manly countenance
A ghostly form should lack,
He took a little chimney soot,
And smeared it grim and black.

Then stealing down the narrow stair,
Which he went up before,
He stood, and with a ghastly grin,
He groaned outside the door.

And conscience being not precise,
To spare the gamesters' gains,
He took the cash they left behind,
To pay him for his pains.

And ere those three affrighted men
Back to the table crept,
He'd found the haunted room again,
And soundly there he slept.

At dawn the three men went away,
And 'twas their future boast,
That *once* they had the luck to see
A veritable Ghost.

The traveller's steed is at the door,
But ere he rode away,
He pointed to the severed branch,
And smiling thus did say-

"Your fare is good, your bed is warm,
And you, my worthy host,
May henceforth lodge your weary
   guests,
For there, I've laid your Ghost."

Crazed.

"LAST night I saw your spirit, John,
'Twas standing on the sea,
And all your clothes were dripping wet,
As wet as they could be;
I saw you smile across the waves,
And beckon unto me.

"Oh! I've been very lonely, dear,
The world is cold to me,
They've buried both our pretty babes
Beneath the churchyard tree,—
The pretty babes you left behind,
 When you went o'er the sea.

"When you went o'er the sea, my love,
My heart was nigh to break;
And when you kept so long away,
My sense began to shake;
I walked about upon the shore,
My rest I could not take.

"All night I walked upon the shore,
And watched the raging sea,
And oh! I prayed that God would send
My husband back to me;
The salt spray dashed upon my face,—
You never came to me.

"The sea-gull screamed above my head,
I thought I heard you cry,
There was no moonlight on the sea,
Nor starlight in the sky;
I shrieked across the billow's roar,
In frenzied agony.

"When morning light came slowly back,
I sought my lonely bed;
Then tidings came your ship was lost,
And all the crew were dead;
Oh! then my heart grew icy cold,
Strange visions filled my head.

"I worked for our two lovely babes,
But I could never speak,
There never rolled a quiet tear
Upon your Susan's cheek;
My heart kept swelling more and more,
As if it meant to break.

"I always heard the billows roar,
My heart would stop, and beat—
If Bessie called her father's name,
I started from my seat;
At last I could not bear to hear
A footfall in the street.

"But still I worked—I worked for
 bread—
I did the best I could;
They did not like my work, they said,
It was not very good;
And so they took the work away—
It had a spot of blood.

"Oh! if those people could have seen
How I toiled at the shirt,
And tried to keep it nice and clean,
Without a speck of dirt,
And worked till midnight all alone,—
Could they have had the heart!

"I do not know—the world is cold;
Then stranger people came
And took me from my little babes;
My brain was turned to flame—
And then! I cannot tell you what
Of my poor soul became.

"All night I thought I heard them cry,
It was the same all day,
I heard them weep so bitterly,
I heard them sob and pray;
But oh, I never saw them once,
They took me quite away.

"I thought they beat the little dears,
Because they cried for me,
And then I knew they'd laid them both
Beneath the churchyard tree;
But I could never see the grave,
They would not set me free.

"I thought if I could cool my brain,
Upon their quiet bed,
And press my heart upon the place
Where they were lying dead,
The tears would rush into my eyes
That I had never shed.

"I beat my breast, I tore my hair,
I never thought to pray,
I heard your drowning cry, my love,
My brain went all astray;
A boiling sea of raging woe,
No words of mine can say.

"But yesternight I saw you, John,
You stood upon the sea,
And all your clothes were dripping wet,
As wet as they could be;
I saw you smile across the waves,
And beckon unto me,
And I am coming, husband dear,
To rest along with thee."

The Two Noblemen.

ONE bright summer day, in the village of B——,
Six miles from the musical voice of the sea,
Two fine little babies were born;
One came to the castle that stood on the hill,
And one to the hut by the old watermill
That grinds all the villagers' corn.

The bells rang as though they would gladden the earth,
Proclaiming the news of a nobleman's birth,
The heir of a great British Peer;
And tidings that flew from the old castle door
Were eagerly caught up, and made into more,
   To gratify every ear.

The babe was a beauty, with never a spot—
One seldom has heard of a babe that was not;
But this was a beauty indeed;
The nurse would not hear of the slightest denial;
When every feature was put upon trial,
'Twas "angel" or "cherub" decreed.

The family honour, the family fame,
The wealth all entailed to the family name,
Were his, by the law of descent.
The roads were all closed to contumely and scorn,
For he was expected, before he was born,
To sit in the great Parliament.

Claude Reginald Vane was the name that he bore,
And great admiration it won from the Poor,
'Twas the prettiest name they had known;
And the very next babe that was brought to the font,
When the minister symbolled a cross on its front,
   Took one of the names for its own.

It was not the child that was born in the hut,
On him all the highways to greatness were shut,
Except the great highway of toil;
'Twas the eighth time his parents had christened a child,
It mattered but little what this should be styled,
As there was no fortune to spoil.

And so, Milly Barker, she christened him Nat,
A beautiful name!—she thought nothing of that,
Now she had so many small heirs.
Her little one now that was joined to the rest
Must trust to his labour, and not to a crest,
   To prosper in worldly affairs.

His clothes were too poor to be worthy a scoff,
They chiefly were garments by others left off,
The gift of the minister's wife;
She knew Milly Barker had nothing to spare,
And yet was content with the homeliest fare,
And never had begged in her life.

Poor Natty, he wrangled, and struggled his best,
'Gainst charity clothing to make his protest,
Then quietly sank into sleep;
And thenceforth he took to his forefathers' fate,
As little lords take to their princely estate,
Both fated to laugh and to weep.

Of wondrous contrivances men now devise
To make a man "healthy, and wealthy, and wise,"
Too many will miss of their aim;
Whilst old Mother Nature, with fostering rude,
With plenty of air and the commonest food,
Will build up a vigorous frame.

And thus in the castle that rose on the hill,
Though art and the sciences never stood still,
They missed of the healthier training;
And the sweet little lord, with his beautiful face,
And every limb the perfection of grace,
Was oftentimes sick and complaining.

But little Nat Barker grew sturdy and strong;
By the side of his mother he gambolled along,
And almost could anything talk;
He hacked at great slices of pudding and bread,
Before the young noble, more daintily fed,
Could handle his knife and his fork.

His eyes were as brown as a ripe hazel-nut,
His chin had a little determinate cut,
His laughter was catchingly merry;
His cheeks were as red as a fine damask rose,
And he had—we must own it—a little snub nose,
And a skin that was brown as a berry.

The little lord's nerves were pronounced to be weak,
The colour so often would change on his cheek,
And doctors advised mountain air;
Whilst Milly remembered her grandmother said,
That nerves were but fancies from luxury bred,
Best cured by hard labour and fare.

When she saw the young boy riding down the green lane,
The groom walking by him and holding the rein,
Attending to every word,—
She thought how her own little Natty would dare
To jog off alone on the miller's old mare,
And sighing, said, "Poor little lord!"

But Time he flew by, as he constantly does,
And at the same pace that he constantly goes,
And bore the lads equally on;
And then by a common, but curious rule,
At the time the young nobleman went to his school
The working boy's schooling was done;

And he was dressed out in a drab corduroy,
And got himself into a farmer's employ,
To work at whatever he could;
No picking or choosing was offered to him,
No thought of a fancy, a whimper, or whim,—
But Nat had a will that was good.

And that's the main thing for a man after all,
If he would succeed, whatsoever his call,
And gain for himself a good name;
And labouring men may be honoured and great,
Though never entitled to wealth or estate,
Or writ in the annals of fame.

So Natty went on in his own humble way,
Still making advancement, as day followed day,
In a practical sound education.
And many remarked, who had noticed the lad,
That an excellent prospect he certainly had
Of standing right well in his station.

His master soon ordered him under the groom
(Another young lad being put in his room),
He said that young Barker was steady;
He could trust him at home, he could trust him abroad,
He could trust to his honesty, trust to his word,
And found him good-natured and ready.

Meantime, the young lord worked at Latin and Greek,
And many learned tongues he was able to speak,
Not gained without much application;
For he had determined to add to the fame
And lustre that hung to the family name,
The gem of a fine education.

But dearly he paid for this excellent wealth,
In loss of sound spirits and vigorous health,
To meet the great battle of life:
For scholars who climb to the temple of Fame
Too often have found it a perilous game,
That weakens the nerve for the strife.

And Milly remarked, as the young noble passed,
That he was too pale, and had run up too fast—
She liked the young gentleman well;
He was the same age as her youngest boy, Nat—
She took greater interest in him for that,
His birthday she always could tell.

It chanced on a day that young Reginald came
To bathe in the stream by the upper mill-dam,
But had not been used to the river.
The mill-stream was rapid, and steady, and strong,
And, ere he could master it, bore him along,
His courage beginning to waver.

He strove and he struggled with might and with main;
He's sinking! But no—he is rising again;
Strive—strive, lad, it is for your life!
Ah! what now to him are wealth, title, and land?
He would give them all up for the grasp of a hand,
To help in this terrible strife.

He's sinking again! Is there nobody near,
To save the young noble, the son of the peer?—
Must he have a watery grave?
A splashing is heard; there has sprung from the bank
A youth who appears of the working-man's rank;
Thank God! he is able to save.

And who was courageous enough to do that?
The youth was no other than Barker's son, Nat,
Who this deed of daring had done;
And when the lad swam with the body ashore,
He was cheered as a hero, or great commodore,
For saving the nobleman's son.

His lordship came down, with his purse full of gold
(Forgetting true courage can never be sold),
And offered some money to Nat;
But he, glowing fresh from the glorious strife,
And proud to have saved the young nobleman's life,
Said, "No, sir, I cannot take that."

His lordship was struck with the noble young chap,
And quickly put on his considering cap,
To think what was best to be done.
He could not rest easy, he said, for a day,
Without finding out proper means to repay
The youth who had rescued his son.

"Very odd," thought his lordship, "I don't understand
What made the young fellow refuse me off hand,
'Tis well known the Barkers are poor.
Five sovereigns I offered him there on the spot,
A sum not despised by such people, I wot,
He'd hardly be thinking of more."

But still it perplexed him and puzzled his head,—
"How can I reward that young fellow?" he said;
"Such scruples I never have met."
He found himself standing on delicate ground,
And turned the thing over, and all round and round;
But still he was thoroughly beat.

At last, he determined to send for young Nat,
He thought he should see his way clearer by that,
And come at the lad's proper mind;
So down went a message that evening to say
That Nat should come up to the castle next day,
If he were himself so inclined.

Of course, in his very best clothes he was drest;
His mother considered he looked at his best,
And watched him away from the door;
His face was so honest, his step light and free,
No servile behaviour, nor speeches had he,
Indeed, he forgot he was poor.

He had not that paltry and pitiful pride,
That looks upon toil as a thing one should hide,
He knew 'twas his lot upon earth.
And when in the nobleman's presence he stood,
He made him the very best bow that he could,
As due to high station and birth.

"Young man," said his lordship, "the deed you have done,
In risking your own life, and saving my son,
Demands the best thanks I can give;
But 'tis not with thanks that I purpose to pay,
If you will yourself put me into the way
To forward your prospects in life."

'Twas Nat Barker's turn to be puzzling now,
The back of his hand he passed over his brow,
He hardly knew what to reply;
He hoped that "My lord would not mention the thing,
'Twas nothing for him in the water to spring,
He had done it so frequently."

He had plenty of work, and his service was good,
He reckoned he did not want clothing or food,—
The youth was contented, in fact;
And then he looked straight in the nobleman's face,
And said he "should count it a cruel disgrace
To have payment for that sort of act."

The old noble smiled; he was sorry, he said,
"That conduct so praiseworthy should not be paid,
Though money could never repay it;
But if a good friend he e'er wanted to find,
Or some way to serve him came into his mind,
He would not a moment delay it."

The nobleman's manner was courteous and bland,
But Reginald took the young lad's honest hand,
And shook it with cordial grace;
With feelings he had not the power to hide,
He gratefully spoke, until pleasure and pride
Glowed warm in the working man's face.

So noble young Barker went forth from the Hall,
And left not a servant there feeling so tall,
He was every inch a man;
He stood in his shoes only five feet eight,
But he carried his head and his body so straight,
He might have been five feet ten.

He put on again his own brown corduroy,
And returned to his stable and daily employ
But a new life had over him come;
His horses that day got a large feed of corn,
His own life seemed all for prosperity born,
He whistled away to his broom.

It is not a ring, nor a gentleman's coat,
It is not the odds between castle or cot,
Between riding in carriage or cart,
That gives what we all are so anxious to find,
A true independence of body and mind—
A true satisfaction of heart.

Now Nat was a peer in the pith of his soul,
And true as the needle is true to the pole,
He was generous, gentle, and kind;
And there was a something Nathaniel had got,
Which was not put on with his best Sunday coat,
Nor left on the Monday behind.

We never observed that he pulled a long face,
Or spoke with a whine, or made any grimace;
    In fact, he did nought of the kind,
Though girls looked surprised, and the young fellows laughed
And winked at each other, and tittered and chaffed,
One day when he spoke out his mind.

"Our Saviour," he said, "was a pattern for man,
That people should copy as near as they can,
    If they would be noble and true;
And he did not care what a scoffer might say,
He knew 'twas the wisest and happiest way,
And there was not another would do."

But now let us see him and Milly that night,
With his pocket so empty and spirit so light,
What was it the good woman said?
She said, "that it made her as proud as a queen,
That her son a true benefactor had been,
And had not with money been paid.

"She wished all the 'quality' could understand
That a working man's heart is as free as his hand,
As ready to give as receive;
And that 'tis a pleasure, for many a day,
When he can a favour, or kindness repay
By some little thing he can give."

So Nat and his mother were glad and agreed,
And liked the great nobleman better, indeed,
Than ever they had done before;
That fact, the Benevolent soon could explain,
And they would not hasten to pay back again
The favour that laid at their door.

When one has been doing an action that's kind,
Such pleasant sensations spring up in the mind,
We long to be doing another;
And though it may have a presumptuous sound,
Ever since the young lord was so near being drowned,
Nat loved him almost like a brother.

"I often think, mother," said he, and he smiled,
"Of what you said to me when I was a child,
I should say I was seven years old;
I opened the gate for a carriage to pass,
The lady who rode in it let down the glass,
And threw me a penny like gold.

"It was a fine penny, quite fresh from the Mint—
I ran to the door just to give you a glint,
Little thinking what followed so pat;
I think I see now the dark frown on your face,
As if I had brought on your name a disgrace,—
'Can't you do a good turn without that?'

"You seized on the penny without more ado,
And into the mill-dam it speedily flew;
I stood like a man in a stound,
Looking hard at the place, where the money had sank,
And seeing the circles flow up to the bank,
Running after each other all round.

"I don't think I spoke, for I felt so ashamed,
Like a mean little urchin, deservedly blamed,
Though I hardly knew what I had done;
So I watched the tall reeds, and the long river grass,
As they grew upside down in that clear looking glass,
And wavered about in the sun.

"But *that* was a lesson that took deep effect,
And taught me the meaning of true self-respect—
To help folks without any pay;
And now I feel hampered, when they offer me
Reward for a service that ought to be free,
I want to get out of their way.

"They're free to my service—no one shall say, Nat
Is backward in helping his neighbours to *that*—
I think 'tis the pleasure of life;
I wish everybody was friendly and kind—
A different lot in this world we should find,
Which often cuts sharp as a knife."

More sturdy grew Barker, more stalwart his frame,
More honoured and trusted his unblemished name,
Though only to labour akin.
The Queen may give title, and rank, and estate,
But the true noble-man she can never create—
The true Noble-man is within.

And in our dark alleys, our fields, and our mines,
Where the sun of prosperity scantily shines,
Unheard of by fortune or fame,
We have fine manly hearts that in solitude bleed,
Yet leave to their country a right noble seed,
To inherit a patriot's name.

You are needed, brave hearts, that are facing the toil,
And bearing unnoticed the wearisome moil,
That presses on every day.
We want the great souls that will suffer and dare,
And all the inglorious martyrdom bear
Of poverty's dreary decay.

Bear up for awhile, ye are warriors good;
Be true to your country, yourselves, and your God,—
The day of account draweth nigh;
Then ye, who work hard in obscurity now,
May find a bright crown is prepared for your brow,
And a home in the mansions on high.

THE END

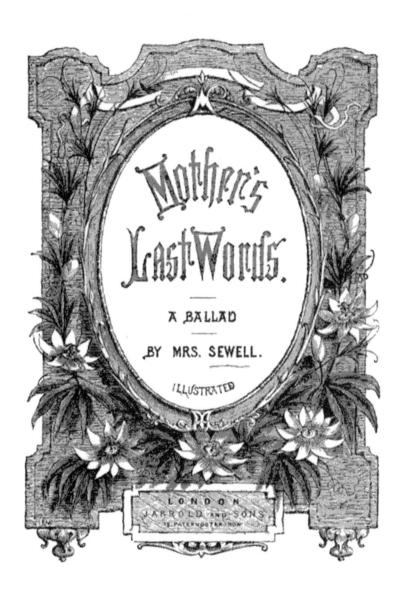

Mother's Last Words.

A BALLAD

BY MRS. SEWELL.

ILLUSTRATED

LONDON
JARROLD and SONS,
12, PATERNOSTER ROW.

First Part

THE yellow fog lay thick and dim
O'er London city, far and wide;
It filled the spacious parks and squares,
Where noble lords and ladies ride.

It filled the streets, the shops were dark,
The gas was burning through the day;
The monument was blotted out,
And lost in gloom the river lay.

But thicker still, and darker far,
The noisome smoke-cloud grimly fell
Amongst the narrow courts and lanes,
Where toiling people poorly dwell.

No sun above, no lofty sky,
No breezy breath of living air,
The heavy, stagnant, stifling fog,
Crept here and there, and everywhere.

Down seven steep and broken stairs,
Its chill unwelcome way it found,
And darkened with a deeper gloom,
A low, damp chamber, underground.

A glimmering light was burning there,
Beside a woman on a bed;
A worn-out woman, ghastly pale,
Departing to the peaceful dead.

Two little boys in threadbare clothes,
Stood white and trembling by her side,
And listening to his mother's words,
The youngest of them sadly cried.

The elder boy shed not a tear,
Nor stirred a moment from his place,
But with a corner of the sheet
He wiped his mother's cold damp face.

"Ah, John!" she said, "my own dear boy,
You'll soon be in this world alone;
But you must do the best you can,
And be good children when I'm gone.

"And listen, John, before 'tis night,
My weary spirit will be free;
Then go, and tell the overseer,
For he must see to bury me.

"You'll walk behind my coffin, dears,
There's little more I have to crave,
But I should like to have my boys
Just drop a tear beside my grave.

"And then you'll have to leave this room,
Because the rent is not all paid,
Since I've been ill, I've let it run;
You know, I've barely earned your bread.

"I don't owe much, I've minded that,
And paid it up, though hardly pressed,
The man must take the little things,
And sell the bed to pay the rest.

"I've mended up your bits of clothes,
It is not much you've left to wear,
But keep as decent as you can,
And don't neglect the house of prayer.

"I can't speak of your father, John,
You know that he has been my death;
If he comes back—you'll say, 'his wife
Forgave him with her dying breath.'

"But oh, my children! when I'm gone,
Do mind your mother's warning well,
And shun all drinking, swearing ways,
As you would shun the pit of hell.

"I'm going to a happy place,
So beautiful and dazzling bright,
'Twas in a vision or a dream,
It passed before me in the night,

"I felt my spirit caught away,
From all the crowd of toiling folk,
Above the cross upon St. Paul's,
And far above the fog and smoke.

"And higher, higher, up I went,
Until I reached a golden gate,
Where all about in shining rows,
I saw the holy angels wait.

"At once, they bid me welcome there,
And all at once began to sing,
'Come in, thou blessed of the Lord,
For thou art welcome to the King.'

"Then one stepped forth and took my
    hand,
And spake like music passing sweet,
'We have been watching for thee long,
To bring thee to our Master's feet.'

"Then hand in hand we floated on,
Through glowing fields of lovely flowers,
And saw ten thousand happy souls
At rest among the shining bowers.

"Our Saviour walked among them, John,
Most beautiful He was to see,
And such a heavenly smile He gave,
When first He saw poor worthless me.

"And oh! the gracious things He spoke,
I hardly could believe the word;
'Come in, thou faithful one,' He said,
'And rest thee now beside thy Lord.'

"Then all around, I heard the sound
Of joyous voices, singing praise,
And I stood there, and joined the song,
And looked upon His blessed face.

"And as I looked my heart grew strong,
And then I fell before His feet;
'Dear Lord,' I said, 'I pray Thee send
An angel to our wicked street.

"'I've left two little boys behind,
To get through this bad world alone,
And much, I fear, they'll miss their way;
And never reach Thy glorious throne.'

"'I will,' He said, and then He called
A beauteous Angel by his name,
And swifter than an arrow flies,
That beauteous Angel to Him came.

"And as I knelt before His feet,
I heard the order plainly given,
That he should guard my little boys,
And bring them safe to me in heaven.

"I saw the Angel bow his head,
And cast on me a look of love,
Then spread his snowy wings to leave
His blissful seat in heaven above.

"So do not fret about my death,
I know you'll not be left alone,
For God will send the Angel down,
To care for you, when I am gone.

"I'm sure you will have daily bread,
For *that* the King gave strict command,
And all the wealth of London town
Is in the power of His hand.

"So never join with wicked lads
To steal, and swear, and drink, and lie;
For though you are but orphans here,
You'll have a Father in the sky.

"I can't see plain, what you should do,
But God, I think, will make your way,
So don't go to the workhouse, dears,
But try for work, and always pray."

The woman ceased, and closed her eyes,
And long she lay, as if at rest,
Then opened wide her feeble arms,
And clasped her children to her breast.

And then aloft her hands she raised,
And heavenward gazed with beaming
    eyes,
"I see, I see, the Angel come,
I see him coming from the skies.

Good-bye—good bye, my children dear,
My happy soul is caught away;
I hear, I hear, my Saviour call,
He calls me up, I cannot stay."

Then soared her soul from that dark
    room,
Above the crowd of toiling folk,
Above the cross upon St. Paul's,
Above the fog, above the smoke.

And higher, higher, up she went,
Until she saw the golden gate,
Where night and day, in shining bands,
The holy angels watch and wait.

And she went in, and saw the King,
And heard the gracious words He spoke
To her, who in this sinful world,
Had meekly borne her daily yoke.

But sadly sobbed the little boys,
As from the bed of death they crept;
Upon the floor they sat them down,
And long and piteously they wept.

The dreary walls around them closed,
No father came to share their grief,
No friendly neighbour heard their cry,
None came with pity or relief.

They cried, until their tears were spent,
And darker still the chamber grew;
And then said little Christopher,
"Now mother's dead, what shall we do?"

Then John rose up, and with his sleeve,
He wiped away the last sad tear:
"Well, we must go, as mother said,
And tell the parish overseer."

"But won't the Angel come to us?
"I cannot tell you," John replied:
"I think he will," said Christopher,
"My mother saw him, when she died."

They stumbled up the broken stairs,
And pushed their way along the street,
Whilst out of sight, an Angel bright,
Walked close behind with shining feet.

He stood beside them at the door,
And heard the growling overseer,
Then touched his heart with sudden
    smart,
And brought an unexpected tear.

"Here, lads," he said, "divide this bread,
You both look hungry, any way;
We'll see about the body, child,
And bury it on Wednesday."

The hungry children ate the loaf,
And then the younger brother said,
"Our mother told us right, you see,
That was all true about the bread."

"It does seem so," was John's reply;
"I say, Chris, shan't you be afraid
To go and sleep at home to-night,
All in the dark there, with the dead?"

'Why should we, John? dead folks don't
   hurt,
She would not hurt us, if she could;
And as she laid upon the bed,
She looked so happy and so good."

"Well, come down then—I'm not afraid."
They entered in, and shut the door,
And made a bed, as best they could,
And laid them down upon the floor.

And soundly slept those little boys,
And dreamt about a far-off land,
With shining bowers, and lovely flowers,
And angels flying at command.

They'd never been beyond the town,
To see the beauteous works of God,
Not even seen the daisies spring
By thousands on the level sod.

They had not seen a robin's nest,
Nor plucked a violet in the shade,
Nor stood beside a running brook,
And heard the pleasant sound it made.

They had not seen young lambs at play,
Nor gleaned among the autumn
   sheaves,
Nor listened to the pattering sound
Of falling rain upon the leaves.

The cuckoo's note was strange to them,
They'd never heard a wild bird sing,
Nor seen the yellow cowslips grow
About the meadows in the spring.

Nor had they run with rosy boys,
At early morning to the school,
Nor spent the pleasant holidays
In catching minnows in the pool.

Ah, no! and yet they were not left
With nought but death and darkness
   there;
A minister of love was sent,
In answer to their mother's prayer.

But little thought those orphan boys,
When to their wretched bed they crept,
That all the night, an Angel bright,
Would watch beside them, as they slept.

When dimly dawned the light, they rose,
And Chris looked round with chattering
   teeth;
The sheet was spread from foot to head,
He knew his mother lay beneath.

"Let's go out to the pump and wash,
As she would always have us do;
We'd better mind about her words,
I think," said John; "Chris, what say
   you?"

"Let's go," said Chris, "beside, you know,
We've got our breakfast now to find."
They went out in the narrow street,
The shining Angel went behind.

A woman at a chandler's shop,
Who knew the children of the dead,
Was touched with pity as they passed,
And gave them each a slice of bread.

"'Tis true," said little Christopher,
"You may be sure the Angel's come,
She never gave us bread before,
No, not the value of a crumb."

The next day, and the next to that,
The promise of the King was kept,
And every night that Angel bright,
Stood by, to guard them as they slept.

On Wednesday the people came,
And took the woman's corpse away;
Two little mourners walked behind,
And saw the grave wherein it lay.

Fast fell the tears upon their cheeks,
When little Christy raised his eyes,
And said, "Oh, mother! how I wish
I was with you above the skies."

'Twas but the thought passed through
  his mind,
When soft a whisper seemed to come
"Be patient, little Christopher,
You are not very far from home."

The minister said, "Dust to dust;"
And then the poor boys left the place—
Two friendless boys in London town;
Oh! was not theirs a hapless case?

They wandered up and down the streets,
And then went home to sleep once more,
And in the morning left the room,
And took the key and locked the door.

They found the landlord at his house,
And said, "Please, sir, our mother's dead;
She could not pay up all the rent,
And we have got to earn our bread.

"But please, Sir, we have brought the
  key,
And left some things upon the shelf,
And there's the blanket and the bed,
My mother thought you'd pay yourself."

"And so she's gone!" the landlord said,
"And you are left to face the strife:
Well, I will say, I never knew
A better woman in my life.

"Of course, I'll take the things, my boy,
For right is right, and so I must;
But there's a sixpence for you both:
You'll find it hard to earn your crust."

They thanked the man, and left the
  house,
"I'll tell you what we'll do," said John,
"This sixpence here will buy a broom,
We'll sweep a crossing of our own.

"We won't go to the workhouse, Chris,
But act like men, and do our best;
Our mother said, 'A crust well earned,
Was sweeter than a pauper's feast.'"

"Oh, yes; we'll work like honest boys,
And if our mother should look down,
She'd like to see us with a broom,
And with a crossing of our own."

Away they went, with anxious hopes,
And long they hunted here and there,
Until they found a dirty place,
Not very far from Leicester Square.

And here at once they took their stand,
And swept a pathway broad and neat,
Where ladies, in their silken gowns,
Might cross, and hardly soil their feet.

The people hurried to and fro,
And 'midst the jostle, jar, and noise,
And thinking of their own affairs,
They hardly saw the little boys.

Not so with all, some caught a sight
Of little Christy's anxious eyes,
And put a penny in his cap;
And every penny was a prize.

At last the streets began to clear,
And people dropped off, one by one;
"Let's go," said little Christopher,
"My pocket is quite heavy, John."

They counted up their pence with glee,
And went away to buy some bread,
And had a little left to pay
For lodging in a decent bed.

Next day John kept his crossing clean,
Swept off the mud, and left it dry,
And little Christy held his cap,
But did not tease the passers-by.

And many a one a penny gave,
Who marked the pale child's modest
  way,
And thus they'd sixpence left in hand,
When they went home on Saturday.

The woman at the chandler's shop,
In kind remembrance of the dead,
Had found the boys a lodging-place,
Where they could have a decent bed.

"Let's go to church," said Christopher,
"She'd be so glad to see us there;
You recollect she often said,
'Boys, don't neglect the house of
  prayer.'"

"We're very shabby," John replied,
"And hardly fit for such a place;
But I will do the best I can
To polish up my hands and face."

Clear rung the bells that Sabbath morn,
As they went briskly up the street;
And out of sight the Angel bright,
Walked close behind with shining feet.

Some idle boys, who played about,
Threw stones and mocked, as they went
  in;
"Aye, let them mock away," said John,
We need not care for them a pin."

A lady watched them, as they sat,
And when the service all was done,
Said, "Do you go to Sunday school?"
"No, ma'am, but we should like," said
  John.

She told them both the place and time;
They went that afternoon to school;
The boys were playing in the street,
And said to John, "You are a fool

"To go to that old stupid place;
We know a trick worth two of that."
Said John, "I mean to be a man,
And that's the trick I'm aiming at."

Second Part

THE second week was bleak and cold,
A drizzling rain fell day by day,
And with their wet umbrellas up,
The people hurried on their way.

And no one thought about the boys,
Who patiently stood sweeping there;
And sometimes over Christy's face,
There fell a shade of blank despair.

Discouraged, wet, and weary oft,
Cold, shivering, to their bed they crept;
But still at night, that Angel bright,
Stood by to guard them as they slept.

And these poor boys would sleep as
    well
As rich men, on their beds of down,
And wake up with a lighter heart
Than many a king who wears a crown.

But winter time came on apace,
And colder still the weather grew,
And when they left the street at night,
Their clothes were often wetted
    through.

Their coats were almost worn to rags,
Their bare feet went upon the stones;
But still they always went to church,
And to the school on afternoons.

And never joined with wicked boys,
And never stopped away to play,
But tried to do their very best,
And swept the crossing every day.

One day a boy came up, and said,
"I know a dodge worth two of that;
Just take to picking pockets, lad,
And don't hold out that ragged hat."

"What, thieve!" said little Christopher,
"Our dodge is twice as good as that,
We earn our bread like honest folks;"
And so he answered, tit for tat.

"Well, that's your own look-out, of course;
For my part, I don't see the fun
Of starving at this crossing here,
When money is so easy won."

"How do you manage that?" said John.
"Oh! come with us, we'll have you taught,
You've but a trick or two to learn,
To grip the things, and not be caught."

"But if you should be caught?" said
    John,
"The end of that would spoil your fun."
"Oh! we know how to manage that;
Come on, I'll show you how 'tis done."

"What do you get to eat?" said John,
Who pondered on these boasting words.
"What get to eat!—just what we choose—
We eat and drink away like lords.

"Now, what d'ye say?—make up your
    mind;
I'm waited for, and must be gone,
We've pretty work to-day, on hand."
"Well, I shan't help to-day," said John.

"The more fool you," replied the boy,
And went off whistling down the street;
And black as night, a wicked Sprite,
Went after him with rapid feet.

John went back slowly to his place,
And grumbling to himself, he said,
"I half repent I didn't go,
It is so hard to earn one's bread.

"I dare say he gets in a day
As much as we earn in a week;
I wish I'd gone." John muttered this;
To Christopher he did not speak.

At night, as he went sauntering home,
He loitered round a pastry-cook's,
Till Christy called, "John, come along,
You'll eat the cakes up with your looks!"

"Well, Chris, I say 'tis very hard,
We never have good things to eat;
I'm tired of nothing else than bread,
I long for something nice and sweet."

"They do look nice," said little Chris,
And lingered near with hankering eyes;
"Which would you have, John, if you
    could?
I'd have these jolly Christmas pies."

John answered in a grumbling tone,
"Oh! I don't know, so let 'em be;
Some boys do get nice things to eat;
Not *honest* boys, like you and me."

"Well, never mind," said little Chris,
"You're out of sorts this evening, John;
We'll both be rich maybe some day,
And then we'll eat 'em up like fun."

"No chance of that, for us," said John,
"Our feet are now upon the stones;
We can't earn food and clothing too,
And you are only skin and bones."

"'Tis hard to work and not to eat;
But, John, you would not do what's
    bad!"
"No; I don't mean to thieve—not I;
But when thieves feast it makes one
    mad."

And so John grumbled day by day,
And longed for something good to eat,
And sometimes looked out for the boy
Who went off whistling down the street.

And oh! indeed, 'twas very hard,
When tired, hungry, cold, and wet,
To pass by all the eating-shops,
That looked so tempting in the street:

To see the people going in,
To buy the sausage-rolls and pies,
Whilst they could only stand outside,
And look at them with longing eyes.

'Twas hard to see the smoking meat,
And smell the vapours floating round
Of roasting joints and savoury steaks,
From steaming kitchens under-ground.

And sometimes little Christy cried,
When limping on with chilblained toes,
He saw fine windows full of boots,
And children's shoes in shining rows.

But still he never would complain,
And sometimes said, if John was sad,
"We got on bravely yesterday,
Why should you take to moping, lad?"

"But, John, I think, if you and I
Were rich, as these great people are,
We'd just look out for orphan boys,
And give them nice warm clothes to
    wear."

"Just so," said John, "and we would
    give
Poor little sweepers in the street
A famous lot of halfpennies,
To buy them something good to eat.

"They'd never miss the little things,
That would make kings of me and you;
I wish that we were rich men, Chris,
We'd shew 'em what rich men should
    do."

One night between the dark and light,
As they were going down a lane,
And Christopher, with bleeding feet,
Was slowly hobbling on with pain:

John saw some shoes, outside a door,—
"They'll just keep my poor Christy
    warm!"
And quick as thought, he snatched
    them up,
And tucked them underneath his arm.

Then pale as ashes grew his face,
And sudden fears rushed on his mind,
He hurried on with quicker pace,
Lest some one should be close behind.

"Do stop a bit," his brother cried,
"Don't be in such a hurry, John.'
John darted round a frightened look,
And from a walk began to run.

He thought he heard the cry of "Thief!"
And swifter down the street he fled;
And black as night, a wicked Sprite,
With rapid feet, behind him sped.

The cry of "Thief" was in his ears,
Through all the bustle and the din;
And when he reached the
    lodging-house,
The wicked Spirit followed in.

He sat down pale, and out of breath,
And locked the door into the street,
And trembled when he only heard
The sound of little Christy's feet.

"There, Christy, boy—there's shoes for
    you,
And now you'll cut away like fun;
Come, let us see, how well they fit—
Just give a tug, and they'll be on."

Then Christopher did laugh outright,
Hurra! hurra!—now I am shod;
But, John, where did you get the shoes?"
John put him off, and gave a nod.

The little boy was tired out,
And quickly to his bed he crept,
And knew not that a wicked Sprite
Scowled on his brother as he slept.

John could not rest; the faintest noise
Made all the flesh upon him creep;
He turned, and turned, and turned
    again,
But could not get a wink of sleep.

He strained his ears to catch the sound
Of footsteps in the silent night,
And when they came close by the door,
His hair almost rose up with fright.

At last his fear became so great,
That in a cold damp sweat he lay,
And then the thought came in his mind,
That he had better try and pray.

"They tell us at the Sunday School,
That we must beg to be forgiven;
My mother used to say the same,
Before she went away to heaven.

"I wish I'd let the shoes alone;
I wonder what I'd better do!—
If I should take them back again,
Poor Christy would not have a shoe.

"Though I don't think he'd care for that,
For he's a better boy than I,
And he would sooner starve to death
Than steal a thing or tell a lie."

"Are you asleep, Chris? Can't you wake?
I want to tell you something bad;
I've counted all the hours to-night;
I say, Chris, can't you wake up, lad?"

Just then, the child screamed in his
 sleep,
And started upright in his bed;—
"Are you there, John? Who's in the
 room?
Oh, John! I dreamt that you were dead.

"I'm glad enough that I woke up,
I'm glad you're all alive and well;
I'd such an ugly dream—I saw
The devil taking you to hell."

"And so he will, if I don't mind,
As far as that your dream is right;
And as to going off to hell,
I think I've been in hell all night."

"What have you done?"—"Why, stole
 some shoes,
That very pair I gave to you;
But I can't rest about it, Chris,
I want to know what we shall do."

'Why, take them back, of course," said
 Chris,
"And put them where they were before;
Let's go at once."—"No, stop," said
 John,
"The clock has only just struck four.

"There's no one stirring in the street,
The shops will not be open yet,
And we should have to wait about
For hours in the cold and wet.

"And now that I've made up my mind,
I don't feel half so much afraid."
Then took to flight that evil Sprite,
And John lay down his weary head.

At six o'clock the boys went out,
The snow was falling in the street,
And through the bitter morning air
They ran along with naked feet.

They watched the busy town wake up,
Undoing shutter, bolt, and bar;
But two full hours they stopped about,
Before *that* door was set ajar.

John quickly slipped the shoes inside,
And then as quickly walked away,
And with a lighter heart he went
To face the labours of the day.

Fast fell the feathery floating snow,
In whirling currents driven round,
Or fluttered down in silent showers
Of fleecy flakes upon the ground.

With broom in hand, and shivering
 limbs,
The little sweepers bravely stood,
And faced the cutting north-east wind,
That seemed to chill their very blood.

A lady, in a house close by,
Who often watched the little boys,
Heard many times that stormy day,
A deep cough mingling with the noise.

She rose up from her blazing fire,
And from the window looked about,
And hard at work amongst the snow,
She spied the ragged sweepers out.

"Do, Geraldine, look here," she said,
"How thin that youngest boy has grown;
Poor little wretch!—how cold he looks,
He's little more than skin and bone."

"Poor little boy!" said Geraldine,
"I never saw a whiter face;
I think they must be honest boys,
They keep so constant to their place.

"There's Frank and Freddy's worn-out
    shoes,
I think, mamma, would fit them well."
"Perhaps they would, I'll have them
    brought,
My dear, if you will ring the bell.

"And there's your brothers' old great
    coats,
They'll never put them on again;
But they will keep these children warm,
In many a storm of wind and rain."

"And give them something nice to eat;
I don't mean dry old crusts of bread,
But good mince pies," said Geraldine,
"You know we've such a number made."

"Well, do so, if you like, my dear."
"Oh! thank you; they shall have some
    pies."
Poor John, and little Christopher,
They hardly could believe their eyes.

They took the clothes and nice mince
    pies,
They bowed, and thanked, and bowed
    again,
Then scampered down the splashy
    streets,
And reached their own dull dirty lane.

And there they fitted on the coats,
And turned the pockets inside out,
Stuck up the collars round their ears,
Put on the shoes, and marched about.

They rubbed their hands and laughed
    amain,
And twisted one another round,
And then John turned a somerset,
And cleared the bedstead with a bound.

"But now for these fine Christmas pies,"
He said, and smacked his lips with glee,
"They're just the things you wanted, Chris,
There's two for you and two for me.

"We never had such luck before,
We never dreamt of such a thing."
"I think 'twas mother's Angel, John,
Who had that order from the King."

"You don't mean that in earnest, Chris?"
"Why not?" said Chris. "I'm sure I do.
I say, John, if we died to-night,
Should we both go to heaven, too?"

"Well, Christopher, last night, I thought
I should be sure to go to hell;
What sort of place that's like to be,
I've now a notion I could tell.

"I'm pretty sure if I had died
Last night, without my sins forgiven,
I'd not a single chance to go,
To be with mother up in heaven.

"I wish I'd never touched the shoes;
To steal is such a shameful sin,
And though they're taken back again,
I don't feel yet all right within.

"It was so bad, to go and steal!
Four months to-day you know *she* died;
And though we've fared quite hard
   enough,
Our wants have mostly been supplied.

"Some boys, we know, have had no bed,
A deal worse off than you and I,
For we have always had some bread,
And just a place where we could lie.

"And now, we've got some clothes to
   wear,
And days will soon be getting long,
And then, old boy, we'll shortly see
You picking up, and getting strong."

"I don't know, John—I fancy not,
I sometimes think I'm going to die;
I dream so much about the place
Where mother went—I don't know why.

"Except, maybe, I'm going too:
I saw one night, John, in a dose,
That Angel, that my mother saw,
With snowy wings and shining clothes.

"He looked at me, and then he smiled,
And said, 'Your time will soon be come;
Be patient, little Christopher,
You're going to a better home.'

"You know, last Sunday, at the school,
The lady told us how to pray,
And said, 'that Jesus Christ had come,
To die, and take our sins away.'

"And so I begged He'd take all mine,
And, Johnny, I believe He will;
And now I shouldn't mind to die,
If we could be together still."

"Oh! Christy, boy, you must not die:
What should I do without you here?
Oh! do get well—you must get well,"
And John brushed off a starting tear.

The winter passed, and spring-time
   came,
And summer days grew warm and long;
But little Christy weaker grew,
And soon could hardly creep along.

And then he stopped all day at home,
And soon he hardly left his bed,
And John was forced to leave him there,
To earn for both their daily bread.

Sometimes the lady at the house
Gave John some little jobs to do,
And when she found he did them well,
She sent him on her errands too.

And now when Christopher was ill,
And John was leaving for the night,
She gave them little dainty things,
To please his brother's appetite.

The woman at the chandler's shop
Had always been a faithful friend,
And often came to see the child,
And staid awhile to wash and mend.

The lady at the Sunday school,
Found out the little orphans' home,
And she would come and read to Chris,
And he was glad to see her come.

She talked about the heavenly King,
And she would kneel and softly pray;
And thus he lingered on awhile,
Still getting weaker day by day.

'Twas on a sultry summer's night,
When heavy lay the stifling air,
As John was dropping off to sleep,
He heard a softly whispered prayer.

He knew 'twas Chris, and did not stir,
And then he heard a gentle sigh;
It was the dear boy's happy soul,
Escaping to its home on high.

He left behind his wasted form,
He rose above the toiling folk,
Above the cross upon St. Paul's,
Above the fog, above the smoke.

And higher, higher, up he went,
Until he reached the golden gate,
Where night and day, in shining bands,
The holy angels watch and wait.

And he went in, and saw the King,
The Saviour, who for him had died,
And found once more, his mother dear;
And little Chris was satisfied.

And there they both together wait,
Till John shall reach that happy home,
And often from the golden gate,
They watch in hopes to see him come.

But John had many years to live,
For he had useful work to do,
And he grew up an honest man,
A sober man and Christian too.

His friend, the lady at the house,
When little Chris was dead and gone,
Bound John apprentice to a trade,
And so he did not feel alone.

And that bright Minister of Love,
Appointed by the Saviour King
To guard those orphan boys on earth,
And then to heavenly glory bring,

Still walked with John his journey
    through,
And though unseen was ever nigh,
Nor left him till his work was done,
And then went up with him on high.

And there, in everlasting joy,
The mother and the brothers meet,
To part no more, and weep no more,
Nor dwell in that dark, dirty street;

To toil no more with bleeding feet,
Nor hungering long for something nice;
For they are clothed as angels are,
And eat the fruits of Paradise.

No more the cold shall freeze their
    limbs,
Nor darkness chill their dreary night;
It is eternal summer there,
And all the blessed rest in light:

And there, with thousand thousand
    souls,
All saved from sorrow, fear, and shame,
They join to sing the happy song
Of praise to God, and to the Lamb,

Dear boys, who read the simple tale
Of these poor sweepers in the street,
The gracious God, who cared for them,
Will also guide your willing feet.

THE

CHILDREN OF SUMMERBROOK:

SCENES OF VILLAGE LIFE,

DESCRIBED IN SIMPLE VERSE.

BY MRS. SEWELL,

Author of " Homely Ballads."

LONDON: JARROLD AND SONS,
47, ST. PAUL'S CHURCHYARD.

Summerbrook.

Away from all the noise and stir
Of cities and of towns,
A little village lay concealed,
Amongst the Sussex Downs.

Its history was never writ
In any learned book;
Few people even knew the name
Of pleasant Summerbrook.

The houses stood about the fields,
Or near a winding road,
That skirted now a chalky hill,
And now a beechen wood.

It passed the school-house and the mill,
Down to a sunny glen,
Where stood the clustered cottages
Of many labouring men.

And then with many a pleasant turn,
Kept on its winding way,
And snug farm-house or mossy cot,
On either side there lay.

It passed the shop, it crossed the brook,
And by the church it ran,
And there you saw the handsome house,
Of Squire Tyerman.

But we will go into the glen,
So quiet and so fair,
That one would think, Content herself,
Might come and settle there.

At early dawn they heard the doves,
When all the vale was still.

At eventide the tinkling sound,
Of sheep bells on the hill.

The rooks dwelt in their ancient trees,
The blackbird in the dell,
And there in spring, the nightingale,
His sweet notes warbled well.

And all about, the primroses
Were thick as they could grow,
And pretty little wood-sorrel,
As white as flakes of snow.

The merry children laughed and played,
Beside their cottage door,
And never thought, young happy things,
If they were rich or poor.

The lambs, the birds, the honey-bees,
The squirrels in the wood,
Were all content at Summerbrook;
Were children there, as good?

Dear little people, you for whom,
I write this story book;
The children were not always good,
Who lived at Summerbrook.

In truth as far as I could see,
The children in the Downs,
Were in their hearts exactly like
The children in the towns.

But if you wish to know them well,
Then you must come with me,
And I will take you first of all,
To see good Jenny Lee.

Jenny Lee.

An orphan child was Jenny Lee,
Her father, he was dead,
And very hard her mother worked,
To get the children bread.

In winter time, she often rose
Long ere the day was light,
And left her orphan family,
Till dark again at night.

And she would always say to Jane,
Before she went away,
"Be sure you mind the little ones,
And don't go out to play.

"Keep baby quiet in his bed,
As long as he will lie,
Then take him up, and dance him well,
Don't leave him there to cry.

"And don't let little Christopher,
Get down into the street,
For fear he meets an accident
Beneath the horses' feet.

"And mind about the fire, child,
And keep a tidy floor;
We never need be dirty, Jane,
Although we may be poor.

" Good-bye, my precious comforter,
For all the neighbours say,
That I can trust my little maid,
Whenever I'm away."

Then Jenny she was quite as proud
As England's noble Queen,
And she resolved to do the work,
And keep the dwelling clean.

She did not stop to waste her time,
But very brisk was she;
And worked as hard and cheerfully,
As any busy bee.

If down upon the cottage floor,
Her little brother fell,
She stroked the places tenderly,
And kissed and made them well.

And when the little babe was cross,
As little babes will be,
She nursed and danced it merrily,
And fed it on her knee.

But when they both were safe in bed,
She neatly swept the hearth,
And waited till her mother's step,
Came sounding up the path.

Then open flew the cottage door,
The weary mother smiled;
"Ah! Jenny dear, what should I do,
Without my precious child!"

The Shepherd's Child.

Across the road, just opposite
The house of Jenny Lee,
Another pleasant dwelling stood,
Beneath a chesnut tree.

It was the home of Jesse Miles,
A shepherd on the hill;
His little girl was Katherine,
His wife was often ill.

Young Kitty Miles and Jenny Lee,
Were faithful friends and true,
And helped each other cheerfully,
Though both had much to do.

Before the cock had called the hens,
That roosted in the shed,
Young Katharine had dressed herself,
And shaken up her bed.

She threw the window open wide,
To breathe the morning air,
She washed her round and rosy cheeks,
And brushed her shining hair.

Then briskly down the stairs she went,
And when the fire was made,
She swept the room and dusted it,
And then the breakfast laid.

And up she took a cup of tea,
And nicely buttered bread,
To tempt her mother's appetite,
As she lay ill in bed.

She was not loud and boisterous,
But gently moved and smiled,
You might have fancied her a nurse,
If you had seen the child.

And when 'twas nearly nine o'clock,
And Kitty heard the chime,
She put her shawl and bonnet on,
To be at school in time.

She did not loiter by the way,
But briskly on she goes,
And if 'twas dirty in the road,
She tripped upon her toes.

She always was in school the first,
In spite of work or rain;
The mistress then would smile and say,
"Here's Kitty first again!"

And she cap nicely write and read,
And neatly hem and sew;
But now I'll tell you what I've heard,
Of little Sally Slow.

The Lazy Girl.

Her sister would come to the bedside and call,
"Do you mean to sleep here all the day?
I saw Kitty Miles up two hours ago,
A-washing and working away.

"And I have been milking the old spotted cow,
As she stood by the sycamore tree,
And brought a great handful of Lent lilies home;
That grew on the slope of the lea.

"The water is boiling, the table is spread,
Your father is just at the door;
If you are not quick, we shall eat all the bread,
And you will not find any more."

Then Sally sat up, and half opened her eyes,
And gave both a grunt and a groan,
And yawning, she said, in a quarrelsome voice,
"I wish you would let me alone."

But though she was lazy, she always could eat,
And wished for a plentiful share,
So tumbled her clothes on, and smeared her white face,
Forgetting her hands and her hair.

Her frock was all crumpled and twisted awry,
Her hair was entangled and wild,
Her stockings were down, and her shoes were untied,
She looked a most slovenly child.

She sauntered about, till the old village clock
Had sounded, and then died away,
Before she put on her torn bonnet, and went
To school without further delay.

But soon as she came to the little cake shop,
She loitered with lingering eyes,
Just wishing that she had a penny to spend,
For one of the pretty jam pies.

Again she went on and she loitered again,
In the same foolish way as before,
And the clock in the school, was just warning for ten,
As she lifted the latch of the door.

The governess frowned as she went to her place,
She had spoken so often in vain,
And now only said with a sorrowful sigh,
"There's Sally the latest again!"

She hated her reading and never would write,
She neither could cipher nor sew,
And little girls whispered, "We never will be
So silly as Miss Sally Slow."

The Dirty Lane.

Beyond the house of Simon Slow,
There is a narrow lane,
So dirty, that I never wish
To go that way again.

Here lived a man called Joseph Brand,
With Margery his wife,
And such bad management and waste,
I ne'er saw in my life.

There was a puddle at the door,
In which the children played,
And ashes, sticks, and broken pots,
Before the house were laid.

The clothes were hanging on the
    hedge,
All tattered and torn out,
Not fairly worn and mended up,
But slit and frayed about.

A little rough ill-favoured boy,
Was stamping in the mud,
To make himself from head to foot,
As dirty as he could.

His mother came and caught him there,
And with an angry cuff,
She snatched him up, and then he
    roared,
And kicked with noise enough.

The other little ragged things,
Were squabbling in the lane;
But as I said, I never wish
To see that place again.

So let us go and see the home,
Of Mr. Andrew White,
Where things as far as I could tell,
Were always going right.

The house stood in a pretty croft,
Where Andrew kept a cow;
And when his orchard was in bloom,
'Twas like a sheet of snow.

The hens and chickens ran about,
The cock crowed on the wall,
The little pond looked quite alive,
With ducklings great and small

His wife was quiet, clean, and good,
Industrious and kind,
One thought seemed ever uppermost,
In this good woman's mind.

To do to others, as you would
That they should do to you,
This was the thought which Martha
    White
Kept constantly in view.

She ne'er spoke ill of any one,
She thought it was not right;
She would not hear of neighbours' faults,
In that she'd no delight.

But where distress or illness came,
The people all were sure
That neighbour White would try her best
To comfort or to cure.

And she could speak with winning
  words,
Of God the Saviour's love;
And sometimes led her suffering friends,
To place their hopes above.

In Summerbrook churchyard there are
Three small graves in a row,
And on the stone you read the names
Of those who rest below.

Four little children used to play
Round Andrew's cottage door;
Now little Nelly plays alone,
The three play there no more.

Their happy faces in this world
Will never more be seen;
Their nimble feet will bound no more
Across the village green.

For they are gone to Paradise,
Where comes no toil nor pain;
And oh! they would not like to live
In Summerbrook again.

They sit beneath the Tree of Life,
Or wander hand in hand,
And sing amongst the lilies,
In that blessed sunny land.

They talk of little Nelly there,
And wish her time was come
To leave the house in Summerbrook,
For their delightsome home.

But Nelly White must stay awhile,
Until the Lord of love
Shall fit that little tender lamb,
To dwell with them above.

Nelly White.

The first day Nelly went to school,
She was but five years old,
A pretty little gentle child,
And never rude or bold.

She sat upon the lowest form,
Not far from Lucy Bell,
A girl of more than twelve years old,
Of whom we've much to tell.

She was not like good Jenny Lee,
Her words and looks were sour;
And children, if they wanted help,
Would never come to her.

Now Nelly had not learned to read,
She could not hem or sew,
Nor even thread her needle well,
So little did she know.

And as she sat upon the form,
She tried and tried again,
To thread the needle's little eye,
But still she tried in vain.

At last she said to Lucy Bell,
"My cotton won't go through;
The needle's eye is very small,
I don't know what to do."

"Why! you must do like other girls,
And not be sitting still,
And if it won't go through at first,
Then try it, till it will."

Then Nelly bit the cotton end,
And earnestly she tried;
But always at the little eye,
The cotton slipped aside.

At last the tears rose in her eyes,
And trickled down her face,
And she began to think that school
Was not a happy place.

But very soon she changed her mind,
When smiling Mary Day
Just lifted up her pinafore,
And wiped the tears away.

"What ails you, dear?" she kindly said,
"What is it makes you cry?"
"I cannot make the cotton go
Into the needle's eye."

"And is that all? well give it me,
 I soon will set it right;"
And through the eye the cotton went,
Almost as quick as light.

Then Nelly with a happy face,
Some little stitches made,
But then she found a tiresome knot,
Had tangled up her thread.

Her little fingers pulled the knot,
It would not stir for them;
The cotton stuck upon its way.
And would not hem the hem.

"Please Lucy Bell," she softly said,
"Undo this knot for me;"
"Why, child, how troublesome you are!
I wish you'd let me be."

"If you make knots to please yourself,
You must undo them too;
Nor waste the time of other girls,
Who've something else to do."

"Come, give it me," said Mary Day,
"I'll manage it, my dear;"
She soon undid the tiresome knot,
And set the cotton clear.

When Nelly home to dinner went,
She then began to tell
Her parents about Mary Day,
And peevish Lucy Bell:

And how the scholars in the school,
Looked up to Mary Day;
And how when Lucy Bell came near,
They often ran away.

And Nelly said, "I'll try to be
As kind as Mary Day,
And not be cross to any one,
In school time or at play."

Then Andrew praised his little girl,
And kissed her bonny face,
And said, the Days were all of them,
A credit to the place.

Daniel Day.

A seaman good was Daniel Day,
A noble British tar,
Who served her Majesty in peace,
And fought for her in war.

He loved his native country well,
He gloried in her fame,
And said a true-born Englishman,
Should guard her honoured name.

But sad was Daniel's manly heart,
When last he left his Jane;
It would be many weary months,
Before they met again.

And she was ill and could not work,
What would she do alone!
How will she bear a life of care,
He thought,—when I am gone?

Then to his children dear, he said,
(George was but twelve years old,)
"Care for your mother, George, my boy,
She's worth her weight in gold.

"And Mary, dear, don't let her want
A loving daughter's care;
And may the Lord reward you both,
That is your father's prayer."

Then Daniel Day, he went away,
To sail upon the sea;
And left to God's protecting care,
His little family.

The Happy Home.

When first I went to visit Mistress Day,
(Her husband then had been six months away,)
I saw her sitting, as was then her rule,
Watching for Mary till she came from school;
And when she hears her tripping foot so light,
Her face looks cheerful, and her eyes grow bright;
She lays her work upon her knee awhile,
To welcome Mary with a loving smile.
"How are you, mother? I'm afraid you're worse,
Do let me stay at home and be your nurse;
And then perhaps you would get well again,
And not be always in such dreadful pain."
"No, no, dear Mary, that can never be,
You must not grow up ignorant for me;
You'll have to earn your livelihood, you know,
And so must learn betimes to read and sew.
I've had the doctor calling in to day;"
"Oh, have you, mother—and what did he say?"
"He said 'twas little use for him to try,
Unless I gave up work and could lay by;
Were I a lady, he had little fear,
To make me well in less than half a year."
"Did he, indeed—well then, you must be still,
And George and I will work with right good will;
And George has grown a very handy boy,
And always ready for some fresh employ;
It is so good of George, whate'er you ask,
He'll do it as a pleasure, not a task."
As Mary spoke, her brother George came in,
A merry boy with rosy cheeks and chin,
Just twelve years old, and lively as the day,
And quite as ready for his work as play.
He had been whistling as he came along,
Trying to imitate the blackbird's song.
His mother heard him give his music o'er,
And scrape his shoes, beside the cottage door.

"Well, George, my boy"—"Well, mother, how are you?
You've got some job for me, I guess to do."
But long before his mother made reply,
He caught his sister's quick and speaking eye,
Who through the low-back door in silence passed,
Whilst full on George, a beckoning look she cast.
"Now, George," she said, as soon as he had come,
 I want to speak to you about our home;
The doctor came, and mother's leg he dressed,
And said, he'd cure it, if she could have rest:
Now, brother, I believe that you and I
Could do the work if we were both to try."
"Of course we could," said George, "no fear of me,
I'll do my part right well and handsomely;
But we must share the work you know, and take
What suits us best—so, Mary, you must bake;
And you must wash, that's plain enough to tell,
But I will draw the water from the well."
"Yes, Georgy dear, and don't run in the dirt,
Your stockings are so black and so's your shirt,
They take such soap and rubbing to get clean,
To make them white, and proper to be seen."
"Well, you shall see, I'll have another plan,
And be as clean as any gentleman;
Then I will run the errands that you need;
'Tis pretty clear too we must make good speed,
For mother will not have us late at school,
She's such a woman not to break a rule."
"Ah, George, she is a mother!—very few
Have such advantages as I and you.
Oh, how I hope she will get well again;
I cannot bear to see her suffer pain."
"Well, Mary, you and I will do our best,
And if we do the work, then she can rest,
And may perhaps get better, who can tell?
I'd work both, day and night to make her well."

This being fixed, these happy children went
To tell their mother what was their intent;
And when they had explained, and made it clear,
And George protested that he had no fear,
She laid a hand upon each youthful head,
And looking in their eager eyes, she said,
"Well, my dear children, you shall have your way,

And do the work for me, and I will play,
And be a lady."—"So you shall indeed,
And we will be your servants, and give heed
To every little thing you may desire;
So now, dear mother, shall we mend the fire,
And put the kettle on and get the tea,
And shew how quick and useful we can be?"

Little Patty.

As I drew near the house of Mistress Bell,
I heard some words that I'm ashamed to tell.
"I won't," said Lucy, to her mother's call—
"You won't. Miss, won't you? then we'll see—that's all;
If you don't mind that child—I say again,
I'll tell your father—and you know what then."
And then, I saw (of course I was not seen,)
Lucy come out, I don't know where she'd been;
But she came forward with a crawling pace,
Just like a snail—and such a sulky face;
She muttered something—and then tossed her head,
I did not understand the words she said;
But I could see she hated to obey,
And meant if possible to get her way.
A little child was just outside the door,
Playing with dust, and wanted nothing more;
For though she was too dirty to be seen,
She was as happy as a little queen.
She kicked the dust and shook her curly head,
Laughing to see the smother she had made;
But when she saw her sister drawing nigh,
She puckered up her little face to cry.
"What are you doing there?—a pretty sight!
How dare you make yourself in such a plight?"
She snatched the frightened infant by the hand,
And plucked her up, and roughly bid her stand.
"Look what you've done! I'll whip you, Miss, right well,
You naughty child, I will," said Lucy Bell,
And then she shook and slapped the little thing,
And by the sound, I'm sure the slap would sting;
Then rudely pushed and sharply jerked her round,
Of course again she fell upon the ground.
"Now, can't you stand?—I'll teach you how to play,
And make yourself this mess another day!
And if you cry, I'll call the sweep to come;
The black old man to take you to his home."

The frightened child clung close to Lucy's side,
But vainly tried its swelling sobs to hide.
Poor little Patty was but three years old,
And knew not how her childish grief to hold;
And sobbing, Lucy dragged her up the road,
Threat'ning to whip her if she was not good.

The case was this, that Lucy Bell had planned,
To steal away to walk with Susan Brand.
So, when her mother wanted her to stay
To mind the child, she wished to disobey;
But still she would not have her father know,
For he could give a very heavy blow,
Which Lucy felt sometimes, and was afraid
Her mother's promise was too truly made.
Now Mistress Bell she ruled her house by fear,
Scolding or beating you might always hear;
And as the children grew, they did the same,
Had little love, and very little shame;
And thus you hear of Lucy's cruel spite
To little Patty in her dirty plight.
But let me ask each little girl by name,
Have you been so unkind, and done the same?
Make answer to yourself, quite true and plain,
And if you have, then don't do so again.
I think I hear you say, you would not be
Like Lucy Bell for all that you could see.
Well there she is, and now we see her stand
Upon the road, and there is Susan Brand.
She had been waiting long to join her friend,
And little thinking how their walk would end.
"Why have you brought the child? she cannot go!
If you take her you'll have to walk so slow!"
"I could not help it.—We will leave her here.
We sha'nt be long, and there's no danger near."
Then threatening Patty, if she dared to stir,
She set her on the bank, and left her there;
And both the girls jumped o'er a gate close by,
Glad to escape, and laughing heartily.
Frightened to find itself left all alone,
The child began to scream when they were gone,
Fearing to see the black old man come by—
She did not know that Lucy told a lie;
Afraid to stir, afraid to look or peep,

She sobbed and sobbed, until she fell asleep.
Surely 'tis cruel—wicked, if you please,
To frighten children with such tales as these.
As the poor infant near the footpath lay,
Mary and George came trudging home that way;
They'd been to shop, to buy their weekly store,
And a great basket they between them bore.
They stopped, surprised to find the child out there,
And not to see her sister anywhere;
So Mary carried little Patty home,
And told her brother she would quickly come.
Now Mistress Bell was much displeased indeed,
And would not hear a word that Lucy said;
She told her father as she said she would,
And he beat Lucy, but it did no good;
For when the beating and the pain were o'er,
She grew more hardened then she was before.
So now, dear children, you have heard me tell,
Of this sad visit unto Mistress Bell.

The Cross Girls.

The school was closed one afternoon,
And all the girls were gone;
Some walked away in company,
And some walked on alone.

Some plucked the flowers upon the banks,
Some chattered very fast,
And some were talking secretly,
And whispered as you passed.

And if, perchance, a girl came near,
Then one of these would say,
"Don't listen to our secrets, Miss,
You'll please to go away."

As Nelly White ran home from school,
Her work-bag in her hand;
She came close np to Lucy Bell,
And her friend Susan Brand.

"We don't want you," said Lucy Bell,
You little tiresome chit;
Our secrets are not meant for you,
You little Tell-tale-tit."

Then both the girls cried "Tell-tale-tit,"
And pushed her roughly by;
Poor Nelly said, "I'm no such thing,"
And then began to cry.

She walked on slowly by herself,
Then heard a footstep near;
And turning round, was glad to see
Kind Mary Day appear.

"Well, what's the matter, little Nell?
You look so dull to day;

Come walk with me and tell me all,
And wipe these tears away."

"I can't bear Lucy Bell at all,
She is so cross to me;
And I shall not be kind to her,
And that I'll let her see."

"Oh, Nell, that is a foolish way,
You'll be as bad as she;
If you are cross and she is cross,
You never will agree.

"If she is cross, you must be kind,
That is the only way;
And if you do but persevere,
She may be kind some day."

"I'm sure I wish she would be kind,
And that friend Susan too;
Dear Mary Day, do take my part,
And tell me what to do."

"Well then, if you'll take my advice,
We soon will let them see,
That we can still be kind to them.
However cross they be."

"Yes, so we will, if you will help,
I shall not mind them then,
And if they call me "Tell-tale-tit,"
I will not speak again."

'Twas thus they parted on that day,
Resolving to do right;
And very proud of her good friend,
Was little Nelly White.

The Butterfly.

As Mary Day and Nelly White
Went off to school next day,
The morning sun was shining bright,
And every thing was gay.

The dew was sparkling on the grass,
The lark was in the sky;
And dancing on before them went
A yellow butterfly.

"Oh! let us catch it, Mary, do,
I'll try and beat it down;
See now! 'tis settled on that leaf,
Ah! silly thing, 'tis gone."

"Oh! Nelly, pray don't beat it down,
You'll hurt the little thing;
Why should you want to catch it, dear?
You'll spoil its pretty wing."

"I never thought that it would feel,
Or suffer any pain;
But if you really think it will,
I won't do so again.

"But are you sure they can be hurt,
As much as you and I;
Such things as beetles, frogs, and toads,
And little things that fly?"

"I'm very sure they suffer pain,
How much I cannot say;
But I can't bear to have them hurt,
Or see them run away.

"Beside they live so happily,
If they are let alone;
They never wish to trouble us,
Nor injure any one.

"I often watch them at their work,
And feel such great surprise,
That such small creatures as they are,
Should be so very wise."

"Well, I should like to watch them too,
To see how wise they are."
"Then just look at this cobweb, made
By that small spider there."

"That nasty spider! you don't mean
To say that he is wise!"
"Dear Nelly, watch a little bit,
And try and use your eyes.

"See, how he draws his thread along,
That's finer than a hair,
And seems to join it with a touch,
At every little square.

"And look how very fast he works,
And yet the work is strong,
And though he never has been taught,
He never does it wrong.

"He has no pattern there to show,
Where he should draw his thread;
The pattern and the working too,
Are in his little head."

"How did it get into his head?
I wonder if you know."
"Yes; God who made him put it there,
But I can't tell you how.

"I only know they're always right,
And never go astray;
And all the work they have to do,
Is done the neatest way.

"Whilst you and I are often wrong,
And many a blunder make;
A little spider weaves a web,
Without the least mistake.

"My mother says that we may learn,
From e'en the smallest thing,
That all God's creatures every where,
A useful lesson bring."

But now they're at the school-room door,
And soon they take their place;
And many girls looked pleased to see
Dear Mary's happy face.

Good for Evil.

"Bring up your slates," the mistress said,
"And all stand up in class,
The cipherers may come to me,
The second class may parse."

Then with their slates, and pencils
    sharp,
The scholars gathered round;
But Lucy Bell was looking down
For something on the ground.

"Come, Lucy Bell, what makes you stay?"
The Mistress looked severe;
"The class is waiting here for you,
We have no time to spare."

"I've lost my pencil, Ma'am," said she.
"Yes—that is just your way,
And I shall punish you this time,
And keep you in from play.

"I have to find more fault with you,
Than any girl in school,
And if you do not come at once,
You'll stand up on the stool."

With reddened cheeks, she once more
    turned
Her work-bag inside out;
The pencil was not to be found,
And she began to pout.

That moment a most happy thought
Came into Nelly's mind;
"She shall have my slate-pencil now,
For that is being kind."

And so she softly left her place,
And went to Lucy Bell;
"Here is my pencil, if you like,
Perhaps 'twill do as well."

Then Lucy snatched it from her hand,
And went and took her place;
But never once thanked Nelly White,
Who saved her from disgrace.

The friends met after school again,
As they had done before;
And hand in hand together walked,
As far as Nelly's door.

"Well, Mary, did you see how good
I was to Lucy Bell?
I am so glad I thought of it,
So glad, I cannot tell.

"But she was rough, and did not smile,
Nor even 'thank you,' say;
She snatched the pencil from my hand,
And quickly turned away."

"Well, Nelly, never care for that,
You know you have been kind,
And so you may be satisfied,
One day she'll change her mind."

The Wreath of Roses.

"I'll tell you what I mean to do,"
Said Lucy to her friend;
"I've been to Charmin's shop to day,
Just at the village end.

"You should have seen how splendidly
The window was set out,
And how the ribbons and the gowns,
Were hung and spread about!

"But oh! the flowers, I never saw
Such beauties as they had;
If I can't get some for myself,
'Twill almost drive me mad.

"The thing I long for is a wreath
Of rose-buds, white and red;
I asked the man the lowest price,
And what do you think he said?"

"Perhaps 'twas sixpence, I don't know."
"I see you do not. Sue;
Why, child, 'twas just as much again,
And quite a bargain too!

"I've set my mind to get that wreath,
But how, I do not know;
I'll turn it over in my head,
And manage it somehow.

"I am to have a lovely frock,
With flounces, and so wide,
And that will be made up, you know,
In time for Whitsuntide.

"It is the sweetest light sky-blue,
Just fit for summer wear;
And I'm to have a ribbon sash!
Yes, Susan, you may stare!

"And I'm to have a bonnet too,
With *little* strings to tie;
And on each side a small rosette.
And ribbon strings to fly.

"Then if I get that rose-bud wreath,
And just a little lace,
It will become me very much;
The colour suits my face.

"And little Pat will be so fine,
You'll hardly know her, Sue,
For she's to have a new white frock,
And handsome trowsers too.

"My mother says the frock won't come
Quite down to Patty's knee;
And so the work and little tucks
Will all be shown, you see.

"I mean to make myself some sleeves,
Like Nancy at the hall;
And she has worked a collar too,
A petticoat and all.

"I do delight in fancy work,
I hate to hem and sew;
If I could choose I would not set
Another stitch, I know.

"My mother likes to see us smart,
She'd count it quite a shame,
To go to church like somebody,
That you and I could name."

Then both the girls laughed heartily,
And joked at Mary Day;
"A little prim, old-fashioned thing,"
The worst that they could say.

"But how you ever get such clothes,
I cannot understand!
I wish that I could have the chance,
I know," said Susan Brand.

"My father scolds in such a way,
If mother goes on trust;
But if we bought such handsome
   clothes.
Of course you know we must.

"He says, that useful decent things,
Are all that he can stand;
That finery and beggary
Go mostly hand in hand.

"Now wife," says he, "I charge you well,
Don't get a beggar's name;
Fine clothes and drinking are the things
That bring a man to shame."

"He talked of that fine feather too,
In little Patty's hat;
And said, 'You'll see that Mrs. Bell
Will *beg* to pay for that' "

"Perhaps your father may be right,
Perhaps he may be wrong;
But I don't care for that, I'll have
My wreath, before 'tis long."

Lucy Bell's Dream.

The latest thought of Lucy Bell,
As she lay down that night,
Was how to get the pretty wreath
Of rose-buds, red and white.

When Lucy's eyes were closed in sleep,
And all were gone to bed,
In dreams she still distinctly saw,
The rose-buds, white and red.

The door was locked, the shutters
   closed,
And very dark the night,
But still the wreath of pretty buds,
Was always in her sight.

When Mistress Bell woke in the night,
She heard her daughter say,
"Oh! they have got the pretty wreath,
And taken it away."

"A foolish child," said Mistress Bell,
"She's dreaming now of that,
But she can't have it, I'm in debt
For Patty's tuscan hat.

"For Lucy's frock, and bonnet too,
And several little things;
Beside, I want a Sunday cap,
As well as bonnet strings.

"And Charmin spoke quite short to day,
About my small account;
And said lie wasn't warranted,
To add to the amount.

"I can't say that I see just how,
The payment will be met;
But that will come another day,
I shall not pay him yet.

"I hope my Jem won't get to know,
I must take care of that;
He thinks I earned the cash to pay
For Patty's tuscan hat"

'Twas very long ere Mistress Bell,
These anxious thoughts could still;
And when she went to sleep again,
She dreamt about the bill.

Lucy a Thief.

How brightly does the morning sun,
Shine down upon the earth;
To waken every living thing,
To gratitude and mirth.

The sweet fresh air is all astir,
To scatter rosy health;
And brings it to the working man,
As well as man of wealth.

But at the door of Mistress Bell,
No welcome could it win;
For though it was so bright without,
There was a cloud within.

'Twas Lucy's plan to fret and tease,
And now it was her thought,
That if she teased and sulked enough,
The roses would be bought.

But Lucy was mistaken here,
The bill was still to pay;
And angrily her mother said,
She'd take her sash away.

So Lucy Bell went off to school,
Exclaiming with a frown,
"I will contrive some way, I will,
To get it for my own."

She did not care about her work,
She lost her place in class,
The wreath was plain before her eyes,
As in a looking glass.

"Are you asleep?" the Mistress said,
"What makes you blunder so?
You cannot say your tasks at all,
Not one of them you know!"

Now Lucy's place upon the form
Was next to Mary Day;
And Mary left her work-bag there,—
Upon the desk it lay.

Then Lucy took it carelessly,
And just undrew the string,
And saw a silver shilling there,
Said she, "That's just the thing!"

And almost ere an eye could wink,
Or e'en her thought be known,
She whipped it out of Mary's bag,
And popped it in her own.

"There now—I'll buy that charming
  wreath!
The price will just be right;"
And then her face turned very red,
And then turned very white.

Mary Day's Secret.

"I wonder what you're going to buy,
Do tell me, Mary, dear;
If 'tis a secret, I won't tell,
I should so like to hear."

"Well, Nelly, no one knows it yet,
But I will trust to you;
There are not many girls I'd tell,
But you speak always true."

"Then, tell me first, how you could get,
A shilling for to spend?
You may be sure I shall not tell,
Because I am you friend."

"I've earned it all at different times,
You soon may do the same;
I hemmed some pocket handkerchiefs,
And marked them with the name.

"And I have sometimes cleaned the
    school,
And one or two things more;
So, Nelly, you may plainly see,
How I have made my store."

"Well, shall you buy some gingerbread,
Or puffs—they are so nice;
Or oranges, or peppermint,
Or cakes of licorice?"

"No; nothing of that kind at all,
The taste so soon is past;
I mean to lay my money out
In something that will last."

"Then, shall you buy some pretty
    clothes,
A collar or a bow;
Or pretty pink silk handkerchief,
Like Lucy Bell's, you know?"

Then Mary laughed out heartily,
And slackening her pace;
Took little Nelly by the hand,
And looking in her face,

Said—"Now I'll tell you, Nelly, dear,
Because we're friends, you see;
And when you have a secret too,
Why, you can tell it me."

"Yes; that I will," said Nelly White,
"I wish I had one now;
But come, do tell me, what you'll buy,
I want so much to know."

Then Mary Day looked round to see
If any one was near;
And only spoke out loud enough
For Nelly White to hear.

"Well; I've two sixpences to spend;
With one, I mean to buy
A present for my brother George,—
A pretty blue neck-tie.

"And with the other, I intend
(Because I've been to see,)
To buy a little tea-caddy,
To hold my mother's tea."

"I know she does so wish to have
A tidy little box;
And there is one of black japan,
And more than that—it locks!"

"But then, what will you have yourself?"
Said little Nelly White;
"Oh! I shall have the fun, you know,
Of seeing their delight.

"I just can see my brother George,
He'll laugh and jump and shout,
And say, 'There's no one like our Poll
The country round about.'

"And then my mother she will smile,
And give me such a kiss;
Oh! Nell, no puffs nor peppermint,
Could be so sweet as this."

"I should so like to go with you,
To see the things you buy;
And I can bring the pretty box,
And you the blue neck-tie."

"Well, so you shall, but let's make haste,
We have no time to stop;"
And so they skipped along the road
To Mr. Charmin's shop.

Mr. Charmin's Shop.

The little girls set off and did not stop,
Till they arrived at Mr. Charmin's shop;
And as you do not know it, I will try,
To tell you something of its history.
For many years this shop had been the place
Where all the working people bought their dress;
Their grocery; their pots and pans; their cheese,
Butter, and treacle, bacon, flour, and peas,
Matches, and shot, tin-ware, and balls of string;
A little, one might say, of every thing,
Small store of each, because the shop was small,
But still for years, it quite contented all;
It was nine miles to reach the nearest town,
And few went there to buy a cap or gown.
But just twelve months before the time I write,
The village people saw a wondrous sight;
The little low shop front had given place
To one, three times the size, of fine plate glass;
And the small parlour at the back, was laid
Into the shop, to suit a larger trade.
Then off to London Mr. Charmin went,
To buy a stock for taste and ornament;
And when the window was in full display,
It was as fine as tulip beds in May;
And wives and maidens, wondering at the sight,
Gave up their senses to a new delight.
Some aged people, by experience wise,
Looked at the matter with regretful eyes;
And said, that decent clothes would soon give place
To flowers and fringes, parasols and lace.
There were two things, which spoiled a poor man's life—
Drink for himself, and dressing for his wife;
They shook their heads, whene'er they had to pass,
Foreboding ill to many a village lass.
Oh dear! how all the little girls did stop,
To feast their eyes at Mr. Charmin's shop.

They loved the ribbons, all, except the brown,
And how they wished they'd money of their own,
So many pretty things they'd like to buy,
To make themselves a heap of finery.
Then off they ran to school, afraid to stay,
And talked about the ribbons all the way.
To elder girls, it was a greater snare,
Full half their thoughts were sure to wander there;
And more than half their talk whene'er they met,
Concerned the handsome things they meant to get.
A book of fashions in the window laid,
A charming book to every village maid.
When the young servant on an errand went,
To Charmin's shop her steps were often bent,
To ask the price of something, or to buy
Some tempting bit of useless finery;
Or read the fashion book to get a hint,
To make the sleeve, or body of her print,
Then hastening home, and questioned, why delayed,
A ready falsehood often came to aid.
'Twas odd to see, how very soon arose
A call for dressmakers to make the clothes,
Before the fashion book had come to town,
Mothers and daughters always made their own;
But not now, not e'en the sharpest could detect
The proper *cut*, to give the right effect.
Thus in the space of just twelve months, or less.
Town hands found work in making village dress.
And some gave up—for instance, Mistress Bell—
To wash at home, she could not iron well:
And flounces must be stiff and well set out,
Or else they draggle down, or cling about.
So, whilst the love of finery increased,
Home comforts dwindled to the very least;
And household management grew worse and worse,
And debts increased upon an empty purse.
For as the wages kept the same, of course
The under-clothing, and the fare were worse;
And children staid from school, for want of pence,
And thus grew up in shameful ignorance;
And others walked with bold undaunted eye,
To shew their clothes to every passer by.
All would be fine; the passion grew apace,
The dirtiest girl had flowers about her face,

Mixed in with gaudy bows and dingy strings,
The most unsightly, of unsightly things;
But there were consequences, worse than these,
Some other day, I'll tell you, if you please.
I don't believe the words so often said,
That all this finery is good for trade;
But my long history must have a stop,
For now we're all at Mr. Charmin's shop.

The Loss.

The shop was full as usual,
So Mary had to wait,
And felt a little anxious too,
For fear they should be late.

"I'll get my money out," she said,
"And when my turn is come,
I know the things I mean to buy,
And then we'll scamper home.

"There stands the caddy on the shelf,
There's George's tie, you see."
And little Nelly clapped her hands,
And jumped about with glee.

They stood just at the counter's end,
Not far from Lucy Bell;
And saw her looking at a wreath,
The wreath she loved so well.

Then Mary Day undrew her bag,
To take the shilling out;
But soon the whole contents were
  turned,
And scattered all about.

"My shilling's gone! it is not here,
Oh dear! where can it be;
I must have lost it on the road,
Do let us run and see."

Away they went, with eager eyes,
Examining the road;
Now running here, now running there;
Alas! it was no good.

But still they hunted up and down,
And up and down again;
We all know where the shilling was,
And that the search was vain.

At last e'en little Nelly talked
In sad despairing tones;
But still she looked among the grass,
And even moved the stones.

"Oh! here comes Lucy Bell," she said,
"Sure now—she can't be cross;"
And off she ran to Lucy Bell,
To tell of Mary's loss.

And such a piteous history
She made of Mary's case;
Whilst all the time the sparkling tears,
Were rolling down her face;

That even Lucy Bell looked grieved,
But said she could not stay;
Though Nelly begged she'd help to
  look,
Before she went away.

"Well, we must give it up for lost,"
Said Mary with a sigh;
"I did so wish to please them both;"
And she began to cry.

And freely ran the trickling tears,
Upon her mournful face;
She was not crying for herself,
And so, 'twas no disgrace.

"Poor mother will not have her box,
Nor George his nice neck-tie;
But 'tis no use to fret, I know,
So Nelly, dear, good-bye."

And all these little girls went home;
Which would you be, I pray—
Proud Lucy, with her stolen wreath,
Or weeping Mary Day?

The Guilty Conscience.

'Twas very long ere Lucy Bell,
Could get to sleep that night;
For just as she began to doze,
She woke up in affright.

And when she slept, she started oft,
Then fetched a heavy sigh;
And dreamed that something had been
   lost,
And heard poor Mary cry.

If Lucy's mother had been there,
And watching at her side;
She might have learned the very thing,
That Lucy wished to hide.

For Lucy dreamt that she was caught,
And then she gave a scream;
No one can tell what they may say,
When they are in a dream.

And as she at her breakfast sat,
Upon the morrow morn,
She scarcely said a word, but seemed
Dejected and forlorn.

At last her mother spoke, and said,
"What is the matter, child?
'Twas but a day or two ago,
That you were nearly wild;

"Because the day was close at hand,
When all the scholars meet
At Squire Tyerman's, at the hall,
To have the yearly treat.

"I can't think what has happened now,
To make you look so dull;
Your clothes I'm sure are to your mind,
They're very beautiful.

"I know that not a scholar there,
Will look so well as you;"
But at each word her mother spoke,
More gloomy Lucy grew:

Still said, she was not dull at all,
Though she was fit to cry;
So very close upon a theft,
Is sure to hang a lie.

"How came you by that pretty wreath?"
Again, said Mistress Bell;
And Lucy said 'twas given her,
Oh! Lucy—Lucy Bell!

And then afraid, that she might have
To answer something more,
She said, 'twas time to go to school,
And started from the door.

And as she went along the road,
She was in great affright,
Lest she should see poor Mary Day,
Or little Nelly White.

There was a terror on her mind,
She could not drive away;
She made mistakes in all her work;
She did not care to play.

The wicked thing that she had done,
Lay on her heart like lead;
When people spoke, her colour
　changed,
And down she hung her head.

But most of all she feared to meet
The eye of Mary Day;
And at each turn she tried to keep
Quite out of Mary's way.

And when the school broke up, she
　chose
To walk away alone;
She had a secret now, she dare
Not tell to any one.

Some girls came up to her and said,
"Why! this is something new;
What is the matter, Lucy Bell?"
Said she, "What's that to you?"

And when they talked about the feast,
She scarcely spoke at all;
She felt afraid to shew her wreath
To-morrow at the hall.

So passed the day—a heavy day,
And as the night drew on,
She started up at every sound,
She feared to be alone.

For still the deed that she had done,
Lay on her heart like lead;
And when her mother spoke to her,
She scarcely raised her head.

"Come, tell me now about that wreath!
For I must know it all;"
And Lucy said, "'Twas given her,
By Nancy, at the hall."

Now Nancy was a dressy girl,
And Lucy's cousin too;
So Mistress Bell was satisfied,
And thought the tale was true.

She took the wreath, and pinned it in,
And said, "Look! that is nice;"
But Lucy shivered as she looked,
She felt as cold as ice.

How peacefully good children sleep!
Who nothing wrong have done;
They're not afraid to speak the truth,
Nor fear to be alone.

And when dear Mary Day had prayed
Her prayer beside her bed;
She lay down happily to sleep,
No trouble filled her head.

For that great God, who made us all,
Who rules the earth and sky,
Keeps every good and praying child
Beneath his watchful eye.

The School Feast.

The thrush sung loud, the lark rose high,
It was a glorious morn;
The dew-drops hung like diamonds,
Upon the springing corn.

The sun rode through the clear blue sky,
No cloud was sailing there,
And sunshine lay on all the flowers,
And sweetness filled the air.

And bright young eyes from cottage
    doors,
Looked out upon the sight;
And glad young hearts were beating
    fast,
Forestalling their delight.

And busy hands up at the Hall,
Were cutting piles of cake,
And called on all, both great and small,
Some work to undertake.

And so the hours flew quickly by
Until the afternoon;
And then with flag and flageolet,
And fiddle and bassoon.

The children marched up to the Hall,
All in their best array,
And every face, excepting one,
Was satisfied and gay.

Some games had kindly been contrived,
The merry hours to pass;
They played at ball and races ran,
Upon the level grass.

Some children played at
    blindman's-buff,
Some swung upon a tree;
Until 'twas time to sing the grace,
And then sit down to tea.

'Twas wonderful to see the lumps
The little ones would take;
And what an appetite they had
For Squire Tyerman's cake.

The tea went round, the buttered bread,
Then cake again was tried;
Till every little hungry child
Was fully satisfied.

Then off again they went to play,
Or walk about the grounds;
And gentlefolks who came to tea,
They also took the rounds.

A gentleman and lady walked,
Through all the happy band;
And children smiled and curtsied low,
To pretty Mistress Bland.

And as they passed by Mary Day,
The gentleman spoke low—
"There, that's the girl, you'd like to
    nurse
Your little Maud, I know."

"That very thought," the lady said,
"Was passing through my mind;
The sweetest face I ever saw,
So modest and so kind."

"We'll ask her if she wants a place;"
And then without delay,
He asked the question pleasantly,
Of gentle Mary Day.

"When mother's better, sir, I shall,"
She said with blushing face;
"Well, then, you'll come to Mistress
 Bland,
And ask her for a place."

He put a shilling in her hand,
And smiling then, he said,
"There, now you see, I've hired you
To be our little maid."

Then walking on they joined a group,
Where Lucy Bell was queen,
And there she stood dressed out so
 fine,
Expecting to be seen.

"How different!" the lady said,
"What foolish airs she has,
Do, Harry, dear, observe that girl,
Do just look at her dress!"

"Oh! she's not worth a second look,
So tawdry and so vain;
I like that little rosy girl,
Who dressed so neat and plain."

"That smart girl's mother came to beg
Last winter at our door;
And such a dismal tale she told,
I thought them very poor."

"Aye, Fanny, dear," the husband said,
"You've yet to understand,
That finery and beggary
Go often hand in hand."

Just as he spoke, he felt a drop,
And looked up in the sky,
"The clouds are gathering fast," he
 said,
A thunder-storm is nigh."

Then off he went with quickened step,
The little girls to call.
And told them all to hasten home,
Before the rain should fall.

Away they ran in haste, pell-mell,
Their different homes to find;
And in less time than you would think,
Not one was left behind.

The Thunder-Storm.

The first large drops fell wide apart,
Like those of summer heat,
And seemed as if they'd not the heart,
To spoil the children's treat.

Thus many girls, whose homes were
   near
Squire Tyerman's at the hall,
Just reached their parents' doors
   before
The rain began to fall.

But Lucy Bell and Mary Day
Had full a mile to go,
And partly through the standing corn,
And by the tall hedge-row.

Now Lucy started off at once,
She thought about her dress;
And as she'd but a parasol,
She felt no small distress.

But Mary stopped to pin the frocks
Of many little friends;
And ere she reached the outer gate,
The heavy rain descends.

But having pinned her tippet tight,
And turned her frock up high;
Her large umbrella sheltered her,
And kept her nearly dry.

Still fast and faster fell the rain,
It dropped from off the trees,
And suddenly the quiet air,
Sprung up into a breeze.

It blew the slender corn about,
Through which she had to pass,
And scattered showers of rain-drops
   down,
Upon the heavy grass.

Still fast, and faster fell the rain,
It was a tempest shower,
And Mary now distinctly heard
The distant thunder roar.

But on she went, she did not fear
To hear the thunder roar;
And now she saw poor Lucy Bell,
A little way before.

Her parasol, too small to shield,
From either rain or sun,
Was dripping now from every point;
Far better had she none.

Her flying ribbons, late so gay,
Hung down in dabbled strings,
The colour run and smudged about,
Most miserable things!

The flounces of her dress were soaked,
Much higher than her knee;
And such a dirty draggle-tail,
'Twas pitiful to see.

"Stop, stop," said Mary, "till I come,
For I can shelter you;
My large umbrella here, you see,
Is big enough for two."

Poor Lucy sobbed just like a child,
She was in such a plight,
And still more vexed that Mary Day
Should come and see the sight.

For Mary's kind and friendly voice,
Increased her inward shame.
"I do not want to have her help,
I'd rather have her blame."

But Mary knew not Lucy's thoughts,
And would not be denied,
So held the large umbrella still,
Quite over Lucy's side.

"My frock is only print, she said,
And so it will not hurt;
But yours I doubt will never wash,
To clean it from the dirt.

"'Twas such a pity that you came
So early from the feast,
I might have kept you almost dry,
Your bonnet at the least.

Your pretty flowers are almost spoiled,
And those nice ribbon strings."
"Oh! I don't care about the flowers;
I hate the nasty things."

As Mary did not know the cause,
Nor could a reason find;
She only thought 'twas Lucy's way,
When things weren't to her mind.

So then she talked about the treat
They'd had up at the hall;
And Lucy said, 'twas very dull,
She was not pleased at all.

Then Mary talked of other things,
Still guarding Lucy's dress;
Until her proud and stubborn heart,
Was melted to confess.

"How kind," she said, "you are to me!"
And sighed a heavy sigh;
"I'm sure *I* had no right to think
That *you* would keep me dry."

"Why not?" said Mary, and she looked
At Lucy with surprise;
And Lucy looked upon the ground,
She dared not raise her eyes.

"What made you think that I should be
So spiteful and unkind?
I'm sorry that I had to stay
So very long behind."

"Oh I don't be sorry—'tis not that—
I did not think of spite—
If you had left me in the rain,
You would have served me right.

"I don't deserve a thought from you"—
And Lucy gasped for breath—
"Oh, Mary! it was I who took
Your shilling for this wreath.

"I have not had a moment's peace,
Since I saw you and Nell;
I've wished it back a thousand times,
But then I dare not tell.

"I'm sure you never can forgive
The wicked thing I've done;
But pray don't let the others know,
Nor yet tell any one."

"I won't, indeed," said Mary Day,
"You need not have a fear."
"Then you're an angel, that is all.
I always knew you were."

But now they're come to Lucy's door,
And there they bid farewell.
"If I don't copy Mary Day,
My name's not Lucy Bell"

George the Gentleman.

George was the prince of boys! morn, noon, or night,
Whate'er he had to do, 't was always right;
No murmur, nor excuses, nor debate,
That 'twas too early, or it was too late;
For when by George his mother's will was known,
In little time, his mother's will was done.
And as to Mary, that dear girl, and he,
Were just as happy as they well could be.
"Our little Polly," was the name she bore,
And when her brother heard her at the door,
He went like any Squire of the land,
And took the wet umbrella from her hand,
And changed her shoes, and gently shook her dress,
Till Mary laughed at George's carefulness,
And gave him such a kiss, as sisters can,
And said, "Ah! George, you are a gentleman!"
"And how's dear mother?" "Oh, she's charmingly.
We've been so merry, Polly, she and I.
She says, she has not half the pain she had,
And that her leg is nothing like so bad;
So there's encouragement for you and me,
To persevere and go on steadily."
"And I declare, George, I have seen this week,
That she has quite a colour on her cheek."
"She's beautiful," said George; "oh, trust to me,
We'll have her strong, when father comes from sea;
We've still some months; that gives a famous chance,
If, as she says, she always makes advance;
And that she shall, if we can have our way,
I think such work is just as good as play."
I think so too; and Father *will* be glad;
When last he left us, he was very sad,
And how he charged us to be kind and good,
And begged us both to help her all we could."
"And so we have, and so we will, and then,
Mary you know, he'll trust us both again;

That's what I like, it makes one feel so pleased,
Instead of being scolded, snubbed and teased,
Like young Tom Bell; there's always such a noise:"
"Yes, George; but he's the very worst of boys."
"Well, so he is, but he's not all to blame;
If I'd his mother, I should be the same;
You can't think how they quarrel and go on,
I'm finely glad that I am not her son:
For *little* things she always chides him so,
But when he's really wrong, she lets it go."
"I pity Lucy," Mary said, and sighed.
"Well, pray don't mention her," young George replied,
"The most unpleasant girl all round about;
Were you like her, we should be falling out."
And then George laughed, as if 't were possible,
That Mary Day should be like Lucy Bell.
And so they sat, and chatted for awhile.
Till Mary said, with a mysterious smile,
"I have a little business of my own
I wish to do, before our mother's down,
And want to get beforehand with my work;
So when you wake, if't is a little dark,
Do call me, George."—"A secret, Mary, hey?"
"Now do not question, brother George, I pray,
You'll know in time;" and Mary shook her head,
And lit the candle, and went up to bed.

Mary's Shopping.

Full many times, I've heard it said,
I do not say 'tis true,
That children's money has a trick
Of burning pockets through.

But whether it be true or not,
'Tis certain Mary Day
Lay planning in her bed that night,
To pay her own away.

And long before her brother George
Came tapping at the door,
She'd cleaned the grate and lit the fire,
And swept the kitchen floor.

For Mary had made up her mind,
To go without delay,
To buy the caddy and the tie,
Upon that very day.

She set the kettle on to boil,
And then she did not stop;
But with a light and bounding step,
Set off to Charmin's shop.

The morning air was calm and sweet,
Refreshed by tempest showers;
And heavy lay the glistening dew,
Upon the grass and flowers.

A light mist from the meadows rose,
Drawn upward to the sky;
And every bush and leafy tree,
Was full of melody.

And Mary sometimes checked her pace,
To try if she could see
What little birds they were that sung
So sweetly in the tree.

"How beautiful it is!" she said,
And raised her beaming eyes,
And turned her honest rosy face
Full upward to the skies.

And God, who fills the earth and sky,
Looked down on Mary there;
And as she walked along the way,
His Spirit walked with her,

And filled her heart brim-full of love
To every creature round;
She could not for the world have hurt
An insect on the ground.

A bright green beetle, burnished gold,
Ran swiftly o'er the road;
"You pretty little thing," she said,
"I'm sure you must be good."

The bees hummed on from flower to
    flower,
To sip the fragrant dew;
"You clever, little busy bees,
I'm not so wise as you."

A rabbit next sprung o'er the path,
To gain the nearest shade;
"You little darling dear," she said,
You need not be afraid:"

"I would not hurt you for the world.
Nor shoot you with a gun;
Not even though you eat our peas,
You little hungry one."

And then she said, "Poor Lucy Bell,
How sorry she must be!
I'll never tell to any one
The secret she told me.

"If I had not been better taught,
I might have done just so;
And I am sure I should not like
That any one should know.

"I wish her mother was like mine,
How happy she might be;
I'll ask my mother, if I may
Invite her in to tea,

"And then perhaps she'd speak to her,
And give her good advice;
And if she grew a better girl,
Oh dear, that would be nice!"

So Mary Day talked to herself,
And wanted no replies;
But when she thought of Lucy Bell,
The tears rose in her eyes.

At last, before the fine shop door
She makes a sudden stop;
She is the earliest customer
At Mr. Charmin's shop.

He soon brought out the very things
That Mary came to buy;
But wished to know how *she* could want
A caddy and a tie?

He liked to talk to Mary Day,
He said she'd turn out well,
And she was very ready too,
Her errand there to tell.

What Mr. Bland had given her,
And what she meant to do,
And what a great surprise 't would be
To George and mother too.

"That's right, my little maid," said he,
And gave her chin a chuck,
Then filled the caddy full of tea,
And said, "it was for luck."

I need not tell you, then, how fast
She ran to reach her home;
Lest she should find her mother down,
Or George to breakfast come.

She is in time—he is not in,
Her mother is not there;
So, quick she took her bonnet off,
And placed her mother's chair.

And then beside the pot she set
The caddy full of tea,
And laid the neck-tie in a place,
Where George was sure to see.

The happiness and joy there was,
I really could not tell;
But families who dwell in love,
They know it very well.

And sure our blessed Saviour feels
Joy in his home above,
When here upon this earth he sees
A dwelling full of love.

The Gleaners.

Some busy weeks had passed away,
With all the summer heat;
And autumn came and harvest time,
With sheaves of golden wheat.

And blackberries were in the hedge,
And nuts were in the wood,
And children with their baskets went
To get them where they could.

And apples hung with rosy cheeks,
In all the gardens round,
And laughing boys climbed up the
  trees,
To shake them to the ground.

The village school was broken up,
That all might lend a hand
To gather in the ripened corn,
That gladdened all the land.

And oh! it was a pleasant sight,
To see the gleaners come,
At evening with their sheaves of corn,
Rejoicing to their home.

And oh! it was a pleasant sight,
O'er all the sunny plain,
To see the children picking up
The scattered ears of grain.

Then sitting underneath a tree,
To eat their meal at noon;
Then singing home at eventide,
Beneath the harvest moon.

Both Mary Day and Lucy Bell,
And little Nelly White,
Were mostly gleaning in the fields,
From early morn till night.

For Mary said that she must work,
And never think of play,
That they might have some corn to
  grind,
Against the winter's day.

And wheresoever Mary gleaned,
There Lucy you might see
At work beside her in the field,
And talking earnestly.

The other girls seemed much surprised;
They all were at a loss,
What could be come to Lucy Bell!
She was not half so cross.

"I don't think so," said Susan Brand,
"She's very cross, I say;
She hardly ever speaks to me,
And goes with Mary Day."

"Well, all the girls like Mary Day,
Of course," said Jenny Lee,
"I think she is as nice a girl.
As you would ever see."

"Oh yes; she's very nice, no doubt,"
Retorted Susan Brand,
"I call her a deceitful snake,
To steal away my friend."

The girls disliked sharp Susan Brand,
They knew her temper well;
And that she'd always been the friend
Of peevish Lucy Bell.

And did not for a moment think
That Mary was to blame;
And when they heard her called a
    snake,
They said it was a shame.

But Nelly White burst into tears,
Her face was in a glow;
"Oh! Mary Day is not a snake,
No one shall call her so!"

Then all the girls laughed heartily,
And said that she was right,
"That Mary Day was not a snake,"
Nor little Nelly White."

Then Susan Brand walked further off,
And cried, "I do not care!"
Oh, little boys and little girls!
Of these bad words beware.

For those who do not care to-day,
Will have to care to-morrow;
It is the nearest way that leads
To sin, and shame, and sorrow.

The Earnest Talk.

Lucy.
And do you quite believe that God
Hears every word I say?
I always think that heaven seems
So very far away.

When I look in the sky at night,
And all is still and clear,
And fancy God above the stars,
I think He cannot hear.

Mary.
The Bible says He's everywhere,
Although we cannot see;
Yes, even in this harvest field,
Observing you and me.

Lucy.
But you don't think so, I suppose,
It never can be true,
That God would listen to the words,
That now I say to you.

I should be quite afraid to speak,
If this could really be;
But 'tis not likely He would watch
Young girls like you and me.

Mary.
The Bible says that every thought,
As well as every word,
Of every person in the world,
Is known unto the Lord.

Lucy.
That's very dreadful! don't you think,
If we were in a mine,
Down in the earth, far out of sight,
Where sun could never shine.

That we could well be hidden there?
Because in such a hole,
No one could possibly look down,
To see into your soul.

Mary.
The Bible says in heaven or hell,
Or on the furthest sea,
Where darkness covers every thing,
Still He will present be.

He sees us when we rise at morn,
And in our beds at night,
And whether we're at work or play,
We're always in His sight.

Lucy.
I hope He does not watch me so,
It makes me quite afraid,
I should not like to think that God
Was close beside my bed.

My mother says when I do wrong,
Or e'en a falsehood tell,
He will be sure to punish me,
And shut me up in hell.

And that He keeps a dreadful book,
That He will judge me by,
Where all my sins are written down,
With every little lie.

Mary.
My mother does not speak like that,
It is her great delight,
To know that God will condescend
To keep us in His sight.

He does not watch to punish us,
Or shut us out of heaven;
Because you know He gave his Son,
That we might be forgiven.

And don't you think that Jesus Christ,
Was very full of love,
When for our sakes He came to earth,
And left His home above;

And lived for more than thirty years.
Like any poor man's child?
A humble life of poverty,
And like a poor man toiled.

When *I* think of the love He shewed,
It makes me fit to cry,
To know that He should lose His life,
For such an one as I.

I often tell Him how I long
To please Him if I could;
And how I'll try to copy Him,
By being kind and good.

And how I hope that I shall grow
More patient every day,
And learn to think of others first,
Nor wish to get my way.

Oh! if we could but grow like Christ,
How happy we should be,
And I should like to live for Him,
Who is so kind to me.

I am so sorry, when I've been
Unkind to any one;
Or been put out, or done a thing
That I should not have done.

Lucy.
I want to ask you something more,
But now 'tis getting late;
My mother said I should be home,
Before the sun was set.

Mary.
Then let us set off instantly,
But only do behold
The sunshine coming through the trees,
Like glittering rays of gold.

I always like to see the sun
Sink down into the west,
He drops so still and peacefully.
As if he went to rest.

And all the clouds are in a glow,
Of purple, gold, and green,
And sometimes there's a bit of sky,
Of clear blue sky between.

With little golden clouds at rest,
So beautifully bright;
I often think that heaven's gate,
Must there be just in sight."

And thus they chatted on their way,
Of things that Mary knew,
Nor heeded that their footprints lay
Upon the evening dew.

The Moonlight Walk.

And now the harvest time is past,
And all the golden corn
Had been cut down and stored away
In stacks, or in the barn.

The gleaner left the stubble field,
And with her latest store,
Walked wearily and thankfully
To her own cottage door.

The full round moon looked calmly down,
'Twas almost light as day,
Except where shadows of the trees
Across the footpath lay.

And Mary Day and Lucy Bell,
Paced on with quiet feet,
As loth to break the silent calm,
That fell so pure and sweet.

The beetle's wing cut through the air,
And made a ringing sound,
And bats went flitting to and fi-o,
And circling round and round.

But still the girls walked side by side,
And neither cared to speak,
Till Mary saw a twinkling tear
Slide down poor Lucy's cheek.

Mary. "What was it, dear, the other night,
You said you wished to ask?"
But Lucy answered with a sigh,
To speak, was now a task.

Again she sighed, and then she spoke,
Her words were very low—
Lucy. "Can you forgive me, what I did?
That wicked thing, you know."

Mary. "Oh yes! I have, indeed, I have,
Pray do not cry and grieve;
I'll never think of it again,
I won't, you may believe.

"I did forgive you from the first."
Lucy. "Oh! that was good of you,
I thought that you would hate me so,
Directly that you knew."

Mary. "Oh! don't say so, I could not hate
A person if I tried;
And then you looked so very sad,
And were so vexed beside.

"I would have told you so before,
But I knew very well,
That you were never fond of me,
Now were you, Lucy Bell?"

Lucy. "No, Mary! I was so provoked,
Because you were so good,
And many a spiteful thing I've done,
To harm you if I could,

"But when the rain came down that night,
And you took so much care
To shelter me, and not yourself,
Well, that I could not bear!

"And then I thought that I would try
At once to copy you;
And every day I've loved you more,
And now, indeed, I do.

"But oh! 'tis hard to be like you,
I'm always doing wrong;
My temper is so bad, you know,
And then, my will is strong."

255

Mary. "Then don't you ever pray to God,
    To take your will away!"
Lucy. "No! that I've never done at all,
    I don't know how to pray.

    "But will you teach me, if you know?
    I really wish to try;
    But God perhaps won't notice me,
    I've often told a lie."

Mary. "Oh yes! He will, for Jesus' sake,
    Who shed His precious blood,
    On purpose to wash out our sins,
    And make us true and good.

    "And if you ask Him earnestly,
    And mean the thing you say,
    I'm very sure that you will find,
    He'll hear you when you pray.

    "Because God is our Father, dear,
    And not our enemy,
    And 'tis His will and pleasure too
    To fit us for the sky.

    "So when you find your will is strong,
    Or temper hard to break,
    Say, 'Help me, by thy Spirit, Lord,
    For Christ my Saviour's sake.'

    "I've often found, when things were hard,
    And I could not get through,
    That when I prayed, I did them soon,
    And found them pleasant too.

    "You need not be at all afraid,
    Don't think it is a task;
    For God is far more quick to help,
    Than we are free to ask."

Lucy's Prayer.

Perhaps you think that Lucy Bell
Was now quite satisfied;
As Mary had forgiven her,
And no one knew beside.

But she was not—she truly said,
"Her money I have had,
And I shall not be satisfied,
Until it is repaid.

"My mother has some shirts to make
For Dr. James, I know."
Now Mistress Bell had been well taught,
When she was young to sew;

And being very sharply pressed
To settle Charmin's bill,
She took the Doctor's shirts to make,
And worked with right good will.

And Lucy, though she hated work,
Could use her needle well,
And when she chose, few girls could
  sew
So quick as Lucy Bell.

"Mother," she said, "you won't object
To let me make a shirt;
I'll promise you to do it well,
And keep it free from dirt."

Her mother quickly raised her head,
She was not sure she heard;
"You make a shirt, and keep it clean!
Child, don't be so absurd!"

"Mother, I mean what I have said,
You know I can work well;
'Tis money that I want to earn:"
"For what?" said Mistress Bell.

"Some foolish nonsense, I suppose,
But you may have your way;
And this industrious fit, I guess,
Will last you just a day.

"However, if you make the shirt,
The money I'll advance;"
And Mistress Bell laughed heartily,
To think how small the chance.

But Lucy made her no reply,
She knew 't would be a trial,
The hardest lesson she had had
In real self-denial.

And thus she reasoned with herself,
"I know that Mary Day,
If she had such a thing to do,
Would think 'twas best to pray.

"She said when things were difficult,
And what she could not bear,
She managed them quite easily,
If first she went to prayer.

"I'll do the same;" and Lucy sank
Down gently on her knee:
"Help me, Lord! to work, that I
An honest girl may be."

"And give me patience to get through
This work I undertake;
And bless me with thy Spirit, Lord,
For Christ my Saviour's sake."

Then Lucy rose up from her knees,
A tear was in her eye;
And yet she felt much happier;
We know the reason why.

For God had heard that secret prayer,
And answered it in love,
And quick as lightning came to her,
His Spirit from above.

And Lucy then sat down to sew,
Her heart felt very light;
"My work is pleasant now," she said,
"And Mary Day was right."

When little Patty came and pulled
The cotton off her lap,
She took it gently from her hand,
Without a word or slap.

'Twas not at all an easy task
That Lucy had to do;
And had she not both worked and
    prayed,
She would not have got through.

She had to go to school each day,
And make the shirt, you know;
So all her play-time she gave up,
That she might sit and sew.

Her mother was surprised indeed,
And thought it would not last;
Still wondered what could make the
    child
Work on so very fast.

She fancied Lucy's temper too,
Was not so rough and cross;
But what had made the difference,
She still was at a loss.

And still the work went briskly on,
For still did Lucy ask
For patience, and a right good will,
To help her through the task.

When she had prayed she went to work,
She did not loiter then;
And if she found her temper rise,
She prayed, and tried again.

And every time that Lucy prayed,
God heard her earnest prayer,
And His good Spirit came to help,
The patient worker there.

Nelly's Secret.

"I've got a little secret now,
That you will like to hear;"
And Nelly put her rosy mouth
Close up to Mary's ear.

"As I was running home from school,
I tripped my foot and fell,
And then I cried, and close behind
Was coming Lucy Bell.

"She ran at once and helped me up,
And said, 'Nell, are you hurt?
Come, let me wipe your frock and hands,
They're covered with the dirt.'

"So then she rubbed them nice and clean,
And spoke so very kind;
'But look,' she said, 'you've torn a slit
Down in your frock behind.

"'But I have got my needle here,
I'll mend it in a trice;'
And then she ran it quickly up—
Do look! so neat and nice.

"And when I thanked her, then she said,
'My thanks I owe to you;
Don't you remember lending me,
Your pencil long ago?

"'I was so very cross and rude,
I did not thank you then;
Forgive me, Nelly, and I wont
Reward you so again.'"

"Well, dear, and then, what did you say,
When she talked of reward?"

"I put my arms about her neck,
And hugged her very hard."

"And then she said, 'I've often been
Unkind to you before;'
Don't mind, I said, you will not be
Ill-natured any more."

"And she said, 'No; I mean to be
Like your friend, Mary Day;'
And then she kissed my face again,
And so she went away.

"You said she would be good at last,
If I would only wait;
And she was very good to day,
And has been so of late."

"Yes, I do really think she means
To gain a better name;
And all the girls observe the change,
And say she's not the same.

"And she was gathering blackberries
Along the hedge one day,
To take them home for little Pat;
That was not Lucy's way.

"This week she's sitting very close
At needle-work, I know;
I can't think why she's doing that,
She never liked to sew."

"Oh! let's be kind to every one,"
Said little Nelly White;
And her sweet happy childish face,
Glowed crimson with delight.

Lucy an Honest Girl.

Now autumn days were growing short,
With heavy dews at night;
And often in the early morn,
The grass was frosty white.

And woodland paths were damp and still,
Save when the rustling breeze
Shook down the yellow, withered leaves,
In showers from the trees.

And all the little birds that sung
So gaily in the spring,
Were gone away to foreign parts,
Or did not choose to sing;

Except the robin, who abides
With us the seasons round,
And comes still closer to our door,
When snow is on the ground.

Then he will sing and sing again,
His sweet and mellow lay,
Till evening shades steal o'er the sky,
And daylight fades away.

I often think that God has tuned
That little robin's voice,
To bid us keep a thankful heart,
And evermore rejoice.

And often Lucy heard him sing,
When it was nearly dark,
As with a patient industry
She laboured at her work.

At last the Doctor's shirt was done,
In every part complete.

And even Mistress Bell confessed
The work was very neat.

"Well, mother, after all, I think,
I rather like to sew."
"Yes, child, you've worked with right
   good will,
And have the habit now;

"And that makes all the difference
Of liking it or no,
Which you will find in many things,
As through the world you go."

And now her mother paid her well,
She fully kept her word,
And Lucy with her money, was
As happy as a bird.

"I now shall be an honest girl,
At least I'll pay my debt,
And this hard lesson I have learned,
I never shall forget.

At school next day, the work-bag lay,
As it before had done,
And Lucy popped the shilling in,
Observed by only one.

But Lucy saw dear Mary's look
Of pleased and glad surprise.
And quickly said, "Don't say a word,"
While tears filled both their eyes.

Not tears of grief, but tears of joy,
They loved each other more,
Now each had done her duty well,
Than ere they did before.

The Day of Rest.

It was the day of rest—a pleasant day,
The quiet sunshine in the churchyard lay,
Where the old stones, with moss and ivy crowned,
Watched o'er the loved ones, sleeping in the ground.
The bells ceased ringing, and you then might hear
The organ's peal rise solemnly and clear,
And then the low confession and the prayer,
That God, our Father, would be present there.
The children of the Sunday School took part,
Chanting the anthems, they had learned by heart;
'Twas sweet to hear their youthful voices raise,
The grand Te Deum and the psalm of praise;
And see them lowly on the bended knee,
Making responses to the Litany:
And then to hear the general "Amen,"
Where children's voices intermixed again.
The Pastor was a minister who gave
His anxious care that little flock to save;
It was their hearts' consent he wished to gain,
And therefore always made his sermons plain,
That even children when they went away,
Could many portions of the sermon say:
And many thought they certainly would try
To gain that home eternal in the sky,
Which he described so beautiful and blest,
So full of happiness and peaceful rest;—
And other hearers as they left the place,
Resolved to seek their Heavenly Father's face.
This day the minister addressed the young,
And kind persuasive words flowed from his tongue;
He counselled them to seek the Lord betimes,
Ere strong temptation led to deeper crimes;
He told of God's free love, and how he sent
His own dear Son, to bear sin's punishment,
And begged that all, who then his counsel heard,—
Would give their hearts in earnest to the Lord.

When all was over, and the people gone,
Mary and Lucy sauntered home alone.
No need to hasten, and it soon was clear
Lucy had thoughts for Mary's willing ear;
"Mary," she said, "I'm trying to be good,
I really wish to give my heart to God.
What does that mean? How can I give my heart,
Take up the cross, and choose the better part?
And what's the meaning of the Christian's walk?
Is it the things they *do*, as well as talk?
What should they do? and what's the difference
Between the good, and those who make pretence?"

Mary.
Good people love the Lord who died for men,
And think they cannot do enough again;
They always wish His precepts to obey,
And copy His example every day.

Lucy.
Well, do describe it very clear and plain,
And if I'm stupid, tell it me again.

Mary.
I'll do the best I'm able, Lucy Bell,
My mother knows it, and explains it well.
She teaches me, when we are at our work,
I only wish that you could hear *her* talk;
Religion seems so pleasant and so good,
You would not do without it, if you could.

Lucy.
That's how I feel when I'm along with you,
Which makes me wish to know just what you do,
And what religion is.

Mary.
Well, let me see.
It's very plain as mother talks to me;
It all is love, and being good and kind,
And meek and patient with a humble mind:
Not discontented, though we may be poor,
And glad that other people should have more,
And never to be proud of what we know,

Or scorning others, who are dull and slow;—
But to assist them, and without pretence,
And never looking for a recompense.
And mother says, we always should be glad
When folks do right, and sorry if they are bad:
Nor should we talk about their evil ways,
But still be always pleased if we can praise;
She says we should go on, and persevere,
And keep a cheerful face, and never fear;
And if things do not happen as we would,
To bear it patiently, and trust in God;
Because He's able, if 'tis best to cure,
If not, He'll give us power to endure.
And mother says, it never is a loss,
To follow Jesus and take up our cross;
For if we do His will, then we shall know
His blessed truth, and like our Saviour grow.

Lucy.
Do you do all these things? said Lucy Bell.

Mary.
I wish to do, but cannot do them well.
I wish I could, but still I mean to try,
And hope at last to gain the victory;
Because you know we are not left alone,
We have the Spirit of the Blessed One;
He speaks within our hearts as with a tongue,
And says, "Now this is right, and that is wrong."

Lucy.
Oh yes! I know it— I have felt just so,
Since I determined I would better grow.
Is that the Spirit? It is very near,
It seems as if it spoke within your ear;
Then I suppose we should not disobey?

Mary.
No I never, Lucy, lest He go away;
And we be left without a friend to guide,
And Satan watching us, to make us slide.

Lucy.

But if we do go wrong, and errors make,
Will God forgive us then for Jesus' sake?

Mary.

Yes, if we are sorry, and confess our sin,
And still are earnest and sincere within.

Lucy.

I hope I shall be earnest, Mary Day;
I am so glad you taught me how to pray,
For when I've prayed, I really feel as though
I'd gained a better mind and will, you know.

Mary.

Ah, yes!—that's how I feel, so well content;
But Lucy, dear, do read the Testament:
It shews so plainly how we are forgiven,
And how God wishes we should go to heaven,
To live for ever in that glorious place,
And see our blessed Saviour face to face.

Lucy.

But there's one thing you have not mentioned yet,
And that is what I never shall forget;
No—I shall always recollect the hour,
When you o'ertook me in that stormy shower,
And were so kind and helped me all you could,
And thus returned my evil, all with good;
That broke my heart at last, and made me see
The mighty difference between you and me.

Mary.

Oh! I did little, Mary quick replied;
Our Lord did that when He was crucified:
He said, as then his latest breath He drew,
"Father, forgive; they know not what they do.'

And thus the dear companions gently walk,
Their young hearts burning, as of Him they talk;
He joined Himself unto them by the way,
And blessed the children on that Sabbath-day.

Christmas Eve.

'Twas winter time and Christmas Eve,
Long looked for now had come,
And separated families
Were gathering at home.

Where loving hearts and busy hands,
Made neither stop nor stay,
To have a real Christmas feast
On happy Christmas-day.

The boys had been into the woods,
Or down the sandy lane,
For branches from the holly trees
To deck the window-pane.

The sun had set with crimson clouds,
It was a frosty night,
And every little star looked down
With penetrating light.

And all the trees stood stiff and cold,
Their barren branches crossed,
Whilst sparkling lay on every spray,
A feathery fringe of frost.

So bright it was, so clear and still,
That as you listening stood,
You plainly heard the horses feet—
Upon the turnpike road.

From early morn till afternoon
Did George and Mary work,
And swiftly passed the busy hours,
With jokes and merry talk.

George had been down to Charmin's
    shop,
With cash in hand to pay,
For nuts and other dainty things,
To eat on Christmas day.

How cheerful did the dwelling look!
First coming in from night;
With all the shining holly twigs
And scarlet berries bright

And now it is by George proposed,
To which they all agree;
To laugh and chat a little bit,
Before they get their tea.

So round about the glowing fire,
They quickly take their place;
And warmly fell the ruddy light,
On every happy face.

"Do, Mary, look at Mother now,"
Said George with glad surprise,
"She looks so rosy and so well,
I can't take off my eyes."

"And mother says she *is* quite well,"
And Mary kissed her cheek;
"Now are you sure your leg is strong?
And don't you feel it weak?"

"'Tis really strong, my darling girl,
So put away your fears,
I have not felt myself so well,
For nearly twenty years."

"Hurrah!" said George—"now little Poll,
We'll keep her strong—we will;
She shan't be slaving at the work,
Whilst we are sitting still."

"No; no, indeed; were father here,
We should have Christmas fun;"
"He may come yet—trust me," said
  George,
He'll do what can be done."

"I know my mother thinks he'll come,
But won't say so for fear;
Now, mother, tell the honest truth,
You think he will be here?"

"I thought we should have had him
  home,
Before the year was out;
When last he wrote from Trinidad,
There seemed but little doubt."

"He's sure to come; the 'Orient,'
He says, is tight and tough;
I think I'll go to sea, mother,
When I am old enough."

"There, George, don't talk about that
  now,"—
Beside, I hear the gate,
And footsteps coming up the path,
'Tis some one calling late."

George sprung at once to ope the door,
"There now, I told you so;
Here's father all alive and well,
Himself from top to toe."

They fly to bring the good man in,
With cries of glad surprise;
And Mary and her mother say,
They can't believe their eyes.

They take his hat, his rough sea coat,
They pull him to the fire;
And every one has twenty things,
That moment to enquire.

"Well, let me get my breath," said he,
"I'm dazzled with the light;
And let me see your faces first,
For that's the finest sight.

My dear! he said, and kissed his wife,
You're looking charmingly;
Full ten years younger, I should say,
Than when I went to sea."

At this George gave a knowing wink,
And Mary caught his eye;
"He'll hear of all from mother soon,
She'll tell him by and bye."

"And how's my little Polly here?"
The happy father said,
And kissed his daughter's glowing
  cheek,
And fondly stroked her head.

"Upon my word, a bonny lass
Our little maid will be;
And here's my boy run up so tall,
He'll soon be fit for sea.

"I think they've kept my charge right
  well,
To care for you, my dear;
They have not broke their mother's
  heart,
I see that very clear."

The happy wife then spoke, and told
The tale we know so well;
And oh! it was a pleasant tale
To hear, as well as tell.

"God bless them both," the father said;
A tear stood in his eye;
"With such a wife and children too,
A happy man am I.

"God bless you both," he said again,
"God bless us all, I pray.
And let us bless His Providence
That here we meet to day."

A moment's pause of grateful joy,
Then round the board they met;
If there be greater happiness,
I have not seen it yet.

Homely Ballads and Stories in Verse:
The Poetry of Mary Sewell
by Mary Sewell

First published in this edition by UEA Publishing Project, 2024

This anthology and its afterword © Thomas Ruys Smith, 2024
All other contributions © Mary Sewell
Illustrations © Envato Elements

Cover Design and Typesetting by
Emily Benton Book Design
Typeset in Atkinson Hyperlegible and Arnhem

Printed by Lightning Source
Distributed by BookSource

ISBN 978-1-915812-43-8